CONTENTS

THE EUROPEAN ENTERPRISE

GEOPOLITICAL ESSAYS

ROBERT STEUCKERS

Translated by Alexander Jacob

www.manticore.press

The European Enterprise: Geopolitical Essays

Robert Steuckers, translation Alexander Jacob
© Robert Steuckers, Alexander Jacob, 2016

BIC Classification:
JPA (Political Science and Theory), JPSL (Geopolitics), JPFM (Conservatism and Right-of-Centre Democratic Ideologies)

978-0-9945958-2-9

MANTICORE PRESS
WWW.MANTICORE.PRESS

PREFACE

Alexander Jacob

obert Steuckers was born in Uccle near Brussels in 1956 and did his Baccalauréat in Latin, drama and history. He later attended the Université Saint-Louis Bruxelles and the Université Catholique de Louvain studying Germanic philology and did a diploma in translation and interpretation at the Marie Haps institute in Brussels. He was involved in the "Nouvelle Droite" movement of Alain de Benoist in the eighties but broke away from it in 1992 to form his own Belgian grouping in 1994 called 'Synergies Européenes' along with Gilbert Sincyr, another former member of Benoist's G.R.E.C.E.[1]

His main interests are the German Conservative Revolution, on which he has produced a study, *La Révolution conservatrice allemande: Biographies de ses principaux acteurs et textes choisis* (Éditions du Lore, 2014), and geopolitics, in which he was first guided by the Austrian general Heinrich Jordis, Freiherr[2] von Lohausen. He participated in several summer university seminars organised by the Association Universitaire Provence-Europe which were conducted not only in France but also in Italy and Germany between 1993 and 2002. Some of the essays I have translated here were presented as talks at these summer university seminars, while others were presented at other conferences at later dates. The essays

---

[1] ['Groupement de recherches et d'études pour la civilisation européene' (Group for the research and study of European civilisation).]

[2] [Baron.]

I have chosen to translate in this edition will reveal Steuckers' clear, and very comprehensive, geopolitical view of the historical efforts of the European states to ward off or control the Mongol/Turkic invasions as well as of the present dangers that the American hegemonic ambitions pose to the cultural and political integrity of Europe and Russia.

~

In the first essay, on "The Geopolitics and Spirituality of the 'Reich' Principle", Steuckers points to the essential qualities of a "Reich". A Reich is indeed a spiritual principle and not equivalent to a "nation". It is truly "multinational" in that it includes many different ethnies within its fold. Unlike the "multiculturalism" propagated today in the American world-order, an empire is, as the Austrian aristocrat Erik Kuehnelt-Leddihn had demonstrated, informed by a transcendental or spiritual Idea that runs vertically through it and elevates its different constituents at whatever level they may be in the social hierarchy of the empire. As Steuckers puts it:

> Verticality — implies the duty of protection and respect, a duty to serve superiors and a duty of the superiors to protect the inferiors in a relationship comparable to that which exists in, traditional societies and families, between parents and children. (p. 35)

The levelling horizontality of a democratic world-order, on the other hand, has no respect for the Other and seeks rather to corrupt or destroy him.

Steuckers traces the spiritual factor of those who established the first Indo-European empires to the warrior stratum of the proto-Iranian/Scythian horse-riding migrants who gradually moved from Central Asia into Europe. According to Steuckers, these knightly warriors were informed by a simple and austere code of conduct whereby they were "trained to render their thought clearly, to purify their feelings, to consider their duty" (p. 39). Unfortunately, the ancient Indo-European migrations were hindered by the Hunnish invasions of the early centuries A.D. which resulted in the "enclaving" of Europe in the western part of the Eurasian continent ("General reflections on the concept of Eurasia").

The geopolitical basis of the first great European empire, the Roman, was constituted of the mastery of Mediterranean maritime routes, of terrestrial routes of communication which the Roman roads were, and of the river routes starting from the western bank of the Rhine and the southern bank of the Danube. This Roman mastery of the continent was reactivated by the Carolingian Empire in the early Middle Ages. One of the basic problems of any attempt at a unification of Europe, however, is the fact that the historical and cultural foundation of the continent is not uniform. The Germans in particular have had a long-standing aversion to Rome, which ruled them in antiquity, as well as to France, which ruled them in the Napoleonic era, and have always sought to institute new imperial forms directed from the north. Thus Herder advocated a return to Greek traditions rather than Roman as a basis of the unification of the Germanic and Slavic parts of Europe ("*Visions of Europe in the Napoleonic Era - On the sources of Contemporary Europeism*"). The Baron von Aretin however more astutely proposed a Protestant Germanic vision of an independent Europe based on the mediaeval Hanseatic League to counter the economic universalism of the Anglo-Saxon thalassocratic and colonial powers. The Germanic Protestant opposition to the Napoleonic rule found expression also in the political vision of the Romantic writers of nineteenth century Germany who championed a neo-mediaeval Empire antedating the rift between Catholicism and Protestantism. However, since mediaeval Europe was primarily Catholic, Joseph von Görres rather realistically saw the new Europe as a Catholic Germanic one since Germany has, by virtue of its central geographical position on the continent, a greater unifying power than the other states. Franz von Baader, on the other hand, suggested a union of all three branches of Christianity, Catholic, Protestant and Orthodox in a new independent Europe. The German philosopher Constantin

Frantz very pertinently emphasised the dangers of French and British colonialism as causative of the economic destruction of the spiritual integrity of the continent. The disastrous result of these colonial adventures was the Crimean War which pitted France and Britain against Russia when it should have been the concern of all the major European powers to dominate the Ottomans, whose territory is necessary for the liberation of Europe from the western peninsula of the Eurasian continent in which it has been enclaved:

> The Black Sea, an internal sea, is for the Europeans of the west the gate towards Eurasia just as it is for the Russians a potential access to the eastern Mediterranean, a necessity that is postulated by their desire to be at once the heirs of the Greek civilisation (which was a north-south Pontic/eastern Mediterranean axis of which the Bosphorus was a bottle-neck in a central position) and of the Byzantine imperium. (p. 195)

The salutary political unions of the nineteenth century such as the Holy Alliance of 1815 and the Quintuple Alliance, or Pentarchy, of 1818 did allow Europe to develop autarkically rather than colonially. Unfortunately, they were of a short duration and had only a weak continuance in the Three Emperors' League of Prussia, Austria-Hungary and Russia which lasted from 1873 to 1887 but was abandoned due to rivalries between Austria-Hungary and Russia in the Balkans.

The European efforts at expansion outside the continent were, according to Steuckers, mainly attempts at de-enclaving themselves. These include the mediaeval Crusades, the commercial expansions of the Genoese and the Venetian Italians in the Renaissance, the Portuguese and Spanish maritime explorations and the efforts of Tsar Ivan the Terrible to replace the Ottoman Empire with an Orthodox Russo-Byzantine one ruled from the Third Rome, Moscow. This goal may have been latent in the Russian foreign policy of the period of the Crimean War (1853-56) when Britain feared that Tsar Nicholas I and his successor Tsar Alexander II may have had the same designs as Ivan the Terrible in Anatolia. And the fear of such a Russian ambition clearly rules American foreign policy to this day.

The chief opponents of the re-establishment of European hegemony are indeed the Anglo-Saxon powers, first Britain and now America. Britain's refusal to allow Russia to find access to the warm waters of the Mediterranean, or to the Indian Ocean when India was the "jewel" in the British imperial crown, was repeated during the First World War when Germany entered into an alliance with the Ottoman Empire, except that this time Russia too repudiated such an alliance. Germany's industrial advances in the late nineteenth century caused the British too to fear a rival to the colonial empire planned by Cecil Rhodes. Russia, however, was the greater enemy of Britain since it threatened India more directly. America, during all this time, was a supporter of the British enterprise. Like the British imperial policy, the American Monroe Doctrine of 1823 had also been clearly anti-Continental in its prohibition of European intervention in America, a prohibition primarily targeting the Spanish who had colonies on the American continent but also the Russians who were positioned in Alaska.

The weakening of Britain's principal enemy, Russia, was successfully accomplished during the Russo-Japanese War of 1904-05 when Britain and the United States supported Japan against Russia. This debilitation was completed during the subsequent Communist Revolutions of Russia. Since the Second World War, when America has taken over from Britain as a spurious hegemon of the world, the arch-rival of the United States has continued to be Europe, which America seeks to weaken in numerous different ways. The American post-war control of Europe through NATO is reinforced by its efforts to encircle Russia in Central Asia. The means it employs in its anti-European policy are diverse, ranging from media subversion of European culture to the fostering of Islamic terrorism to disturb the economies and societies of the Europeans. The anti-Russian strategy of the Americans after the Second World War began with the establishment of the Cold War and was reinforced in 1971 through the Sino-American rapprochement, which aimed primarily at countering Soviet power and influence.

As Steuckers puts it:

> This diplomacy was based, once again, on the geopolitical
> theories of Mackinder and his disciples: according to these
> theories, it was necessary, if need be, to support a power of
> the "rimland" (or "inner crescent"), or an alliance of smaller
> powers of the rimland, against the ruling power of the "Central
> Land". The Maoists of May '68 would partially swing to the
> American camp against the "Moscowteers". Washington had
> already deployed its own "Communists", mostly of Trotskyist
> faith ...; these were soon joined by Maoists deriving from the
> Washington/Peking alliance. (p. 112)

Given the extraordinary importance of the subversive Trotskyist
factor in both Soviet and American politics – where it is now
disguised as Neoconservatism – it is not difficult to recognise
the true nature of the major divisions in international geopolitics
today. If the cultural, social and economic ills of globalism today
are American and Neoconservative, they are in fact the same that
destroyed the Soviet Union and whatever the latter may have
retained of a European national sensibility. The inclination of
German geopoliticians like Karl Haushofer, Oskar Niedermayer
and Otto Hoetzsch ("*The Themes of Geopolitics and of the
Russian Space in the Cultural Life of Berlin from 1918 to 1945*")
to a cooperation with the Soviets in the twenties, thirties and
forties of the last century was one directed primarily by a desire
to consolidate the Eurasian continent against the Anglo-Saxon
thalassocracy. In this respect, Russia's attempts to break the British
Empire through Afghanistan and India already in the nineteenth
century – before there was any Soviet Union – may be seen as
part of the continuing "Eurasian" effort to dismantle the economic
empire of the Anglo-Saxons. Hoetzsch in particular proposed a
closer alliance of western Europe with the Slavs in order to develop
a "Greater Europe". Unfortunately, the Ribbentrop-Molotov pact
of 1939 to 1941 was the last formal alliance between Germany and
Russia before Hitler's invasion of the Soviet Union foreclosed any,
even tenuous, cooperation between these two powers.

The United States, which has taken over from Britain as hegemon of the world, operates according to a geopolitical vision that was first presented by Admiral Alfred Mahan in the early part of the last century and has been continued by the geostrategist Zbiegniew Brzezinski and the Neoconservative warmongers after him. America's "Alexandrian" strategy of Eurasian expansion indeed became clear during the Yugoslav Wars (for the Balkans are indeed the springboard to the Near East and Central Asia) of 1991 to 2001, under George Bush Sr. and Bill Clinton, and was reinforced during the Afghan invasion in 2001 and the Mesopotamian invasion in 2003 under George Bush Jr. These adventures reveal how Trotsky's ideal of "permanent revolution" in society also entails the conduct of "permanent war" against ideological enemies abroad.

European "intellectual" support for these Trotskyist American wars was provided by the so-called "New Philosophers" in France grouped around the Jewish activist Bernard-Henri Lévy who justified the American intervention in and the Balkanisation of south-eastern Europe. Since the Balkanisation was an American move to establish a "Greater Middle East" that would serve American interests and exclude Europe and Russia from the resources of these regions, these Jewish thinkers were in fact acting, exactly like the Americans themselves, in a blatantly anti-European manner. The political effects of this American-European propaganda were directly observable in the replacement of the German Chancellor Gerhard Schröder – who had dissociated himself from the American invasion of Iraq in 2003 – by Angela Merkel in 2005 and the elimination of Dominique de Villepin – who was the Foreign Minister of Jacques Chirac who had also opposed Bush's Iraq war – from the presidential race of 2007 by the pro-American Nicolas Sarkozy.

The American enterprise that seeks world hegemony today is, in spite of its propaganda platitudes, an essentially destructive one because it completely ignores the importance of the preservation of historical and cultural continuity within the nations that constitute an empire (which America clearly is not). In fact, America can never allow the nations it controls to retain their sovereignty, which includes the right to wage war. America's experiment in the colonisation of Europe has indeed proven to be intolerable because it consists in an unrelenting cultural and social subversion through the agency of the media, multinationals, Mafias and terrorist organisations.

Worse, the strategic associations that America forms today – with the fundamentalist Wahhabis, for instance, and perhaps even the horrifying Islamic State – expose a fundamentalist strain in American culture itself which should be avoided at all costs. This is the Judeo-Puritanical basis of American religion which has rendered Americans incapable of any real artistic or spiritual culture at the same time as their government vigorously spreads a primitivist American "multiculture" (or "cultural Trotksyism") throughout the world that it wishes to rule. The spread of this anti-culture is facilitated by the psychological promotion of the "carnival" or "partying" spirit by the media aimed at preventing the rise of political and historical consciousness among the European citizens. The problem is compounded when this "multicultural", "liberal", "democratic" model is defended with pseudo-ethical imperatives like "human rights" (propagated by President Carter) and the fight against "Evil" (Reagan) or against the "Axis of Evil" (Bush).

Europe's counter-strategy to acquire and assert its independence must necessarily entail a total break with NATO and a development of European forces like OSCE (Organisation for Security and Cooperation in Europe) and military production that is independent of the present debilitating American control. Energy independence too is crucial for the European enterprise and must be developed along the lines suggested in France by President De Gaulle. Germany especially must strengthen its energy cooperation with Russia. Steuckers favours the policies of Henri de Grossouvre ("*The Brzezinski Strategy, the Paris-Berlin-Moscow Axis and Indirect Wars*") centred on a Paris/Berlin/Moscow axis which will be able to counter the American globalist enterprise. Economic development should cease to adhere to the American model of constant change for the acquisition of short-term gains but focus on long-term advantages that are based on production (the "Rhineland" economic model) rather than on speculation.

Following in the footsteps of King Friedrich II of Prussia and the economist Friedrich List every attempt must be made to link all parts of the Eurasian continent through an effective system of roadways and river-ways, just as European satellite communication must be improved to counteract American espionage activities like the ECHELON network ("Europe and the challenge of globalisation"). As Steuckers points out:

> Today we will have again an "empire" in Europe, an imperial (reichisch) system if we optimise our systems of communication (especially the telecommunication satellites), if we succeed in directly perceiving the manoeuvres of obstruction posed by corrupt politicians and combat them immediately and pitilessly. If we had such an attitude, if we had this "spatial memory", we would never have swallowed the American war against Serbia and, ipso facto, the Euro would not have devalued as a result of this war, which was a catastrophe for Europe that the false elites that govern it today did not even notice. (p. 34)

The Pontic space must be considered by Europe as a European one and not to be ruled by American stooges like the present Ukrainian government. As Steuckers declares:

> In a European and Russian perspective the peaceful control of Central Asia, the Caucasus, the Caspian and the Black Seas is an important geopolitical and geostrategic advantage that cannot be undone lightly at the risk of seeing the triumph of the dearest wish of the Anglo-Saxon geopolitics whose foundations were theorised by Halford John Mackinder and Homer Lea n the first decade of the 20th century. (p. 90)

Turkey must be wrested from the arms of America at all costs. Kemalist pan-Turanianism is not a bad idea in itself as long as it is not utilised as a tool by the Americans to dominate Central Asia. The other Islamic powers that must be torn away from American influence are Syrian Baathism and Iran. Baathism was able to maintain a pluralist society in Iraq and Syria until the Americans intervened and some of the Iraqi Baathists were recruited as leaders of the surreptitiously created fundamentalist Islamic State. The position of the Baathist party in Syria remains unstable. Iran, whose Shah once sought to reconcile Iranians with Saudis, suffered a revolution which overthrew its secular rule for an Islamic republic. The present attempted rapprochement between America and Iran should equally be aborted since America's intentions are mainly economic geopolitical ones focussed on Central Asia and Russia rather than inspired by a desire for any pact with the Shias of Iran who are distrusted and feared by the American Jews and the Israelis equally.

The battle against the American hegemon must indeed be waged internationally so that the South American states that have sought to resist American hegemony in their continent must be supported by and allied to the European. In this regard, Steuckers especially favours the model of Hugo Chavez in Venezuela. Steuckers also proposes that Europeans should adopt a supple Confucian politics of syncretism and harmony freed of the ideological obsessions that characterise the fundamentalist forces derived from Abrahamic religion. In fact, Steuckers even proposes a "Grand Alliance" that would include not only European powers but Asiatic ones like China, Japan and India in order to serve as an anti-American force. Steuckers' own European geopolitical interests were derived from the notion of "Jeune Europe" or "Young Europe" developed by Jean Thiriart in the sixties. Thiriart was notably anti-American as well as anti-Soviet though he moved closer to Russia after the fall of Communism.

As for the controlled opposition to globalism represented by the periodic anti-globalist demonstrations around the world these are leftist tactics that lack any territorial base and are therefore to be discounted as real allies in the battle for European independence.

Real resistance to the American hegemony can only come from states or groups of states such as the BRICS organisation. Steuckers point also to the Shanghai Pact as a sensible model of anti-American political organisation. It is also important to bear in mind that the various independence movements that have sprung up recently in Europe are not genuine in spite of their recourse to fashionable "identitarian" disguise since they do not have any sense of the collective identity that Europeans must have as Europeans and never even think of opposing NATO:

> The resistance to the Americanocentric globalist system is not to be found, in fact, in a global "network" of hippy dissidents or thugs stoned on cocaine but derives much more from classical statist and imperialist structures deeply anchored in the past: "the Shanghai Group with a China of thousand year old political traditions, Putin's Russia which is recovering its memory, an Ibero-American independence movement in the spirit of the Mercosul and of the Venezuelan president Chavez." (p. 138)

The independence movements in Catalonia and Brittany are examples of this disintegrating subversion of the European enterprise. As Steuckers puts it:

> The strategy of the permanent partition of the territory aims, in fact, at preventing any reconstitution of an imperial reality in Europe, heir to the empire of Charles Quint or of the "Grand Alliance" (p. 310)

Since the American anti-European strategy is constituted of a policy of "distracting the human imagination at any cost from all tradition or historical reality" Steuckers suggests that an effective European counter-strategy would consist in

> Re-appropriating one's own history, knowing its fecund principles, which allow a consolidation of one's positions, and the perverse principles which lead to implosion; this implies

also exploring the history of the adversary to cause to appear on his territory paralysing conflicts. In plain language, for consistent European strategists, exploiting the anger of the American Blacks or cleverly supporting the protest movements within the United States. (p. 274)

THE GEOPOLITICS AND SPIRITUALITY OF
THE "REICH" PRINCIPLE[1]

The first fundamental idea that I would like to stress today by evoking the principle of the "Reich" is that the latter certainly has a spiritual, symbolic, cultural dimension (which I shall explain) but one must also know that every Reich is a territorial space of large dimensions. The symbols and the spirituality of the Reich need a space to be embodied, to acquire concreteness. That is the reason why a good knowledge of the geographic dynamic of the territory where this Reich should be established is an imperative that one cannot avoid.

That is why it seems important to me to reflect well on the receptacle-space of the idea of a Reich (*regnum*). First, every Reich is a political space whose dimensions correspond to the "*Großraum*" theorised by Carl Schmitt, whose dimensions are continental.[2] Next, this space is organised by means of communications and transport. Every Reich aims at accelerating the relations between the people

---

[1] Talk held at the seminar of Synergon Deutschland, 2000. Published in www. centrostudilaruna.it, 1 January, 2000.

[2] [N.B. All notes in box-brackets are by the translator.] [Carl Schmitt (1888-1985) was a German jurist and very influential political theorist. He was appointed in 1933 as president of the Vereinigung nationalsozialistischer Juristen (Union of National-Socialist Jurists).His concept of "Großraum" was presented in a work published in 1939 called Völkerrechtliche Großraumordnung und Interventionsverbot für raumfremde Mächte. Ein Beitrag zum Reichsbegriff im Völkerrecht.]

living on its territory. This territory is both vast and nevertheless circumscribed by clearly defined limes,[3] even if they are in constant expansion. Some examples: the Roman Empire, the unsurpassed model in European history, was a great constructor of routes, its army, the legions which embodied it, which were its principal instrument, was constituted of combatants, experienced and well trained soldiers, but also of pioneers, troops of technologists who constructed roads, bridges and aqueducts. The British Empire, a maritime empire, more dominating and exploitative in economic terms than the Roman Empire to the point that one can contest its quality as a Reich, equally possessed its instrument of mobility and speed: its navy. Devoid of a constituent spirituality, this mercantile thalassocracy nevertheless organised the maritime routes, especially those that conduct us to India passing through Gibraltar, Malta, Cyprus, Suez and Aden. China, an empire that was unshakeable for millennia, also emerged thanks to the construction of roads and canals and the organisation of a coastal fleet.

Against "Large Spaces": The Thalassocratic Strategy of Sabotaging the Efforts of Territorial Organisation

These contradictory examples allow us to ascertain, on the basis of the henceforth classic distinction between land and sea (Mackinder,[4] Haushofer,[5] Schmitt) that Great Britain and, after it, the United States are going to systematically oppose the grand labours of organisation of routes of communication on the continental spaces. This systematic opposition is aimed at preserving the monopoly of greatest mobility in the transport of men and goods, that is, the monopoly of an exclusively marine mobility. The examples proving this fundamental hostility are abundant:

---

[3] [Frontiers of the Roman Empire.]

[4] [Sir Halford John Mackinder (1861-1947) was an English geographer and geopolitician who developed the significant geopolitical concept of the "heartland" in his 1904 speech "The geographical pivot of history" and in his 1919 work, *Democratic Ideals and Reality: A Study in the Politics of Reconstruction*, London: Constable and Co.]

[5] {See below p. 61]

In 1904, Halford John Mackinder elaborated his theory of the containment of continental powers, in particular, of Russia, because the Tsarist Empire had just realised, under the dynamic impetus of the minister Witte,[6] the trans-Siberian rail connection acquiring for this immense continental empire a mobility which permitted the rapid displacement of troops from the Baltic to the Pacific. Since the realisation of this transcontinental rail route, the Tsar was demonised in the media, Japan was raised against it, the new Japanese navy was financed in order to destroy the Russian navy off the coast of Korea (Tsushima, 1905);[7] an insidious propaganda described him as a bloody autocrat, revolts shook the big cities of the Empire orchestrated by shadowy agitators whose motivations one hardly understood since they were so vague and muddled, etc.

Blocking the Danubian Artery

From 1914 to 1918, the German and Austro-Hungarian politics aimed at organising the Balkans starting from the Danubian artery; this project was combated tacitly by Great Britain, which, as usual, manipulated the crooked French politicians agitated by sub-Voltairean pseudo-philosophers and a pathological Germanophobia in order that the people of France would be bled dry and sacrificed, theoretically, for ideological chimeras conveyed by rabble of the left and the right and, practically, for the blocking of the Danube in the interest of the thalassocratic powers. In geopolitical literature it was precisely the Frenchman, André Chéradame,[8] who expressed most clearly the war aims of

---

[6] [Count Sergei Witte (1849-1815) was a Baltic German Russian statesman who was appointed Minister of Finance in 1892 and was responsible for the industrialisation of the Russian Empire and efficient development of the Trans-Siberian railway project.]

[7] [The Battle of Tsushima was a decisive battle fought during the Russo-Japanese War (1904-05). The Japanese fleet under Admiral Togo Heihachiro destroyed the Russian under Admiral Rozhestvensky.]

[8] [André Chéradame (1871-1948) was a French journalist whose geopolitical writings warned of the dangers of German militarism and expansionism.]

England and established the bases of the Treaty of Versailles which the French politicians enslaved to the ideological follies of 1789 would demand at the top of their voice and which the British and American political strategists would support with hypocritical discretion by throwing the responsibility of the chaos in Central Europe onto France (what the appearances evidently confirmed). Chéradame demanded in this way the division of the Danubian space into as many artificial nations as possible. His historical and geopolitical demonstration implied the reduction of the Great Hungarian Haza[9] into a small enclave state without a coastline, the expulsion of Bulgaria from the Danube delta, the inordinate enlargement of Serbia towards Dalmatia and Slovenia in order to cordon off the Adriatic; the enlargement of Romania in order that it would be an ally of France (misled by the sly propaganda of the British), which controlled the delta of the great European river. The idea of dividing and blocking the course of the Danube returned at full gallop during the events of Yugoslavia in the 90s.culminating in the destruction of the bridges of Novi Sad[10] and Belgrade followed by an attempt to demonise Austria after the entry of the populist liberals of Jörg Haider[11] into the government.

From 1904 to 1915, the Oriental question arose, following the treaties of alliance between the Hohenzollern Reich (which was not the traditional Reich born after the victory of Otto over the Hungarians in 955) and the Ottoman Empire. England disapproved of the construction of a Berlin-Baghdad railway and the inauguration of air routes on the same track. The Middle East could not on any account become the backyard of a European continent regrouped around Germany and Austria-Hungary, a fortiori if this method of cooperation were to end on a coast of the Indian Ocean, the Central Ocean considered as an internal British sea.

---

[9] [Homeland.]

[10] [The second largest city of Serbia, situated on the banks of the Danube.]

[11] [Jörg Haider (1950-2008) was the leader of the Freiheitliche Partei Österreichs (Austrian Freedom Party) from 1986 and, from 2005, of his own breakaway party, the Bündnis Zukunft Österreich (Alliance for the future of Austria).

Even France, cannon-fodder reserve for the City of London, every time that Illuminist politicians directed it, underwent indirect pressures when it constructed the large-scale canal between the Atlantic (Bordeaux on the Gironde) and the Mediterranean, a work of civil engineering which ipso facto relativised the position of Gibraltar.

As regards the National Socialist Third Reich (which was not a Reich in the traditional sense of the term), it is necessary to state that the policy of constructing Autobahns, of wanting to establish a Main-Danube connection (considered as a war-signal by the London press in 1942, which published a suggestive and revealing map in this context), of establishing a first trans-Atlantic flight on a Focke-Wulf Condor in 1938 after the dramatic accident of the Zeppelin 'Hindenburg' in 1937, of preparing broad-gauge fast-train projects on the Paris-Berlin-Moscow and Munich-Vienna-Istanbul lines and of realising the plans of Friedrich II of Prussia[12] and the economist List[13] by completing the system of canals between the Elbe and the Rhine (which is in turn connected to the Meuse and the Scheldt by similar works executed in the Netherlands and Belgium) were clear provocations to the thalassocracies hostile to every organisation of communications on the continental space. Such were the objective and verifiable criteria that justified the hostility of Roosevelt and Churchill with regard to the Third Reich: the other reasons are less clear and lead to infinite speculations that obscure the debates between historians.

These works or plans permitted yesterday and a fortiori today (notably on the basis of the Delors Plan[14] which it would be good to realise) the extension of such a notion of the Reich, as the head and motor of "communications" in all of Europe and the creation

---

[12] [Friedrich II, "the Great" (1712-86), was King of Prussia from 1740 and noted for his effective reorganisation of the Prussian armies and patronage of the arts.]

[13] [Friedrich List (1789-1846) was a German economist who stressed the importance of the nation as the basis of economic development.]

[14] [Jacques Delors served as head of three European Commissions, from 1985 until 1994, and supervised the Economic and Monetary Union of the EU that was commenced in 1990.]

of the conditions for a lasting alliance with Russia and the Ukraine, rulers of the Pontic space (Black Sea). The optimal organisation of internal river and maritime routes (Black Sea and Baltic Sea) is henceforth possible in Europe ever since the digging of the Rhine-Main-Danube canal under Chancellor Helmut Kohl. Beyond the potentialities of this connection in western, central and eastern Europe, the complete mastery of the Danube, connected definitely to the Rhine and thus to the Atlantic, very logically permits the extension of the system thus created to the Pontic space and the Russian and Ukrainian rivers, to the Don and, through the Lenin Canal, to the Volga and the Caspian Sea and the revival of the geopolitical and hydropolitical system that the Roman Empire had initiated but its defeat by the Huns and its anarchic Christianisation had interrupted.

From the Proto-Iranians to the Goths

Rome and the Germans were pitted against, or allied with, one another to hold the Rhine-Danube line from the North Sea to the Black Sea. With the former organising all the territories south of this line, the latter massed in the north. The Visigoths, originating from present-day Sweden, occupied the Ukraine and the Crimea – as the Varangians[15] would do later. Since then three Indo-European imperiums were gathered around the Black Sea: the Roman, effective, the Slavo-Germanic, in gestation, and the Persian, the most ancient. The Visigoths, who acquired in the Ukraine the techniques of horse-riding bequeathed by the Scythians and, before them, the Proto-Iranians, were too soon overturned by the Huns who ruined the potential fusion of the three imperiums around the Black Sea. In this sense, Russia, if it succeeded in detaching itself totally from its Bolshevik parenthesis, would be at once the heir of the Scythians (and the Proto-Iranians), the Goths, the

---

[15] [The Varangians were Vikings who, between the 9th and the 11th centuries, ruled the Kievan Rus' federation. Some of them also served as the elite Varangian Guard of the Byzantine Army between the 10th and the 14th centuries.]

Varangians and the Persians (who, first Islamised, then crushed by the Mongols, were not able to reconnect with their deep roots – the diversion attempted by the last Shah[16] being of too brief a duration, before it was reduced to nothing by a newly confected Islamisation) even while remaining, of course, the heir of Byzantine since 1453.

Digression on the Rhône: The Rhône falls into the western basin of the Mediterranean and connects the latter to the nerve-centre of Central Europe, through Geneva; the course of the Saône and the Doubs, which leads it to the Burgundian Gate, that is, to the gap of Basel or of Belfort, close to the Rhine and not far from the source of the Danube. In this respect it has been a primordial geostrategic stake since antiquity. A state of affairs which did not escape the perspicacity of Halford John Mackinder, the founder of British military geopolitics. In his work, Democratic Ideals and Reality (last edition, 1947) he recalls the mistake of the maritime empire of Geiserich (Genseric), king of the Vandals,[17] who was not able to connect his conquests to the Rhône artery, and recounts the adventures of the Saracens who went up the Rhône, the Saône and the Doubs up to the Burgundian Gate, and finally shows the importance of the alliance between Savoy, a Rhône power, Austria and England in the Spanish war of succession.[18]

Ariovistus, Caesar, the Rhône and the Rhine

His German counterpart Hermann Stegemann,[19] author of a military history of the Rhine (*Der Kampf um den Rhein*, 1924) shows that, strategically, the system of the Rhône is connected to the system of the Rhine and that the mastery of the Rhône was the

---

[16] [Mohammed Reza Pahlavi (1919-80) was the Shah of Iran from 1941 until his overthrow by the Islamic Revolution of 1979.]

[17] [Geiseric was King of the Vandals and Alans from 428-77.]

[18] [The War of Spanish Succession lasted from 1701-14.]

[19] [Hermann Stegemann (1870-1945) was a Prussian-Swiss journalist and historian with a markedly nationalist viewpoint.]

first objective of the great Roman strategy from Marius[20] to Caesar. Master of the western Mediterranean since its victories over Carthage, Rome had to ensure a hinterland in Europe: it chose to go up the Rhône and its tributaries where, via the Doubs, it entered the course of the Upper Rhine to the east of Thann and Cernay/ Sennheim. This was the domain of Ariovistus,[21] who managed a Swedish kingdom astride the Rhine, the Doubs and the source of the Danube. The defeat of this Germanic chieftain shows that the Rhine-Rhône line (via the Doubs and the Saône) is the ideal line of penetration towards the north for every power dominating the western basin of the Mediterranean. Ever since his victory over Ariovistus, Caesar made himself master of the basin of the Seine and the Loire but left to future leaders the trouble of crossing to the right bank of the Rhine. His successors would try to unify the course of the Danube from its source to its mouth in the Black Sea: this was the great continental strategy of the Roman Empire, as important as the mastery of the Mare Nostrum.[22]

The great lesson of the Roman Empire, the organiser of communications in Europe, is still valid: Europe, in order to have an imperial structure in the good sense of the term, that is, a structure of internal organisation and not a structure permitting imperial conquests, must have, like Rome in the past, large projects of organisation which, in the economic system that rules today, mobilises workforce and revives internal consumption at the same time as it accelerates communication. Friedrich List,[23] the liberal economist, who is nevertheless claimed by a good number of non-liberal statists, recommended this type of policy in the middle of

---

[20] [Gaius Marius (157 B.C.-86 B.C.) was a Roman general who defeated the Germanic tribes of Cimbri and Teutones in 101 B.C.]

[21] [Ariostivus was the leader of the Suebi who took part in a war in Gaul (58 B.C.) in which they were defeated by Caesar.]

[22] ["Our Sea", the Roman name for the Mediterranean.]

[23] [Friedrich List (1789-1846) was a German economist who developed a system of "national economics" which stressed the importance of the nation as the basis of economics. His major work was entitled *Das nationale System der politischen Ökonomie* (1841).]

the 19th century. In our time, the Delors Plan did not receive the attention that it deserved at the European level, when it suggested the development of rapid railways and the establishment of a programme of telecommunication satellites. Similarly, Europe today does not have the imperial dimensions required today in that its navy is too weak as much on the military level – as the French admiral, Allain Coataena, regrets – as on the level of civil and oceanographic exploitation. Europe does not develop enough large projects for the exploitation of marine and oceanic resources. Quite apart from the connections between Great Britain and the continent, the coastal fleets of hover-crafts or catamarans are not developed enough in the internal seas, including the Mediterranean.

The Historical Dimensions of the Notion of Empire

At Verdun in 843,[24] the grandsons of Charlemagne shared the river basins, insofar as the rivers were at that time the only means of safe and relatively rapid communication. Charles the Bald[25] obtained the basins of the Somme, the Seine, the Loire and the Garonne, with a considerable advantage, peculiar to the Parisian basin. From Paris one can effectively unify the territory thanks to rivers like the Marne and the Oise (which served as the axis of penetration for the Frankish colonisation) and the proximity of the Loire connected to the Seine by a relatively short land route going from Paris to Orleans. This ideal position permitted a rapid centralisation of France. Lothaire[26] obtained the basins of the Rhine and the Meuse, the Rhône and the Po, at the same time as the title of 'Kaiser', in memory of Julius Caesar, who had succeeded in controlling the

---

[24] [The Treaty of Verdun divided the Carolingian Empire among the three sons of Charlemagne's son, Louis the Pious.]

[25] [Charles the Bald (823-77) was King of West Francia, King of Italy and Holy Roman Emperor from 875-77.]

[26] [Lothaire I (795-855) was King of Italy, of Lotharingia and Holy Roman Emperor from 840-55.]

west, along these axes, and in setting up the bases of the future colonisation of the Danubial space (at least its southern side). Louis the German[27] obtained the north, that is, the plain of parallel rivers not connected among themselves from the Scheldt to the Vistula. But also the mission of conquering the Danube in order to establish the Roman order there conferred by the *translatio imperii*[28] upon the Germans, who ipso facto established it in the north and the south. This Danubian mission implied also, from the 10th century, the alliance with Hungary (the ancient Roman Pannonia). The Germano-Hungarian dual alliance – the alliance of the Romano-German imperial crown and the Magyar crown of St. Stephen – would face the Ottomans who wished to conquer the Danube from the Balkans and from its mouth in order to establish the geographical unification of the Danube but not under an imperial and Roman sign but an Islamic. The Ottoman Empire wished to follow the Danubian politics of Byzantium, but without having European geographical legitimacy, the Turkish geographical legitimacy being Central Asian and the Islamic geographical legitimacy being Arabic.

The Proposal of Pius II[29]

This Ottoman ambiguity, where the Sultan was at the same time the Muslim Caliph and the heir, *volens nolens*,[30] of the Byzantine Basileus, did not escape Pope Pius II, also known as the humanist Aeneas Silvius Piccolomini, the former chancellor of the Germanic emperor Friedrich III. Pius II proposed the conversion of the Sultan to Christianity just as the Hungarians had accepted it after their defeat in 955 at the hands of the Germanic army of Otto I.[31]

---

[27] [Louis the German (810-76) was King of Bavaria and King of East Francia.]

[28] [Transfer of rule.]

[29] [Pope Pius II (1405-64) was elected pope in 1458.]

[30] [Willingly or unwillingly.]

[31] [Otto I (912-73) defeated the Magyars in the Battle of Lechfeld and was Holy Roman Emperor from 962.]

The Sultan would have then become at once the heir of Rome and of Byzantium restoring the ancient unity desired by all humanists, extending the re-established European power towards the Iranian space through the Black Sea; with the *sine qua non* condition that the Ottoman elite forget *ipso facto* – like the Hungarians of the 10th century – their pre-European and Central Asian (Turkish ethnic) geographical determination as well as their Arabic nomadic determination transmitted through Islam. This Turko-Mongol "steppe character" or this "desert character" originating in the Arabian peninsula being two matrices totally foreign to Europe, the conversion to Christianity was, in the context that concerns us, not so much the adoption of the evangelical faith as the voluntary abandonment of geopolitical dynamics other than those of the ancient Roman Empire. The Sultan did not accept Pius II's proposal, wanted to foolishly continue in his Turko-Arabic policy, which finally led nowhere after 500 years of efforts. For this reason this Turko-Arabic politics, partly lame and partly inefficient, a useless burst of intemperance and violence, cannot be considered as "sacred" in the same way as the Romano-Germanic imperium (*Sacrum Imperium*) since it ended in an impasse or permanent war (or, to borrow an Iranian and Zoroastrian conceptual model, the Romano-Germanic sacred imperium or the Persian imperium originated from Ahura Mazda, the principle of light, whereas Ottomanism originated from Ahriman, the principle of destruction and darkness, a fortiori if it were allied with the Mammonism of the Bank of England or the American economy).

The conflict between the west and the east of our continent effectively constitutes the major dynamic of our history. This conflict is played out on the Danube. The Romans identified two Danubes, the one starting from its source in the Swabian Black Forest up to its "cataracts" in the Balkans and bearing its Celtic name Danuvius, the other starting from these cataracts up to its mouth and bearing its Greek name Ister. This separation would be equally that of the two Roman empires of the east and the west. This break was based on a hydrographic fact: the break of navigation on the Danube at the "Iron Gates",[32] called "cataracts" in antiquity. The final conflicts between the two empires would have as their object both the Mediterranean and the Danube.

The Missions of Bregenz and Passau

At the time of the Christianisation of Central Europe, the Celtic (Irish-Scottish) missions setting out from Bregenz and champions of a reconciliation with the models of Byzantine monarchy entered into competition and lost to the equally Danubian missions from Passau; the latter were champions of the Roman papal supremacy and so hostile to Byzantium, in the final analysis hostile to the imperial principle of ancient Rome, which the papacy sometimes claimed, even though this constituted a dangerous imposture. The missions of Passau won their cause in Hungary in spite of the existence and persistence of a mixed zone with rites inspired by the Byzantine liturgy but of papist Roman following (Moravia, Croatia). They extended their influence to the Iron Gates. In the east, the Byzantine domination remained. In the west, the Frankish and Roman domination was solidly established. Byzantium was in a worse position because they could win this competition only if they dominated Pannonia from the Moravian border to the Adriatic. This hinge zone remained "Roman", so Rome remained the master of the game. Later, the Ottomans would be very aware of this stake; for them the domination of Europe passed equally through the mastery of Pannonia and of Croatia but the Germanic determination of the European imperium had shifted somewhat to the east the nerve-centre that would ensure this domination. Henceforth it was Vienna, which the Ottomans called the "Golden Apple", that constituted the key to the Danube. The two Ottoman attacks on the imperial capital of Europe ended in painful mistakes. That is why Europe is not Turko-Muslim today in spite of the French treachery. The second mistake at Vienna, in spite of the

---

[32] [The Iron Gates is a gorge on the Danube between Serbia and Romania.]

indecent role played by the "robber-king" Louis XIV[33] (the "king of bandits") in attacking the European imperial troops in the back to assuage the Turks, sealed the definitive decline of the Ottoman power, which stopped harming the European nations.

The Rhône, the Rhine and the Danube

The dynamic of Roman history, to repeat Stegemann's theses, or the politics of Roman territorial expansion was based, in the final analysis, on the strong control of these three river basins of Europe. The object of the Punic Wars[34] was to control the western basin of the Mediterranean, a control solidly ensured by the conquest of Sicily. The latter occupies a position between the eastern and western basins of the Mediterranean. The power that seizes them is potentially capable of controlling with little effort the two basins of the Mediterranean. The Carthaginian Punic forces had important territorial advantages with the Balearics, Spain, the Gallic tributaries in the Rhône basin (which provided excellent mercenaries) and the control of the Alpine passages permitting access to Italy. Hannibal used all these advantages but failed in Italy. After the three Punic wars, the Romans became aware that Italy is defended at the Rhône before the Alpine passes. Rome was therefore going to deploy successively four strategic plans to avoid the return of any Hannibal.

- The colonisation of Spain, which would be a process lasting very long and which would begin with the conquest of the Mediterranean coasts, the Atlantic front not being of any use at that time.

- The colonisation of Provence aiming especially at occupying the mouth of the Rhône and, slowly going up this valley as far as possible.

---

[33] [Louis XIV (1638-1715), also called "the Great", or "the Sun-King".]

[34] [Rome fought three Punic Wars with Carthage between 264 B.C. and 146 B.C.]

- Avoiding a new danger since Provence remained open to peoples not controlled in the north, Gauls or Germans (with the arrival of the Cimbri[35] and the Teutons[36] first, and the Swedes of Ariovistus later).

- Intervening to protect these allies, especially when Ariovistus attacked the Helvetii who sought refuge among the Sequani of Franche-Comté, allies of Rome.

The Basel Gap or the Burgundian Gate[37]

Caesar was therefore obliged to stop the breach through which the Germans, following the Swedes of Ariovistus, could rush into the badly organised territory of the Gauls and thus threaten Provence more seriously than the Cimbri and Teutons had done in the past during the time of Marius. In this campaign against Ariovistus (himself very aware of the hydrographical and geographical stake of the Gallic region that he occupied in the Vosges and on the course of the Doubs, almost up to Besançon. Caesar took into consideration the entire geographical and hydrographical layout of the European hinterland of the western basin of the Mediterranean. Logically, the presence of Ariovistus' troops in the Doubs valley showed Caesar that Provence could be held only if the entire Rhône valley were secured for the benefit of the west Mediterranean empire of Rome, but this very Rhône valley was secure only if the Basel Gap and the Belfort Gap (the Burgundian Gate) were sealed off against the Germans. But to seal the Burgundian Gate well it was necessary to control the Rhine downstream up-to the North Sea. Therefore

---

[35] [The Cimbri were Gallic or Germanic tribes allied with the Teutons in their battles against Rome between 113 B.C. and 101 B.C.]

[36] [The Teutones were a Germanic tribe originating from southern Scandinavia. They were defeated by Gaius Marius at the Battle of Aquae Sextiae, near Aix-en-Provence, in 102 B.C.]

[37] [The Burgundian Gate, also called the Belfort Gap, is a plateau that divides the drainage basin of the Rhine in the east from that of the Rhône in the west.]

Caesar determined very quickly that the Rhine and the Rhône are connected to each other, strategically speaking. Similarly, the Rhône basin gives access, through its principal tributary the Saône, to the Langrès Plateau through which the line of the division of the waters passes and where the Atlantic Seine, as well as the Meuse, has its source. The control of the Rhône implied that of the Saône, which, in turn, implied that of the Seine and its tributaries. Furthermore, the Seine gave access to the English Channel from where the tin of Cornwall came; the control of the Seine implied also the control of the south of Britain. Which Caesar attempted to do and his successors completed.

After Caesar, the proximity of the sources of the Danube and the Burgundian Gate showed that the conquest of the Rhône from Provence led to the necessity of conquering the Rhine and to the opportunity of controlling the Danube. This process was initiated by Augustus[38] and then completed by Trajan,[39] who conquered Dacia (present-day Romania).

Caesar's Strategy is Still Valid

All this is not ancient history. Caesar's strategy was adapted during the Second World War; apparently the English and American strategists did not just follow the advice of their best geopolitician Mackinder but also absorbed the magisterial study of Stegemann. The landing in Provence on 15 August 1944 allowed the Allied troops to quickly seize the Rhône valley only to run into a fierce German resistance at the top of the Burgundian Gate in exactly the same place where Ariovistus had given battle to Caesar. The victory of the Franco-Moroccan and American troops in the Alsatian Vosges led the Allies to seize the Burgundian Gate and the Upper Rhine and then to cross the latter in the direction of the source of the Danube in the Black Forest, in Swabian country ("Swabian"

---

[38] [Augustus (63 B.C.-14 A.D.) was the first Roman Emperor.]

[39] [Trajan (53-117) was Roman Emperor from 98.]

being derived from 'Swedish'', Ariovistus' tribe).[40] The campaign begun with the landing in Provence up to the seizure of Belfort at the end of 1944 is a modern adaptation of Caesar's campaign against Ariovistus.

Unifying the Basins of the Rhône, the Rhine and the Danube

This double historic reference to the conflict that Caesar opposed to Ariostivus and then to the campaign that followed the landing in Provence in August 1944 allows us to understand the geopolitical necessity of unifying the three basins of the Rhine, the Danube and the Rhône as much as possible, or the North Sea (and the Baltic through the new canals of northern Europe), the western Mediterranean and the Black Sea in order that the future European Union may remain master of the large routes of communication in the interior of the lands itself without the possible intervention of a maritime power external to our sub-continent. This necessity should lead us to condemn decisively the obstruction posed by the French Greens, including Mme. Voynet,[41] to the digging of a large-scale canal between the Rhine and the Rhône. Such a criminal and abject political manoeuvre can benefit only the worst enemies of Europe. And was, in the final analysis, certainly "inspired" by them.

In this Roman and Imperial perspective the long war between Austria-Hungary and the Ottomans was also a struggle for the Danube, thus, according to our reasoning, to reinclude the Black Sea in the European sphere, and make it an internal sea without interference, that is, without the intrusion of a geographical dynamic whose starting point would not be European, would not be situated on the line that starts from Denmark (the Scandza

---

[40] [The Swabians, in fact, formed part of the Irminones (east Elbe Germans) and were later equated with the Alemanni.]

[41] [Dominique Voynet (1958-) is a member of the Green movement in France. She was Minister for the Environment in the government of Lionel Jospin between 1997 and 2001, member of the European Parliament from 1989-91 and mayor of Montreuil from 2008-14.]

island, matrix of the nations for the Romans)[42] and ends in Sicily including the space located between Vienna and Budapest. Europe must annul the effects of any external geographical dynamic having as its starting point a badly defined space located beyond the Aral Sea or Lake Baikal (the Turkish or pan-Turanian perspective), or the centre of the Arabian peninsula (the Arabo-Muslim perspective), in the Black Sea, an internal sea, or in the eastern Mediterranean. None of these dynamics can benefit the European sub-continent, can have any *Wachstumspitze* (point of growth, to repeat the vocabulary of Karl Haushofer) within the orbit of the European world, that is, in all the territories which once formed part of the Roman Empire.

The Permanence of Telluric Facts and "Long History"

The mediaeval Hansa[43] extended over the territory of the great northern European plain where parallel rivers flow, at that time not connected to one another. In order to derive an advantage from them, the Hansa had the genius to organise the internal seas of the north (North Sea, Baltic Sea) by taking the merchandise of the interior of the continent from the ports at the mouths to distribute it in the periphery. This view remains valid.

Conclusion: this panorama of historico-geographical facts should lead us to comprehend the permanence of telluric facts, the foundation of "long history" (Braudel).[44] Every viable empire should be borne by men capable of always bearing in mind the permanent factors of this "long history", for no empire can survive

---

[42] [Scandza was the term used by the Gothic historian Jordanes (5th century A.D.) for the Scandinavian home of the Goths.]

[43] [The League of Hansa was a commercial and defensive confederation of merchant guilds that extended along the coast of Northern Europe from the 13th to the 17th centuries.]

[44] [Fernand Braudel (1902-85) was a French historian who stressed the importance of the *"longue durée"*, or continuity, of deep socio-economic and cultural structures in historical development.]

without such a "spatial memory". Today we will have again an "empire" in Europe, an imperial (*reichisch*) system if we optimise our systems of communication (especially the telecommunication satellites), if we succeed in directly perceiving the manoeuvres of obstruction posed by corrupt politicians and combat them immediately and pitilessly. If we had such an attitude, if we had this "spatial memory", we would never have swallowed the American war against Serbia and, ipso facto, the Euro would not have devalued as a result of this war, which was a catastrophe for Europe that the false elites that govern it today did not even notice.

The Political Principles of Every "Reich"

First, it is necessary to specify that a "Reich" is not a nation, even if it is borne in theory by a "populus" (the *populus romanus*) or a "nation" (the *Deutsche Nation*). Erik von Kuehnelt-Leddihn[45] has shown us very well the difference between "Reich" and "nation"; if his position is not a nationalist one, and even anti-nationalist, it has nothing against sentiments of nationalist stamp, against the pride in belonging to a nation. Such sentiments are positive, he writes, but should be transcended by an idea. This transcendence leads to a verticality that is opposed to all modern forms of horizontality, which is, besides, the main idea, the ideal crux, of all traditions, as Julius Evola also stresses. But this traditional and vertical idea sometimes forgets the depth of the soil: by taking this soil into consideration we say that there is no Uranian verticality without Chthonic depth. To resume briefly the traditional position of Erik Kuehnelt-Leddihn: let us say that the modern horizontalities do not permit respect for the Other, the other being. If the Other is judged to be a disturbance, inopportune in his alterity, he can be purely and simply eliminated or brought to heel without the least respect for his alterity, for horizontality makes everybody

---

[45] [Erik, Ritter von Kuehnelt-Leddihn (1909-99) was an Austrian aristocrat whose major anti-democratic works include *The Menace of the Herd*, 1943, and *Liberty or Equality*, 1952.]

an "ontological nothing" deprived of intrinsic value. This is the culmination of the egalitarian logic typical of ideologies and systems that have sought to usurp and eradicate the "reichisch" tradition: if everything is worth everything in the interior of man, or even in his physical constitution, that signifies finally that nothing has specific value any more, and if a specific value seeks to point against everything it will quickly be considered as an anomaly which demands extermination, the fanatic and bloody intervention of "infernal columns". Verticality, on the contrary, implies the duty of protection and respect, a duty to serve superiors and a duty of the superiors to protect the inferiors in a relationship comparable to that which exists in, traditional societies and families, between parents and children. Verticality respects ontological and cultural differences, it does not consider them as "nothings" that deserve neither consideration nor respect.

Servants of the Empire from All the Nations

In an empire diverse communities coexist and, consequently – given the important territorial extent of every empire – diverse peoples whom one does not intend to fuse into an insipid and indifferentiated magma. Empires are generally multi-ethnic. This was the case of the Austro-Hungarian monarchy, the last bearer of the Romano-Germanic imperium, where men of all ethnic origins served, not only the Austrians and the Hungarians but also southern Slavs such as General Bosoiev, and then, during the Second World War, the general of Croatian origin, Rendulic,[46] who was the last to surrender his weapons. During the Thirty Years' War,[47] the Brabantian T'Serclaes, Count of Tilly[48]

---

[46] [Lothar Rendulic (1887-1971) was a general in the Wehrmacht during the Second World War.]

[47] [The Thirty Years' War began as a war between Protestant and Catholic states and lasted from 1618 to 1648.]

[48] [T'Serclaes, Count of Tilly (1559-1648) was a Catholic nobleman born in Brabant (now Belgium) who served as commander of the Catholic League forces in Bavaria during the Thirty Years' War.]

commanded the Bavarian army and later the entire imperial army; his statue still stands in the Feldherrnhalle in Munich; the Lombard Montecuccoh similarly served imperial Austria, not to mention the most illustrious of Savoyards, Prince Eugène.[49] In Russia, the generals were often Germans or Germans from the Baltic countries, including Rennenkampf,[50] who invaded eastern Prussia in 1914. The minister Witte was of Flemish or Dutch origin, Xavier de Maistre, Joseph's brother,[51] similarly had command in the Tsar's army to fight against the Revolutionary and Bonapartist insanities. The Liégeois later founded the Russian armaments factory of which the Nagant pistols are remembered. In Belgium, where the imperial system was maintained up to 1918, where the second Jacobin offensive defeated the secular traditions, the army of 1914 was commanded, in Africa, by a Dane, Colonel Olsen, and, in the country, by Jungbluth, Rhénan, and Bernheim, a Viennese of Jewish origin.

True Multiculturalism and Genocidal Multiculturalism

An empire is thus made up of multiplicities, differences, which have nothing in common with the false multiculturalism boasted of by the media of today. This multiculturalism, an ideological fraud, derives precisely from this horizontality that aims at robbing everybody, indigenous and foreign, of their ontological substance. This multiculturalism kills the essence that lives in man. All politics that seeks to promote it is a criminal genocidal politics in

---

[49] [Prince Eugène of Savoy (1663-1736) was a French general of the Imperial Army of the Holy Roman Emperor who distinguished himself militarily in several European wars.]

[50] [Paul von Rennenkampf (1854-1918) was a Russian general who served in the Imperial Russian Army.]

[51] [Xavier de Maistre (1763-1852) was the younger brother of Joseph de Maistre (1753-1821), the monarchist philosopher, and served briefly in the Tsar's army shortly after his brother was appointed Piedmont-Sardinia's ambassador to the court of Tsar Alexander I in 1803.]

the sense in which it was understood by the American philosopher Thompson. This multiculturalism, a public mask to have modern genocide accepted, must be opposed by the imperial verticality or the sublime idea of Herder, who saw in Europe a "community of historically interconnected ethnic personalities." Following these reflections of Herder on European diversity, the geographical centrality of Germany, still divided, made it – for the Romantics who moved from the Revolutionary and Enlightenment ideal to the ideal of a physical Restoration beyond the abstract and disembodied geometrisms of Jacobinism – the perfect sacrum imperium divided territorially over the Roman, Slavic and Scandinavian peoples and alone suited, through this fact, to allow a European synthesis to blossom and thrive.

Following these two batteries of arguments, the first of an organisational and territorial sort and the second of a philosophical and ethical, it seems to me opportune, before concluding, to pose two important questions:

- What category of men can embody the "Reich"?
- How did such a category of men emerge within European humanity?

The category of men capable of embodying a "Reich" was born from the Persian tradition, which was for a long time an "Orient" (a model by which one "oriented" oneself), but this fact of history and tradition is no longer considered at its full value. In the Persian tradition there is an "eternal winter", a very probable allusion to the beginning of a particularly severe glacial age that surprised the first European peoples in their first habitation. At the time that this "eternal winter" arrived a heroic king, Rama, gathered together the tribes and clans and travelled to the south, towards the Caucasus, Bactriana and Persia (the Iranian high plateaus). This heroic king established castes or, more precisely, the functions that George Dumézil later studied.[52] After having led his people to a good

---

[52] [Georges Dumézil (1898-1986) was a leading French scholar of comparative philology and mythology who focused on the tripartite division of ancient Indo-European societies.]

destination in order to avoid the rigours of this "eternal winter", Rama retired to the mountains. This heroic and royal figure is found in the Avestan and Vedic, where he is called Yama or Yima.[53]

In order to conduct this expedition and this migration, Rama-Yama-Yima used horses and chariots and in this way provided the first organisational principles of a cavalry, principles which remained the privilege of these clans and tribes who mixed to form the Iranian people (Persian or Parthian) of antiquity. Later, Zarathustra (Zoroaster) codified the rules which every knight should follow. The codification properly was the work of his disciple Gathas.[54] Zarathustra's troop, which oversaw the adherence to his practical instruction, was armed with clubs (the "Clave" in the work of Julius Evola). At the top of the troop of Zarathustra's adepts was the caste of warriors, the *kshatriyas* of the Indian tradition, an active caste anchored in political and geographical reality which dominated the caste of priests, contemplative and less inclined to exercise a rigorous discipline over itself.

A Simple and Rigorous Ideal

From the ranks of the kshatriyas emerged the kings, which implies, right from the start of the Indo-European tradition of Iran, the domination (championed by Evola) of the active man over the contemplative man. The Iranian figure of the Sraosha[55] – who produced the St. Michael[56] of mediaeval tradition – operated

---

[53] [This identification of Rāma with Yama/Yima is erroneous. Ram in the Avestan 'Ram Yasht' is a storm-god, the stormy aspect of the solar force, while Yama is an original macro-anthropomorphic form of this force as a Cosmic Man (cf. Alexander Jacob, *Ātman: A Reconstruction of the Solar Cosmology of the Indo-Europeans*, Hildesheim: Georg Olms, 2005, Chs. 14,25]

[54] [*Gathas* (=songs) is the name given to seventeen hymns of the liturgical Yasna, which is part of the greater Zoroastrian Avesta.]

[55] [Sraosha is a sacred being or 'yazata' who represents Obedience (to Conscience).]

[56] [St. Michael, derived from the Old Testament archangel Michael, is a defender of the Catholic Church, just as Sraosha is also a guardian of mankind.]

between heaven and earth, that is, between tradition and reality, which necessitated a rigorous training like that of the disciples of Zarathustra. The latter, as the Iranian tradition was consolidated, were trained to render their thought clearly, to purify their feelings, to consider their duty. Armed with these three cardinal directive principles, the disciples of Zarathustra fought against Ahriman, the incarnation of Evil, that is, of the corruption of feelings which renders one unsuited to work constructively and lastingly in the real world. Only the knights capable of embodying this simple but rigorous ideal would be endowed with a charisma, a radiance, a light, a *kwaranah*. They were bound to one another through an oath.

In 53 B.C., when the Parthian troops of Surena[57] confronted the legions of the triumvir Crassus, a contemptible figure on account of his cupidity and greed for gold, the Romans were horrified – if they were decadent like Crassus[58] – or fascinated – if they still had a feeling for the State – by this rigour. During the long struggle between Romans and Parthians, elements of this Iranian military spirituality were slowly distilled into the western world, especially when some Indo-Iranian cavalries like the Sarmatian cataphracts[59] or the Alans[60] cavalries placed themselves in the service of Rome. The Goths, arriving from Scandinavia, discovered in their turn this kshatriya spirituality when they burst into the Crimea, into Scythian space. They took the traditions and techniques of the mounted peoples of the Pontic zone and introduced them into the Germanic world. The god Odin, with his steed, transmitted some Iranian elements and Loki, a trickster god, inherited traits borrowed from the Persian Ahriman.

---

[57] [Surena (died 53 B.C.) was a Parthian general who defeated the Romans at the Battle of Carrhae in 53 B.C.]

[58] [Marcus Crassus (115 B.C.-53 B.C.) was a Roman general and one of the wealthiest of Romans. His army was defeated at the Battle of Carrhae by the Parthians.]

[59] [Armoured heavy cavalry units used by the peoples of the Eurasian steppe such as the Scythians and Sarmatians.]

[60] [The Alans or Alani were a Scytho-Sarmatian tribe originating in the Caucasus. Their name is an East Iranian variant of Āryan.]

The Iranian Tradition Arrives in Europe Through the Crusades

Among the Franks, the battle-axe, the *framée*,[61] from Clovis (Chlodwig) to the Crusades, implies a transmitted military art, but the west does not yet have a cavalry on the Iranian model. The Franks had at their disposal a militia but not yet a cavalry according to the criteria of later periods. In the course of the Crusades, when the Frankish and Germanic troops entered into contact with the Persian (Islamic) and Armenian (Christian) cavalries, heirs of the traditions of ancient Iran, they progressively reconnected with the lost heritage of the Indo-European east that the Avestan tradition represents, still surviving in spite of the Islamic pseudo-conversion. The *fotowwat* (service, cavalry, youth) of Iran is a transposition of the ancient heritage into an Islamic framework. Jean Tourniac,[62] disciple of Guénon, in his work Lumière d'Orient, explains the progression that led from this cavalry of Iran, whose origins were Zoroastrian and participated in a cult of Light, to the western and Templar cavalries that were constituted in the wake of the Crusades.

The mediaeval cavalry was at once military, medical, and managed a banking system in order that the economic activity be equally imbued with a luminous ethics deriving in the final analysis – going back through the chain of avatars – from the same Iranian and Zoroastrian matrix, originating from the first Indo-European peoples who moved into present-day Persia. Traditional Iran, in spite of its superficial Islamisation, was destroyed later by the Mongols. It was never able to recover from that and could never become an "Orient" again. In the book by Henry Corbin,[63] the greatest French Iranologist and Islamologist of the 20th century, we find more than one homage to the Islamised Persian philosopher

---

[61] [A Frankish lance.]

[62] [Jean Tourniac (pseudonym of Jean Granger) (1919-95) was a specialist in Freemasonry and the works of René Guénon (1886-1951). His work *Lumière d'Orient: Des Chrétientés d'asie Aux Mystères Évangéliques* was published in 1979.]

[63] [Henry Corbin (1903-78) was professor of Islamic Studies at the 'École pratique des hautes études' in Paris.]

Suhrawardi,[64] who, reservoir of the original Iranian wisdom, rebelled, just before the destruction of his country by the Mongols, against bigotry, the restrictive rationalism which is its corollary, and demanded a return to a noble, luminous, archangelic and St. Michael-like attitude which is nothing but the Persian/Avestan tradition of the most remote origins. Sohrawardi demanded a revolt against the caste of restrictive priests and consequently against all thoughts and behaviour implying sterile limits. This attitude always seemed suspicious to the caste of priests or intellectuals interested to impose frozen ideas on the populations that were subjected to them, in the west as well as in the east. Arthur de Gobineau,[65] who is reproached for a Nordicism that is judged to be a caricature and a direct ancestor of Nazism, was the first in Europe to draw the attention of the Europeans of his time to the luminous past of ancient Persia, in his eyes a more fecund model than Greece, which was too intellectual and too speculative. The chivalrous model, whose origins go back to Rama and Zarathustra, entails a practice of the mastery of oneself that is superior, for Gobineau, to the intellectual speculation of the Athenians. And, in fact, when Persia was devastated by the Mongols, Islam as a whole began to decline. Wahhabi fundamentalism is the expression of this decadence insofar as it is an extreme, caricature reaction to the decline of Islam, henceforth deprived of the great Light of Persia – the poor Wahhabi masquerade, of course, never being able to serve as an "Orient".

The "New Imperial Chancellory", According to Carl Schmitt

If the model of the Persian and Armenian cavalry were able to constitute a model for Europe, a traditional working model without

---

[64] [Suhrawardi (1154-91) was the Persian founder of Islamic Illuminationism, which drew on Zoroastrian and Platonic concepts. The second volume of Corbin's *En Islam Iranien: Aspects Spirituels et Philosophiques*, Paris: Gallimard, 1971 was devoted to Sohrawardi et les platoniciens de la Perse.]

[65] [Arthur, Count de Gobineau (1816-82) was a French aristocrat whose famous anthropological work, *Essai Sur l'inégalité des Races Humaines*, was published in 1853-55.]

equal of a "kshatriya" type or "kshatriya" leadership, it cannot be conceived outside the plan of the "new European imperial chancellory" formulated by Carl Schmitt. The latter stressed the necessity of forming an authority of this type, after the catastrophes which struck Europe in the first half of the 20th century, and of preparing the Renaissance that would follow the subjugation of our sub-continent. This chancellory should be based on three groups of ideas:

1. The law, according to the historical school founded by Savigny,[66] where the law is included within a well-mastered historic continuity permitting the continuance of the concrete orders of society.

2. The economy, deriving from the historical school of Rodbertus[67] and, more specifically, based on the corpus bequeathed to us by Schmoller.[68]

3. The rediscovery of the founding tradition deriving from the researches of Bachofen[69] which had an influence on Julius Evola, defender of the "kshatriya" principles, and on Georges Dumézil, who clearly underlined the functions of the traditional Indo-European societies including, of course, the "kshatriya". In the work of Kantorowicz,[70] who

---

[66] [Friedrich Carl von Savigny (1779-1861) was a German jurist and historian who belonged to the historical school of jurisprudence initiated by Gustav von Hugo (1764-1844).]

[67] [Johann Rodbertus (1805-75) was a German economist who founded the conservative school of socialism.]

[68] [Gustav von Schmoller (1838-1917) was a leading member of the Prussian historical school of economics.]

[69] [Johann Jakob Bachofen (1815-87) was a Swiss jurist, philologist and anthropologist one of whose major works was a study of ancient matriarchal society, *Das Mutterrecht: Eine Untersuchung Über die Gynaikokratie der Alten Welt Nach Ihrer Religiösen und Rechtlichen Natur*. 1861.]

[70] [Ernst Kantorowicz (1895-1963) was German Jewish historian famous for his 1927 study, *Kaiser Friedrich der Zweite*, on the Holy Roman Emperor Friedrich of Hohenstaufen (1194-1250).]

rehabilitated in a particularly brilliant manner the figure of the Emperor Friedrich II of Hohenstaufen, we find equally a thread that will lead us to the true Persian/Avestan "Orient" which has nothing to do with the "Orients", small or large, of the criminal and restrictive parodies that led Europe to its fall. The study of the itinerary of Friedrich II leads us inevitably to the active spirituality of the warlike and hospitable Germanic knights and the Armenian and Iranian models encountered during the Crusades, especially through the brilliant personality of Saladin,[71] a Kurdish prince.

The study of this vast domain of traditions is a colossal work, especially if one combines with it the exact study of our own geographical framework (a necessity if one wishes to know the land that our "Reich" must fecundate). A colossal work which we should conduct without ever flinching, up-to our last breath, as Marc Eemans,[72] explorer of the Persian Orient, Germanic traditions and the mysticism of Flanders and the Rhineland, has shown us. But the call of the arch-angelic Light of St. Michael is an imperative which we cannot avoid lest we commit an unpardonable treason particularly against ourselves.

---

[71] [Saladin (Salāh ad-Din) (1137-93) was the first Sultan of Egypt and Syria and founder of the Ayyubid dynasty. He was the leader of the Muslim forces against the Crusaders.]

[72] [Marc Eemans (1907-98) was a Belgian painter and art historian who began as a Surrealist and later moved to a symbolic-mystical style.]

VISIONS OF EUROPE IN THE NAPOLEONIC ERA ON THE SOURCES OF CONTEMPORARY EUROPEISM[73]

The visions of a unified and autarkic Europe do not date from Locarno[74] and Aristide Briand,[75] nor from the Second World War, nor from the founding fathers of the European Communities. They have had antecedents from the age of the philosophy of the Enlightenment. A good number of conceptions were specified in the Napoleonic era.

Europe in the view of the Enlightenment is:

- A space of "civilisation" and "good taste".

- A civilisation marked by decline and maladaptation (due to rising industrialisation).

- A civilisation where reason is in decline.

- A civilisation marked by Gallomania and destabilised by the national reactions to this omnipresent Gallomania.

---

[73] Taken from a talk given at the summer university of "Synergies européenes", Lourmarin, 1995.

[74] [The Locarno Treaties were negotiated between 5-16 October 1925 to secure the post-war territorial arrangements between the Allied powers and Germany.]

[75] [Aristide Briand (1862-1932) was French Prime Minister between 1909 and 1929. He was, along with the German foreign minister, Gustav Stresemann, awarded the Nobel Peace Prize in 1926 for his role in the Locarno Treaties.]

The philosophers of the Enlightenment already considered Europe to be stuck between Russia and America. They were divided into Russophiles and Russiphobes. All however considered America as a New Europe begun on the other side of the Atlantic and where multiple opportunities were waiting to be cultivated.

The Enlightenment and Herder[76]

Within the framework of the Enlightenment and the ubiquitous Gallomania, Herder developed a critical vision of the intellectual situation in Europe and reflected deeply on the significance of the historical individuality of collective constructions, the fruits of long maturation defined and fashioned over time. He posited the bases of a positive critique of Gallomania as an artificial cult of imitated Greco-Roman styles to the exclusion of all others, particularly of the mediaeval Gothic. Rousseau agreed with this view and saw history as a harmonious dialectic between the nations and the world but esteemed that Europe in decline, behind the neo-classical façades of the 18th century, was morally condemnable because it was perverse and corrupt. Herder wished to re-establish more rooted popular cultures, revive autochthonous cultures which the processes of urbanisation and rationalisation typical of civilisation had marginalised or thwarted. For him Europe was a family of nations (of peoples). Contrarily to Rousseau, he esteemed that Europe is not condemnable in itself but that it should consolidate itself and not export to Russia and America an abstract Europeism with a Greco-Roman veneer, the expression of a rootless artificiality permitting all manner of manipulations and engendering despotism. Herder knew Europe physically and sensually having travelled from Riga to Nantes, peregrinations about which he has left us a diary teeming with observations

---

[76] [Johann Herder (1744-1803) was a German philosopher who stressed the relationship between language and cultural tradition and encouraged democratic, or *völkisch,* nationalist thought in Germany.]

relating to the attitudes of the 18th century. He compares in detail the regional cultures of the countries that he travelled through, poses a series of diagnostics combining assessments of decline with hopes of recovery – the recovery of a people through the resurrection of their language, their traditions and the roots of their literature. On the basis of this lived experience he wished to make of the Baltic countries, his homeland, and the Ukraine (along with the Crimea) the workshop of a renovated Europe which would be respectful of both the classical Greek models (but especially Homeric; Herder fully rehabilitates Homeric Greece providing an impetus to later philological researches) and faithful to its non-Greek and non-Roman, mediaeval and barbarian (Slavic and Germanic) ones.

This renovated Europe will be forged by the intervention of a new system of education much more attentive than its predecessors to the most ancient roots, of legal entities, of the law, the physical history of peoples, etc. In this sense, the Europe hoped for by Herder must be not a society of states constituted of persons but a "community of national personalities".

After the troubles and upheavals of the French Revolution, after Napoleon's accession to power, many European political observers began to view Europe as a "Continental Bloc" (Bertrand de Jouvenal published a work on this subject).[77] With the continental blockade the idea of a European economic autarky progressively took shape. It has had especially French proponents but also many German partisans like Dalberg,[78] Krause[79] or the poet Jean Paul[80]

[77] [Bertrand de Jouvenal (1903-87) was a French political economist and sociologist who wrote several books on politics and economics and was one of the founders, along with Friedrich Hayek and Jacques Rueff, of the Mont Pelerin Society for free-market economy and the 'open society'.]

[78] [Karl Theodor von Dalberg (1744-1817) was Archbishop of Mainz and he supported Napoleon's policies as the "Prince primate" of the newly formed Confederation of the Rhine.]

[79] [Karl Christian Krause (1781-1832) was a German philosopher whose system was called 'panentheism', a combination of pantheism and monotheism. He had a strong influence on Spanish political thought in the 19th century.]

[80] [Jean Paul (Johann Paul Richter) (1763-1825) was a German Romantic novelist who also wrote several essays on political subjects.]

(whose direct descendant in the 20th century would be another poet Rudolf Pannwitz).[81]

Baron von Aretin

Johann Adam, Freiherr von Aretin (1733-1824), a Bavarian, considering himself to have a Celtic heritage, was a partisan of Napoleon in whom he saw a champion of Romanism and Catholicism against Prussianism, Anglicism and Protestantism. However, the German Protestants in turn developed a pro-Napoleonic Europe not in the name of an ideological mixture of Celticism, Romanism and Catholicism, but in the name of the Protestant ideal, which consists in systematically opposing all universal powers as the British thalassocratic is understood to be. Protestantism, in this view, was raised formerly against the universalist pretensions of the Roman Church; it is raised today no longer against the Revolution and the Napoleonic Code but against the economic universalism of English thalassocracy. This ideal, at once Protestant and European, was essentially found in the mercantile bourgeoisie of North Germany (Bremen, Hamburg, and also Antwerp). For this category of men it was a question of breaking the English monopolies and replacing them with European monopolies (they prefigure in this way the theories of the economist List). The objective was the development of an autochthonous European industry capable of being developed without the competition of colonial English products sold at low prices.

---

[81] [Rudolf Pannwitz (1881-1969) was a German philosopher and poet who was influenced by Nietzsche and Stefan George.] Cf. Robert Steuckers, "Mort de la Terre: Imperium europæum et conservation créatrice», in *Nouvelles de Synergies Européennes,* n°19, April 1996.

The Memorandum of Theremin[82]

Among the other German theoreticians of Continental European autarky and independence we may cite the Prussian Theremin, who, in his memorandum of 1795 (*On the Interests of the Continental Powers in Relation to England*), declared that England colonised Europe and India commercially and that it constituted in this manner a maritime despotism. (Theremin is clearly a precursor of the geopolitician Haushofer). After 1815, many German theoreticians felt a clear nostalgia for continental autarky. Thus, Welcker pleaded for a Franco-Prussian alliance "in order to organise Europe". Glave, for his part, advocated a Franco-Austrian alliance to exclude Russia and the Ottoman Empire from Europe. Buchholz,[83] in *Der neue Leviathan* (*The New Leviathan*) pleaded for a European unification in order to confront "thalassocratic universalism". Bülow wished to promote a "universal European monarchy" which would have as its goal the conquest of England in order that it may cease to harm the interests of the continent and formulated a "cultural project" of Europeist inspiration in order to neutralise the inconsistencies and centrifugal pressures which local nationalisms generate.

The Count d'Hauterive[84]

The French theoreticians of European autarky in the Napoleonic era definitively abandoned orientalising exotic Romanticism after

---

[82] Karl Theremin was a legation councillor at the Prussian embassy in London. His essay "Des Interets des Puissances Continentales Relativement a l'Angleterre" was published in Paris.

[83] [Friedrich Buchholz (1768-1843) was a socialist who championed the doctrines of August Comte and Saint-Simon. His work *Der neue Leviathan* was published in 1805.]

[84] [Alexandre, Comte d'Hauterive (1754-1830) was a French diplomat who worked in the foreign office and sometimes served as temporary minister of foreign affairs. He wrote *De l'Etat de la France à la fin de l'an VIII* (= 1800) on Napoleon's orders as a manifesto to foreign nations.]

the double failure of the military operations of Napoleon in Egypt and Palestine. From now on the protagonists of the continent argued in exclusively "European", that is, to use an anachronism, "Eurocentric" terms. Reviving the "Testament of Richelieu" in the imperial France of Napoleon, these visionary Frenchmen of the future Europe made France in their plans the basis of continental unification. Against England and its ubiquitous and powerful navy a blockade should be organised, Europe should be closed to English commerce and this closure should be made a "universal system".

Thus the Count d'Hauterive wrote in his work *On the State of France at the End of Year VIII (=1800)* that the ideal for France in Europe had been the situation of 1648 but that this situation had subsequently been overturned by the rise of Prussia and Russia and by the naval dominance of England. France was interested to counter the rise in power of these three factors. Nevertheless, after the Revolutionary wars, a new situation emerged: the Continent as a whole henceforth confronted the sea dominated by England, thanks notably to the victories of Nelson in the Mediterranean (Abukir and Trafalgar). In this context, France was no longer simply a part of Europe opposed to other parts but the hegemon of the continent, the driving force of the new Continental European entity. D'Hauterive, whose ideology was not at all revolutionary, explicitly adopted a Carolingian perspective equally opposed to Protestantism in Europe.

In the camp that was hostile to Napoleon and the hegemony of France people generally championed a "balance of powers", the keystone of the conservative diplomacy of the time. Every state should limit itself, wrote authors like Martens, von Gentz[85] or Ancillon.[86] If the states do not limit themselves, do not control their power and their propensities to expand, the European whole

---

[85] [Friedrich von Gentz (1764-1832) was a German anti-Napoleonic statesman who was appointed in 1802, by the Austrian emperor Franz I, as imperial councillor in Vienna and served as adviser to Metternich and secretary to the Congress of Vienna (1814-15).]

[86] [Friedrich Ancillon 1767-1837) was a Prussian statesman and historian who wrote several works on political philosophy.]

will undergo decline as a consequence of incessant wars exhausting the vitality of the peoples. For these Prussian conservatives it was necessary to elaborate a system of counter-forces and counterpoises (which, contrary to their goodwill, would prove to be productive of war at the beginning of the 20th century). The camp of the anti-Napoleon Europeists was diverse: we find there monarchists of the *ancien régime*, representatives of the peasantry (hostile to the Napoleonic Code and to some of its legal rules), purist Republicans (who see in Bonapartism a return to monarchical forms), representatives of the fraction of the bourgeoisie hurt by the blockade, Revolutionaries disappointed because the ideal of fraternity was not incarnated in Europe.

Fichte, Arndt, Jahn

In this context, the Romantics, among them Novalis,[87] Müller[88] and the Schlegel brothers,[89] recommended a return to mediaeval Christianity, that is, a return to an ideal before the fracture of the Reformation and the Counter-Reformation which they believed capable of overcoming the cruel internal divisions of Europe. The (German) nationalists like Fichte and Jahn[90] were republicans

[87] [Novalis (pseudonym of Georg Philipp Freiherr von Hardenberg) (1772-1801) was German Romantic poet and philosopher. His speech "Die Christenheit oder Europa" (1799), written in response to the French Revolution, called for a return to Christianity as the basis of a new Europe of unity and freedom.]

[88] [Adam Müller (1779-1829) was a political economist who opposed the materialist liberalist economic doctrines of Adam Smith and presented a mediaevalist vision of the state in his *Elemente der Staatskunst* (1809).]

[89] [August Wilhelm Schlegel (1767-1845) was a German poet and translator of Shakespeare as well as of the *Bhagavad Gita* into German. His brother Karl Wilhelm Schlegel (1772-1829) was a philologist and Indologist who also wrote political essays such as "Signatur des Zeitalters" (Signature of the Age) (1820), in which he advocated an organic Christian corporatist state.]

[90] [Friedrich Ludwig Jahn (1778-1852) was a German gymnastics teacher who developed a *Turnverein* (Gymnastics Association) movement in order to strengthen the sense of nationalism among the youth after the humiliation that Prussia had suffered at the hands of Napoleon in 1806.]

hostile to the French form of the Revolution but equally as hostile to a pure and simple restoration of the ancien régime. For Fichte, Arndt[91] and Jahn Prussia was a simple but very efficient instrument for forging a new and powerful German nation. Fichte was a voluntarist: the voluntary constitution of national state systems would lead to a universal *telos*,[92] to a world organised according to as many different modalities as there are nations. Universal harmony would arrive when every national space had obtained, to its own degree, the structure of a state. In this sense, Fichtean universalism was not monolithic but pluralistic. For these nationalists the nation is the people opposed to the arbitrariness of princes and monarchs. To this voluntarism and this nationalism centred on the people was added, especially in Arndt, a North/South dialectic where the North was liberal and the South developed an annoying tendency to obey the Prince and the Church too much. Arndt, for example, proposed for the future unified Germany which he wished for the Swedish model, the model elaborated by a homogeneous nation, the example of a more authentic and very powerful Germanness organised according to solid statist criteria since the civil and military reforms of King Gustav-Adolph[93] in the 17th century, a king who had wished to become the champion of Protestantism – but of an organised Protestantism and not productive of anti-political sects like the English Dissidents and the American Puritans – against Rome and the Catholic empire of the fanatic Ferdinand II[94] who preferred, as he used to say, to reign over a desert than a country populated with heretics! (One can certainly compare the reforms of Gustav-Adolf to certain creations of Richelieu such as

[91] [Ernst Moritz Arndt (1769-1860) was a patriotic German poet and author whose writings express anti-Napoleonic anti-Semitic and anti-Slavic sentiments as well as a desire to restore Germany as a vigorous Protestant Germanic society.]

[92] [Goal.]

[93] [King Gustav Adolph (1594-1632) was king of Sweden from 1611 and his military genius was responsible for Sweden's rise to the status of a great European power during the Thirty Years' War.]

[94] [Ferdinand II (1578-1637) was the Habsburg Holy Roman Emperor during the Thirty Years' War and an ardent Catholic.]

the establishment of a Royal Academy aimed at organising abstract and practical knowledge to consolidate the state).

The Holy Alliance and Franz von Baader[95]

During the Restoration it was the Austrian Metternich who set the tone and tried to definitively forge and establish a reactionary Europe hunting down everywhere all the residues of the French Revolution. The international authority of the era was the Holy Alliance of 1815[96] (Great Britain, Russia, Prussia, Austria) which became the Pentarchy in 1822 (when France joined the four victorious powers of 1814-15). The Restoration permitted the flowering of a counter-revolutionary Romanticism embodied notably in Franz von Baader. It also aimed at organising Europe rationally on the basis of the traditions of the ancien régime that was back in power in 1815. Franz von Baader envisaged a religious Union of the three Christian faiths in Europe (Protestantism, Catholicism, Orthodoxy) to concertedly oppose the lay principles of the Revolution and to smooth out the disputes which could occur among the major members of the Holy Alliance. This project was rejected by the most intransigent Catholics who refused to accept that a common destiny linked them to the Protestants and those of Orthodoxy. Franz von Baader viewed Russia as the bastion of the Restoration and as the final redoubt of religion faced with the surge of modernity. The "Conservative Revolution" of the first decades of the 20th century would take up this idea under the impetus of

---

[95] [Franz von Baader (1765-1841) was a German Catholic philosopher whose metaphysics was partly based on the mystical doctrines of Jakob Böhme. Baader was so impressed by Tsar Alexander I's Holy Alliance of 1815 after the defeat of Napoleon that he visited Russia and promoted there an ecumenical Christian project that would include Orthodoxy along with Protestantism and Catholicism.]

[96] [The Holy Alliance was established between Prussia, Austria and Russia in September 1815; the United Kingdom joined this alliance in November to form the Quadruple Alliance. France joined in 1818 to form the Quintuple Alliance, or Pentarchy.]

Arthur Moeller van den Bruck, the translator of Dostoyevsky,[97] who claimed incidentally that Russia had maintained its anti-liberal instincts intact despite the Bolshevik Revolution. Thereby, in the conservative Moeller van den Bruck's view, Soviet Russia became a potential ally of Germany against the West.

Schmidt-Phiseldeck[98]

The Danish diplomat in the service of Prussia, Schmidt-Phiseldeck, advocated in the context of the Restoration, a centring of Europe around itself – the same idea as that of the Napoleonic Continental Bloc but under different ideological signs – and warned the European nations against all colonial adventures that would dissipate European energies in the four corners of the world, destabilise the continent and provoke rivalries of extra-European origin between Europeans against the interest of Europe itself as a family of nations united by the same geographical destiny. Schmidt-Phiseldeck wished for an "internal integration", thus a structural organisation of Europe, and clearly perceived the American danger (which already appeared in the horizon). For him the only possible expansion of Europe was in the direction of Turkish Anatolia and Mesopotamia. The entire old Byzantine area had to become European again, by force if necessary and an indissoluble union of all the military forces of the Pentarchy capable of destroying the Ottoman armies in a short campaign. One may say a posteriori that Schmidt-Phiseldeck was an (anti-Ottoman) precursor of the Berlin-Baghdad airline and railway but without any hostility towards Russia.

---

[97] [From 1906 to 1922 Moeller van den Bruck edited German translations of Dostoyevsky's works in 22 volumes that were published by Piper Verlag.]

[98] [Konrad von Schmidt-Phiseldeck (1770-1832) was a German Danish political thinker who advocated a federal unification of European states in order to counteract the growing power of America.]

Another theoretician of the time, Constantin Frantz[99] equally criticised colonial expansions in analogous terms prefiguring in this way the theses of Christoph Steding,[100] the geopolitician Arthur Dix[101] and Jäkh, author, during the First World War, of a memorandum justifying the Germano-Ottoman Alliance in the sense of a common exploitation of the space between Constantinople and the Persian Gulf. The Gulf War is thus – in light of these analyses presented successively by Schmidt-Phiseldeck, Frantz, Steding, Dix and Jakh – a preventive war against Europe, whose only possible expansion is in the direction of the south-east, as the principal Indo-European waves of proto-history and antiquity were similarly borne in this direction, founding successively archaic Greece, the Hittite Empire, the Persian and Median Empires, the Aryan kingdoms of India.[102] The fate of Europe is towards the south-east: the power that hinders the path of Europe in this direction is that which thwarts it and prevents its harmonious development. Today, clearly, it is the strategy chosen by the Turko-American alliance which has just reinstalled an Ottoman presence in the Balkans by interposing Bosnia and Albania in order to oppose the peaceful and economic penetrations of Germany, Austria – civil and industrial powers capable of developing the Balkans – and of Russia, capable of giving a military and nuclear guarantee to this project. Worse, it is a matter of a strategy which challenges Russia on its presence in the Black Sea threatening the acquisitions of Catherine the Great.

---

[99] cf. Robert Steuckers, «Constantin Frantz», in *Encyclopédie des Œuvres philosophiques,* PUF, 1992.

[100] [Christoph Steding (1903-38) was a German historian who was influenced by Max Weber and Carl Schmitt.] cf. Robert Steuckers, «Christoph Steding», in *Encyclopédie des Œuvres Philosophiques*, PUF, 1992.

[101] [Arthur Dix (1875-1935) was a German economist and geopolitician who recommended the formation of a United States of Europe that would protect the individual European states from gigantic states like the USA.]

[102] The rest of this paragraph was added to the paper in April 2000.

Görres[103] and German Hegemony

For his part, Görres, another German theoretician of the Restoration era, envisaged a unified and re-Catholicised Germany as the hegemon of Europe, in the place of Napoleonic France. This Germany would be civil and spiritual and not warlike in the Bonapartist manner. It would aim at perpetual peace and would be the powerful unifying state par excellence, having common borders with all the other European nations. The geographical destiny of Germany, the multiplicity of its neighbours, makes it the unifying power of Europe through its geographical destiny. The universality (or catholicity in the etymological sense of the term) of Germany derives precisely from the simple concrete existence of these multiple and diverse neighbours permitting the German intelligentsia to constantly observe the events of the world with a varied and pluralistic viewpoint without wishing to cancel them out with the help of a ready-made ideology. It alone could integrate, assimilate and synthesise better than others, thanks to a territorial and physical proximity that has lasted thousands of years.

Leopold von Ranke,[104] a German nationalist historian, developed, for his part, a more Romano-Germanic vision of Europe that is essentially Christian. He evoked a "western spirit" contrary to Baader who emphasised the virginity of Russia compared to the rationalist decline of the west. For von Ranke the orient is a "dark folly", for neither the state nor the Church penetrates to the depths of the people. The west for him is the most perfect system. This system is God's chosen one on earth. Ranke is thus one of the originators of the westernist formulas of later nationalist Germany.

---

[103] [Joseph von Görres (1776-1848) was a German publicist who fostered German national independence in the face of the Napoleonic threats.]

[104] [Leopold von Ranke (1795-1886) was a major German historian and one of the first to stress the importance of using primary sources in historical writing.]

Constantin Frantz and the Pentarchic Balance

Constantin Frantz was opposed to three major political forces active in the German states of his time: ultramontanism, Catholic particularism in Bavaria, Prussian national liberalism (and therefore capitalism). These political forces were centrifugal, causing a division of the Central European whole because they argued in partisan and fractional terms, For him the modern Reich, the Reich to come after the abrogation of the historical Reich in 1806 under the Napoleonic pressure, should extend to all of Central Europe (Mitteleuropa) and be given a federalist organisation taking into account the diversities of our continent. The European balance, for Frantz, should remain Pentarchic and centripetal within the European geospatial framework. All colonialist extroversions are dangerous even if, in his eyes, England is no longer a European nation but a maritime empire on the periphery of the continent; France too had stopped being fully European ever since it set foot in Algeria and in Africa; it had become a Euroafrican nation which distanced it a fortiori from the specifically European problems and distracted it from the structural tasks which the continent strongly needed when the growth of the population and industrialisation implied a large change and encouraged a political voluntarism and imagination to see that the dark predictions of Malthus would not become the inevitable fate of large uprooted urbanised and proletarianised masses. The social policy of Bismarck and academic Socialism were the responses to this challenge.

Colonial Extroversion

Frantz severely criticised England and France, powers that had already committed the sin of extroversion, for having conducted the Crimean War against Russia. In this way they opposed a constituent state of the European Pentarchy for the benefit of a state that did not form part of it (the Ottoman Empire), which, for Frantz, constituted a serious infringement of the spirit of unity of the Holy Alliance which was considered to bring a definitive peace to Europe, in a way that would make the latter a coherent and solid civilisational bloc extending from the Atlantic to the Pacific. The Crimean War alienated Russia, defeated in relation to the rest of Europe, and a violent anti-western reaction against Germany and Austria, which were neutral in this disgrace, was constituted and consolidated among the Russian intellectuals. The latter did not forgive the other Europeans for this abject betrayal of Russia, which had fought for Europe for a long time by liberating the northern shores of the Black Sea and the Caucasus from the Ottoman yoke between 1750 and 1820.

Incipient Germany and Austria became for their part empires without space stuck between powers with vast extra-European, central Asian or Siberian, spaces at their disposal. Henceforth the task of organising autarkically the part of Europe that remained to them fell to them alone but without the power to extend this constructive principle of structural and territorial organisation to the western and eastern borders of our sub-continent. Since then Europe was dangerously destabilised. The inter-European wars became possible, including those to regulate extra-European problems that occurred in colonial spaces. The Crimean War bore the seeds of the horrible tragedy of 1914-18.

Ernst von Lasaulx[105]

For Ernst von Lasaulx, professor of classical philology at Würzburg and Munich, the European diplomats should recognise the forces at work here and now on the continent and respond to the question: "Where are we now in the flux of history?" Only this interrogation would allow one to make consistent plans for the future. It implied that the serious and efficient statesman should know a maximum of historical facts (if not all of them), for all have an impact, even fortuitous, on the structure of the present. The

[105] [Peter Ernst von Lasaulx (1805-61) was a German philologist who also served in the Bavarian Chamber of Deputies from 1849.]

future is constructed only by resorting to the past, all of the past. One who ignores it or does not know it well or knows it through the filter of propagandistic images is condemned to make trials and errors, to proceed with tentative steps doomed to fail. Catholic in origin, influenced by Baader, Lasaulx was above all a Germanic and "pansophist" mystic. In this viewpoint the true religion of the strong historical periods was the expression of life, of vitality. In Europe, "young nations" had regularly, in cycles, regenerated aging nations. During the collapse of the Roman Empire, this role devolved on the Germans. For Lasaulx the Slavs (especially the Russians) will take up the baton. They will be the *katechon*[106] of Europe which, without them, will be engulfed in decadence accentuated by French and western ideas.

Conclusion

The visions of Europe in the Napoleonic era and in the Restoration retain a definite political relevance; they explain stabilities and groundswells. Knowledge of this record remains, in our view, a "serious" imperative for statesmen.

Our presentation contains seven major ideas, still topical, that one should always bear in mind when one thinks or wishes to think of Europe as a coherent civilisational space:

1. The space extending from the Baltic countries to the Crimea should be organised according to its own methods without hostility towards the rest of Russia (Herder).

2. Europe is (and will remain) a diversity. This diversity is a source of richness on condition that it is harmonised without being sterilised (Herder).

3. The land/sea opposition remains a constant of European history (Theremin, d'Hauterive), and, in the concert of

---

[106] [A biblical Greek term meaning "restrainer", or one who controls the powers of evil until the realisation of the Christian imperium.]

European nations, France oscillates between the two, for it is capable of being sometimes a naval power, at other times a continental power. Carl Schmitt and Karl Haushofer are the intellectual heirs of Theremin and d'Hauterive. In the sixties of our century, Carl Schmitt however perceived a strategic and technological change of order with the rise of air power and the mastery of circumterrestrial spaces.

4. Baader's idea of forging a religious Union and in this way going beyond the confessional divisions productive of war remains an important imperative. The inter-Yugoslav wars of 1991 to our days show clearly that confessions are not neutralised, that they retain a definite conflictual potential. For us, it remains to be seen if the official forms of Christianity can bring about the harmonisation of the continent or if it is not legitimate, as we consider it, to return to pre-Christian values in order to give a more secure base to our civilisational space.

5. With Schmidt-Phiseldeck we are forced to declare that the Ottoman presence is an anomaly in the western Aegean and the Bosphorus preventing our continent from "vertebrating".[107] Every Ottoman presence in the Balkans prohibits the Europeans from organising the Danube. The objective of the Ottomans was to control this big river, at least as far as Vienna, "the golden apple". This plan was defeated thanks to the heroic resistance of the urban militias of Vienna, the Hungarian and Polish imperial armies. This plan almost succeeded through the betrayal of the kings of France, François I and Louis XIV.

6. Görres and Frantz clearly theorised the necessity of conserving at any cost the cohesion of the centre of Europe. This geographic necessity should be the concrete base of a renaissance of the Holy Empire.

---

[107] The rest of the paragraph added in April 2000.

7. Colonial extroversion has ruined Europe and it imported conflicts into Europe whose origins were extra-European. Europe should first become self-centred and then organise its periphery through diplomacy and inter-civilisational dialogue.

These seven points are worth reflecting upon.

THE THEMES OF GEOPOLITICS AND OF THE RUSSIAN SPACE IN THE CULTURAL LIFE OF BERLIN FROM 1918 TO 1945[108]

*I*n 1922, after the Spartacist turmoil that had just shaken Berlin and Munich a year before the Frano-Belgian occupation of the Ruhr, the Bavarian artillery general Karl Haushofer,[109] who had a diploma in geography, was considered, unanimously and rightly, as a specialist on Japan and the oceanic territory of the Pacific. His experience as a military attaché in the Empire of the Rising Sun before 1914 and his university dissertation presented after 1918 allowed him to claim this distinction. In this way Haushofer entered into contact with two Soviet personalities of first rank, the Comintern man in Berlin, Karl Radek,[110] and the Commissar for Foreign Affairs, Georgy Chicherin[111] (who signed

---

[108] August 2002. Published in www.centrostudilaruna.it, 13 April, 2011.

[109] [Karl Haushofer (1869-1946) was the teacher of Rudolf Hess at the University of Munich.]

[110] [Karl Radek (1885-1939) was a Jewish socialist who was active in the Social Democratic movement in Poland and Germany, where he helped found the Communist Party of Germany (KPD). He moved to Russia in the twenties, where he became the Secretary of the Comintern, but was finally prosecuted during the Great Purge of the thirties and sentenced to ten years of penal labour.]

[111] [Georgy Chicherin (1872-1936) served as People's Commissar for Foreign Affairs from 1918 to 1930. He adopted a pro-German and anti-British position in foreign affairs and was involved in the signing of both the Treaty of Brest-Litovsk and the Treaty of Rapallo.]

the Rapallo accords with Rathenau).[112] In what context did this meeting take place? Japan and the USSR sought to smooth the differences by initiating a series of negotiations where the Germans played the role of arbiters. These negotiations essentially dealt with the control of the island of Sakhalin. The Japanese demanded the presence of Haushofer in order to have on their side "an objective person who was informed of the facts". The Soviets accepted that this arbiter be Karl Haushofer because his writings on the Pacific space – neglected by Germany to the point that it lost Micronesia as a consequence of the Versailles Treaty – were read with a sustained interest by the young Soviet diplomatic school. And what is more, with the hagiographical mania of the Bolshevik revolutionaries, Haushofer knew the Ulyanov (Lenin)[113] brothers at Munich before the First World War; he liked to speak of this and related it later in his memoirs. The Soviet interest in General Haushofer lasted until 1938 when, with a sudden change of attitude during the great trials in Moscow, the prosecutor demanded the condemnation of Sergei Bessonov[114] whom he accused of being a German spy in contact, he claimed, with Haushofer, Hess and Niedermayer (see below). The same accusations had been borne against Radek, who was finally executed during the great Stalinist purges.

These three facts of history – the presence of Haushofer during the negotiations between the Japanese and the Soviets, the contact, no doubt very brief and anodyne, between Haushofer and Lenin, the condemnations and executions of Radek and Bessonov – indicate that independently of the ideological labels of "left" or "right" geopolitics, as it was theorised by Haushofer in Munich and Berlin in the twenties, is concerned only with the relationship existing between geography and history; it is therefore considered as a scientific process, as a practical knowledge and not as an ideological or occult speculation conveying fantasies or interests.

---

[112] [Walther Rathenau (1867-1922) was a Jewish German industrialist and politician who served as Foreign Minister during the Weimar Republic.]

[113] ['Lenin' was the alias of Vladimir Ilyich Ulyanov (1870-1924).]

[114] [Sergei Bessonov (1892-1941) was Soviet ambassador in Berlin in the thirties, but was prosecuted in 1937 at the third of the Moscow trials.]

At that time one could speak of a true "Geopolitical International" largely transcending ideological labels exactly as today a knowledge of a geographical sort scattered in a multitude of institutes begins to be formed everywhere in a world where the large geopolitical stakes have become the order of the day: the question of the Balkans, that of Afghanistan, place in the foreground of current affairs all the large subjects of geopolitics, especially those that Mackinder and Haushofer had stressed.

A Factual and Material Process Without any Occultist Slant

From 1924, Haushofer published his *Zeitschrift für Geopolitik* (*Journal for Geopolitics*) where he especially stressed the Pacific space, as his articles and his chronicle, edited mainly from reports sent by Japanese correspondents, attest. The tenor of this journal was thus essentially political and geographical contrary to the rumours which ran in the decades after 1945 and which fortunately are beginning to be reduced; these rumours evoked a fantasmagoric "esoteric" dimension of the *Zeitschrift für Geopolitik*; it was reported that Haushofer belonged to all sorts of esoteric or occult (or occultist) sects. These allegations are certainly completely false. Further, the interest in Haushofer and his theses on the Pacific space evinced by the Radek and Chicherin is a supplementary – and important – evidence that attests to the factual and material nature of his writings; sects being by definition irrational; how could a man who is claimed to be immersed in this universe on the margins of all scientific rationality have sustained the interest and active collaboration of materialistic and historicist Marxists? Of Marxists who attempted to purge all irrationality from their intellectual processes? The accusation of occultism made with regard to Haushofer is thus a propagandistic counter-truth spread by services and powers which have an interest in seeing that his work remains unknown and is no longer consulted in the chancelleries and the general staffs. It is obvious that it is a question of powers who are interested in seeing that the large

Eurasian continent is not organised or managed territorially even in its regions most distant from the sea.

The principal geopolitical and scientific work of Haushofer is thus his *Geopolitik des Pazifischen Raumes* (*Geopolitics of the Pacific Space*), a meticulous reference work which was permanently in the office of Radek in Berlin as well as in Moscow. Karl Radek played the role of diplomat of the CPSU (Communist Party of the Soviet Union). Nevertheless, when the French sentenced to death and shot the German nationalist activist Albert Leo Schlageter,[115] he pleaded, for a common front between nationalists and communists against the Western occupying power. Later Radek was named Chancellor of the Sun-Yat-Sen University in Moscow, nerve-centre of the new international political culture which the Soviets intended to spread all over the globe. Radek organised from this new sort of university a permanent exchange between universities whose knowledge would be able to forge this new international diplomatic culture.

Three Symbolic Figures

Within the framework of this Sun-Yat-Sen University three symbolic figures merit our attention even today insofar as their methods can still have a real influence on all present-day reflections regarding the destiny of Russia, Europe, Central Asia and the general theories of geopolitics: Mylius Dostoyevsky, Richard Sorge and Alexander Radó. Mylius Dostoyevsky was the grandson of the great Russian writer, who, let us recall, laid the foundations of a conservative revolution in Russia beyond the limits of the pan-Slavism of the beginning of the 19th century and consolidated, indirectly, the Russophile dimension of the German conservative revolution through the bias of his reflections in his *A Writer's Diary*,[116] an excellent work that was translated into German

[115] [Albert Leo Schlageter (1894-1923) was a member of the German Freikorps whose sabotaging activities against the French after the First World War led to his arrest and execution by French troops.]

[116] [*A Writer's Diary* was a collection of fictional and non-fictional writings by Dostoyevsky covering the years 1873-81.]

by Arthur Moeller van den Bruck. Mylius Dostoyevsky had specialised in the history and geography of Japan, China and the maritime space of the Pacific. He belonged to the young guard of the Soviet diplomacy and was an attentive reader of the *Zeitschrift für Geopolitik*; to be courteous to these young Soviet geographers, in his habitual courteousness. Karl Haushofer always precisely took into consideration the diverse developments of the new Soviet geopolitics. He considered that the Germans of his time should know the large outlines and dynamic of it.

Richard Sorge,[117] another reader of the *Zeitschrift für Geopolitik*, was a Soviet spy in the Far East. We know his role during the Second World War. In 1933, when Hitler assumed power in Germany, Sorge was in contact with the geopolitical school of Haushofer. He remained that in spite of the change of regime and in spite of the official anti-Communist formulas – a supplementary proof that geopolitics is far beyond ideological differences and politicians. In the course of the years that followed Hitler's "assumption of power" he wrote many substantial articles in the *Zeitschrift für Geopolitik*. His knowledge of the Far Eastern world – and that alone – justified this collaboration.

Alexander Radó and "Pressgeo"

Undoubtedly the chief Soviet disciple of Karl Haushofer was the Hungarian Jew, Alexander Radó, a geographer by training, who served as a spy for the benefit of the young USSR, especially in Switzerland, a meeting point of many official contacts. Radó was the man who forged all the new concepts of Soviet political geography. He was, among others, the one who forged the denomination itself of "Union of Soviet Socialist Republics". Radó was principally a cartographer who began his career by preparing air-traffic maps which obviously constituted an innovation at

[117] [Richard Sorge (1895-1944) was a Soviet spy before and during the Second World War both in Germany and in Japan. He was arrested by the Japanese in 1941 and executed in 1944.]

that time. He taught at the Marxist School for Workers. Later he founded the first cartographic press agency of the world which he christened "Pressgeo", where a future celebrity like Arthur Koestler would notably work. The foundation of this agency corresponded perfectly to the aspirations of Haushofer, who wished to make popular – and diffuse to the maximum to the masses of the population – a pragmatic knowledge of a geopolitical, historical and economic sort matched with a spirit of defence. The map, a succinct outline, a didactic instrument of the first order served the objective of rapidly instructing the executive minds of the armies and of diplomacy as well as teachers of history and political science who had to quickly communicate an essential and vital knowledge to their members.

Haushofer also spoke in this way of *Wehrgeographie* (defence geography) or of "military geography". The objective of this pragmatic science was to synthesise in a brief cartographic glimpse an entire issue of a strategic nature recurring in history. Pedagogy and cartography formed the two major pillars of the political education of the elites and the masses. Today Yves Lacoste[118] follows in France a similar system referring to Elisée Reclus,[119] a dynamic geographer, championing a pedagogy of space in a perspective that he wished to be revolutionary and "anarchic". Lacoste, like Haushofer, is perfectly aware of the military dimension of geography (and *a fortiori* of Wehrgeographie) when he writes in reference to the first military cartographies of ancient China: "Geography helps to make war!"

---

[118] [Yves Lacoste (1929-) is a French geopolitician who is a founding member of the Institut Français de Géopolitique.]

[119] [Élisée Reclus (1830-1905) was a French geographer and anarchist who founded the International Association along with Prince Peter Kropotkin, who also had geographical interests.]

On the Pedagogical Utility of Cartography

Michel Foucher,[120] a professor at Lyons, today directs a geographical and cartographical institute whose maps, very didactic, illustrate the major parts of the French organs of press when the latter indicate the hot spots of the planet. In the same multidisciplinary spirit – with a clearly pedagogical aim – which, in France, runs from Haushofer to Lacoste and Foucher – Alexander Radós, their Soviet precursor, published in the USSR and Germany, in 1930, an *Atlas für Politik, Wirtschaft und Arbeiterbewegung* (*Atlas for Politics, Economics and the Workers' Movement*). Radüs is thus the precursor of an innovating and interesting manner of practising political geography, of mixing in audacious syntheses a spectrum of economic, geographical, military, topographical, geological, hydrographical and historical information. The syntheses which these maps represent help to apprehend in a single glance extremely complex issues that mere written text, which takes very long to assimilate, does not permit to apprehend so quickly, to express without useless digressions. That was a great step forward in scientific and political pedagogy in the sense initiated a century earlier by the geographer Carl Ritter.[121]

This cartography facilitated the work of the military man, the geographer and the statesman, it allowed one, as Karl August Wittfogel[122] emphasised, to get out of an impasse of the old traditional (and "reactionary" for the Marxists) geographical science, where one had systematically neglected the macroprocesses unleashed by human labour and thus the "historic-plastic" character of what one believed to be the "eternal facts of nature" It was this fundamental epistemological position that – beyond ideological divisions, fruits of the "ethics of conviction" with calamitous repercussions – joined

---

[120] [Michel Foucher (1946-) is a leading French geopolitician and diplomat.]

[121] [Carl Ritter (1779-1869) was a German geographer who, along with Alexander von Humboldt, is considered one of the founders of modern geography. He occupied the first chair in geography at the University of Berlin from 1825.]

[122] [Karl August Wittfogel (1896-1988) was a Marxist historian, playwright and Sinologist.]

together Elisée Reclus, Haushofer, Radó, Wittfogel, Lacoste and Foucher. Wittfogel, who presented himself as a revolutionary, recognised this "historic plasticity" in the work of the "bourgeois geopolitician", Karl Haushofer. The two schools, Haushoferian and Marxist, wished to inaugurate a dynamic geography where space was no longer posited as an inert and immobile bloc but was apprehended as a dense network of relations, rapports, movements in perpetual turmoil (one thinks naturally of the "rhizome" of Gilles Deleuze,[123] who influences the Italian "geophilosophers" of today). At the heart of this always agitated network Time can bring epochs of rest, of greater repose, just as it can inject dynamism, violence, upheavals that constrain the important political personalities to work at a redistribution of maps. The work of man, who domesticates certain spaces in managing them and in creating more rapid means of communication, is a really "revolutionary" work; statesmen who refuse to manage space in a spirit of territorial defence or in a spirit of ensuring communications and resources to future generations are "reactionaries", cowards who prefer slow corruption to the dynamic of transformation, defeatists who play in this way the perverse game of the thalassocracies.

Consequently, evoking men like Mylius Dostoyevsky, Richard Serge, Alexander Radó or Karl August Wittfogel appears to us to be very useful intellectually and methodologically, for this proves,

- That the general interest in geopolitics today can no longer be placed on par with an unhealthy interest in the National Socialist past (the context in which Karl Haushofer had to work).

- That no morbidity of an esoteric or occultist sort is detectable in the work of Haushofer and his German or Soviet disciples.

---

[123] [Gilles Deleuze (1925-95) was a French philosopher who propagated a modernist form of individualism. The term "rhizome" appears in the introduction to his collection of essays with the psychoanalyst Félix Guattari, Mille Plateaux (A Thousand Plateaus), 1980.]

- That these schools have established important landmarks in the development of political science, geography and cartography.

- That they have bequeathed a scientific property of the highest importance.

- That we should be interested more in the developments of Soviet geopolitics of the twenties and thirties (and analyse the work of Radó, for example).

Oskar von Niedermayer,[124] the German "Lawrence"

Apart from Haushofer, an approach to geopolitical knowledge as it was deployed in Berlin in the twenties, thirties and forties, cannot omit studying the figure of Oskar von Niedermayer, who was nicknamed the German "Lawrence of Arabia". Born in 1885, Oskar von Niedermayer had the career of an officer, but was not contented with simple military service. He studied at university physical natural science, geography and Iranian languages (which would permit him to have long contacts with the Ba'hai religious community which, at that time, was as it were the only door open for Iran to the west).From 1912 to 1914, he undertook a long travel to Persia and India. He was in this way the first European to cross from side to side the sand desert of Loot (Dasht-e Loot).[125] In 1914, when the First World War broke out, Oskar von Niedermayer, accompanied by Werner Otto von Henting, crossed the mountains of Afghanistan to incite the Afghan tribes to rise against the English and the Russians in order to create an "induced abscess" obliging the two powers hostile to Germany to partially weaken their fronts in Europe, in the Caucausus and in Mesopotamia. This mission was a mistake. In 1919, Niedermayer found himself in the ranks of the Free Corps of Colonel Franz, Ritter von Epp which crushed

---

[124] [Oskar von Niedermayer (1885-1948) was a German general and spy active during both the world wars.]

[125] [Dasht-e Loot is a large salt desert in the Kerman province of Iran.]

the Soviet Republic of Munich. In spite of his role in the adventure of this anti-Communist Free Corps, Niedermayer was named thereafter liaison officer of the Reichswehr with the new Red Army in Moscow. In this context, it is interesting to note that he was, above all, an expert on Afghanistan, Persian dialects and of the entire key zone of international geostrategy which runs from the south bank of the Caspian to the Indus. It was thus Niedermayer who negotiated with Trotsky and who visited on behalf of the Reichswehr, in the context of the future military cooperation between the two countries, the armament factories and the naval works of Petrograd (that had then become Leningrad). Oskar von Niedermayer was thus one of the tools of the Germano-Russian military and military-industrial cooperation in the twenties. In 1930 became professor of Wehrgeographie in Berlin.

The "Swamp" and its Ethics of Conviction

The principal lesson that he drew from his political and diplomatic activities was a challenge to the politicians of the "centre" and the "swamp" incapable of understanding the major springs of international politics, of the "big game". His criticisms were directed especially to the Social democrats and the Centrists of all ideological complexions; with such personages, von Niedermayer stated in a report where he does not hide his bitterness, it is impossible to articulate in the long term a lasting, rational and constant foreign policy. He accused them of criticising everything publicly through the press; in this way no secret diplomacy was possible. Worse, he thought, by the deleterious behaviour of these acrobats without a solid political spine, no customary remit of international diplomacy still functioned in an optimal manner. For the ethics of conviction (*Gesinnungsethik*,[126] the terminology

---

[126] [The concept of "Gesinnungsethik" (attitudinal ethics) was discussed by Max Weber in his 1919 lecture "Politik als Beruf".]

of Max Weber)[127] that informed all the vain political agitations of those men altered the spirit of restraint, seriousness and service that was necessary to make such a traditional diplomacy function. The priority accorded to convictions tended to betray the fundamental interests of the state and the nation. Niedermayer's bitterness was born as a consequence of an incident in the parliament where the Socialist, Scheidemann,[128] informed by an unrealistic pacifism of bad alloy, had denounced a secret military accord between the USSR and the Reich on the pretext that commerce and the exchange of armaments are not "moral". The following day, accidentally as it were, the London press in unison took up the information and began a propaganda against the two continental powers which had bypassed the Versailles clauses relating to embargoes. This incident shows also that a good number of journalists serve interests foreign to their country. In this nothing has changed today: the United States benefits from the unconditional support of the majority of the leading figures of the Parisian press.

Yuri Semionov, a Specialist on Siberia

In the thirties, Niedermayer met Yuri Semionov, a White Russian in exile and specialist on Siberian economics, geography, geology and hydrography. Semionov was the author of a work, still topical, still consulted in high places, on the treasures of the Siberian geology. Equally a specialist of the French colonial empire, Semionov compiled his various reflections in a volume whose last German edition dates from 1975.[129] Born in 1884 in Vladikavkaz in

---

[127] [Max Weber (1864-1920) was a major German sociologist and political economist who wrote several influential works including *Die protestantische Ethik und der Geist des Kapitalismus* (1905) and *Wirtschaft und Gesellschaft* (1922).]

[128] [Philipp Scheidemann (1865-1939) was a German Social Democrat who served as the second head of the Weimar Republic for a short period from February 1919.]

[129] Juri Semjonow, *Erdöl aus dem Osten – Die Geschichte der Erdöl- und Erdgasindustrie in der USSR*, Econ Verlag, Wien/Düsseldorf, 1973 and *Sibirien – Schatzkammer des Ostens*, Econ Verlag, Wien/Düsseldorf, 1975.

the Caucasus, Yuri Semionov studied at the University of Moscow before emigrating in 1922 to Berlin, where he taught Russian history and geography and more particularly those of the Siberian territories. After the fall of the Third Reich, he emigrated in 1947 to Sweden, where he taught in Uppsala and ended his days. In *Siberien – Schatzkammer des Ostens* he retraces all the steps of the history of the Russian conquest of the territories situated beyond the former capital of the Tartars, Kazan. He shows that the conquest of the entire course of the Volga, from Kazan to Astrakhan, allowed Russia to speculate on the eventual conquest of India. Semionov places all these facts of history in a geopolitical perspective, that of the organisation of the Great Continent, from the White Sea to the Pacific. The chapters on the 19th century are particularly interesting, especially when he describes the global situation after the decision of Tsar Alexander III[130] to finance the construction of a Siberian railway.

This extract from Semionov's book (pp.356-7) summarises this situation perfectly:

We know that the entire politics of "concentration of forces on the continent" such as was envisaged in Russia provoked an anxiety caused by jealousy in England. Every movement of Russia in Asia was considered there as a threat weighing on India. Admiral Stirling[131] saw this threat being concretised right from the installation of the Russian presence along the river Amur. The English writer, forgotten today but very well-known in his time, T.T. Meadows,[132] evoked in 1856 in one of his writings a future "Russian Alexander the Great" who would go on to conquer China and then, without any difficulty, would

---

[130] [Alexander III (1845-94) was the conservative son of the more liberal Tsar Alexander II.]

[131] [Admiral Sir James Stirling (1791-1865) signed the Anglo-Japanese Friendship Treaty in 1854 when he was Commander-in-Chief of the East Indies and China Station.]

[132] [T.T. Meadows (1815-68) was a British consular officer in China and author of The Chinese and their Rebellions, London, 1856.]

destroy the British Empire and subjugate the entire world. This pathetic cry of alarm reverberating in the English press suddenly appeared quite realistic when, during the eighties of the 19th century, the Russians advanced into Central Asia and approached the Afghan frontier. In 1884 the famous "Afghan incident" took place; a Russian detachment seized a contested point on the frontier, later the Afghans, who acted on the orders of the English, attacked this post but were defeated and dispersed by the Russians. The British Prime Minister Gladstone declared to the parliament in London that war with Russia was henceforth inevitable. Only the refusal of Bismarck to support the English prevented at that time the outbreak of an Anglo-Russian war.

All recent events seem summarised in this brief extract.

The chapters devoted to Witte, the father of Trans-Siberianism, are equally illuminating. Semionov recalls that Witte was a disciple of the economist Friedrich List, theoretician of the management of large spaces. Before the First World War and the Russo-Japanese War, there existed a truly great continental idea. It was shared in France (Henri de Grossouvre[133] has reminded us of the work of Gabriel Hanotaux),[134] in Germany (with Bismarck) and in China, with Li-Hung Chang,[135] who negotiated with Witte. England succeeded in breaking this unity, which brought in its train the bloody procession of all the wars of the 20th century.

Oskar von Niedermayer met also with Professor Otto Hoetzsch, whose itinerary we shall retrace later in this discussion. In spite of their itineraries quite different from their diverging

---

[133] [Henri de Grossouvre directs the think-tank "Forum Carolus" created in 2006 and is the author of *Paris-Berlin-Moscou, la Voie de l'indépendance et de la Paix*, Paris: Éditions de l'Age d'Homme, 2002.]

[134] [Gabriel Hanotaux (1853-1944) was a French statesman who served as minister for Foreign Affairs between 1894 and 1898.]

[135] [Li Hung Chang (1823-1901) was a Chinese general, politician and diplomat of the Qing Empire who championed the modernisation of China's industries and military.]

ideological choices, Haushofer, Niedermayer, Semionov and Hoetzsch usefully complement one another and the simultaneous reading of their works allows us to understand the Eurasian issue without mutilating it or omitting anything of its complexity.

From Professor to the 162nd Division

In 1937, Hitler ordered the foundation of an "Institut für Allgemeine Wehrlehre" (Institute for the General Defence Doctrine). Niedermayer, though sceptical, loyally served this state institution whose objective, centred on ethnology, given the interest of the National Socialists for racial questions, was to study the mutual relationships between peoples and places. Hostile to the *Gesinnungsethik* of the National Socialists, just as he was hostile to those of the Social Democrats and the Centrists, Niedermayer protested against the defamation campaigns orchestrated against the professors who were described as "apolitical intellectuals", a Hitlerian conduct that finds its perfect appendix in the defamation campaigns orchestrated by a certain contemporary journalism against those who remain sceptical with regard to the plan to eradicate Iraq, Libya and Serbia and that of supporting Mafia groups like those of the UCK[136] or the Turkish military-mafia complex. Today, those who listen to reason are not treated as "apolitical intellectuals" but as "anti-democrats".

From Torgau Prison to Lubyanka

Like the majority of the experts on the Russian question of his time, Niedermayer regretted the German-Soviet war that broke out in June 1941. In 1942, on the suggestion of Claus von Stauffenberg, the future originator of the plot of 20 July 1944 against Hitler, Niedermayer was named chief of the 162nd Infantry Division of

---

[136] ['Ushtria Çlirimtare e Kosovës' is the Albanian name for the Kosovo Liberation Army.]

the Army, in which volunteers and legionnaires of Turkish origin (originating from the Turkic peoples of Central Asia) served. This unit underwent varied fortunes, but the mistake of the National Socialist policy in the east considerably accentuated Niedermayer's scepticism. Stationed in Italy with the remainder of his division, he openly criticised the policy maintained by Hitler on the territory the Soviet Union, which led to his arrest; he was incarcerated in Torgau on the Elbe. When the American troops entered the city he left the prison and was arrested by Soviet soldiers who had him conveyed directly to Moscow, where he stayed in the famous prison of Lubyanka. There he died of tuberculosis in 1948.

Niedermayer's death does not close his "file" in the former USSR. In 1964, the Soviet authorities used the texts of his testimony in Moscow in 1945 to rehabilitate Marshal Tukhachevsky.[137] One had to wait until 1997 for Niedermayer himself to be fully rehabilitated, that is, cleared of all the incongruous accusations that he had been charged with.

The Indian Pivot of History and the Necessity of the "Kontinentalblock"

We have enumerated a good number of biographical facts of Niedermayer in order to better understand the essential crux of his approach as an Iranologist, as explorer of the Dasht-e Loot, as German agitator in Afghanistan and as commander of the Turkophone division of the army. Two basic ideas informed Niedermayer's action:

1. The idea that India is the pivot of world-history.

2. The awareness of the imperative necessity of constructing a Continental (Eurasian) Bloc, the famous Kontinentalblock of Karl Haushofer (a plan that he very probably took from the Japanese

---

[137] [Mikhail Tukhachevsky (1893-1937) was a Soviet military leader who was accused of treason during the Stalinist purges of 1937-8 and shot. His reputation was rehabilitated in 1957 under Nikita Khruschchev.]

statesmen of the beginning of the 20th century such as Prince Ito,[138] Count Goto[139] and the Prime Minister Katsura,[140] advocates of a grand continental Germano-Russo-Japanese alliance).

If Niedermayer doubtlessly takes this idea of a "continental bloc" directly from Haushofer's work without going back to the Japanese sources – which he certainly was ignorant of – the idea of India as the "pivot of history" came to him very probably from General Andrei Snessarev,[141] Tsarist officer who came under the thumb of Trotsky to become the chief of staff of the Red Army. This general, hostile to the Anglo-Saxon thalassocracies, representative of a grand continental geopolitical ideal transcending the white/ red division, used to repeat: "If we wish to knock down the capitalist tyranny that weighs on the world, then we need to chase the English from India."

Thalassocratic principles, liberalism in the western manner, political and moral permissiveness, capitalism whose motivations systematically annihilate the historical and cultural traditions (cf. Dostoyevsky and Moeller van den Bruck) and the market economy were synonyms of abjection for this traditional officer, no matter if they were combated under a white/traditionalist label or under a red/revolutionary one. Labels are "convictions" without substance; the only thing that matters is a constant action aiming at reducing and destroying the disintegrating forces of mercantile modernity for they lead the world to chaos and the nations to a misery without end. As we see much more today than at that time, the industrialist, the merchant and the banker, with their monstrous system of accumulation, appeared as abject or inferior, fundamentally

---

[138] [Prince Itō Hirobumi (1841-1909) was a samurai who served as Prime Minister of Japan for four terms between 1885 and 1901.]

[139] [Count Gotō Shōjirō (1838-97) was a samurai and liberal politician who headed the Freedom and People's Rights movement.]

[140] [Prince Katsura Tarō (1848-1913) was a general in the Imperial Japanese Army and served three times as Prime Minister, between 1901 and 1913.]

[141] [Andrei Snessarev (1865-1937) commanded of the Khorog garrison from 1902 to 1908 and wrote several works on the people of the Pamirs.]

maleficent, beings to this superior Russian and Soviet officer who respected only men of quality – historians, priests, soldiers and revolutionaries. The imperatives of geopolitics are constants in history which the man of long memory – the only valuable man, the only man endowed with unsurpassed qualities – must obey. Following Snessarev, whom he doubtless met during the time when he served as liason officer with the Red Army, Niedermayer – on account of his experience as an Iranologist, explorer of the Dasht-e Loot and specialist on Afghanistan, the key to the access to India since Alexander the Great – equally knew that the destiny of Europe in general, and of Germany, its geographical heart, in particular, was played out in India (and therefore in Persia and in Afghanistan). A lesson that events have proven more true than ever.

Exporting the Revolution and Absorbing the "Rimland"

For Niedermayer, a German officer, this essential role of the Indian territory posed a problem, for its land does not possess any point of support in the region nor in its immediate surroundings. But Tsarist Russia did and, following it, the USSR too. Consequently, the Soviet military positions in Tajikistan and along the Afghan frontier were absolutely necessary advantages for Europe as a whole, for the entire community of peoples of European origin. It was the possession of this strategic advantage in Central Asia which, in Niedermayer's eyes, would justify the unfailing Germano-Russian alliance, the only guarantee of the survival of European culture as a whole. For the followers of revolutionary Bolshevism around Trotsky and Lenin, the solution for causing the downfall of capitalism, the global system of the liberal thalassocracies, resided in the policy of "exporting the revolution", of agitating the colonised and subjected populations with a good dose of nationalism and social revolution. Thus, the continental powers of the "land of the centre" could transfer their energies towards the Indian, Persian and Arab "rimland", realising at a single stroke the fears formulated by Mackinder in his speech of 1904 on the Siberian and Central Asian "pivot" of history. A proposition that he would repeat in his book *Democratic Ideals and Reality* of 1919. However, in order to be able to free India and export the revolution to it, a continental bloc well-bonded by the Germano-Soviet alliance was necessary, the prelude to the liberation of the entire Euroasiatic continental mass.

To Structure Europe: a Broad-Gauge Railway

In order to perfect the organisation of this gigantic continental mass it is necessary to recall and to apply the suggestions recommended the Minister of the Tsar, Sergei Witte, father of the Trans-Siberian. In the Berlin of the twenties a plan already circulated which took shape during the Second World War, that of constructing a broad gauge railway (*Breitspurbahn*) allowing the transport of a maximum of persons and merchandise in a minimum of time. This idea, coming from Witte, is not entirely dead, and still constitutes a major imperative for anyone who wishes truly to work for the European construction: the Delors Plan, sketched in the corridors of the European Union, recently advocated large public works of territorial management including a rapid railway system, now inspired by the French high-speed train. In 1942, Hitler, in invoking Witte's Trans-Siberian, ordered Fritz Todt[142] to study the possibility of constructing a Breitspurbahn with trains running between 150 and 180 kph, for the transport of goods, and between 200 and 250 kph, for the transport of persons. The project, assigned to Todt, did not concern merely Europe, in the limited sense of the term, did not intend to connect merely the large European metropolises to one another but also, through the Ukraine and the Caucasus, the cities of Europe to those of Iran. These projects, which appeared at the time somewhat fantastic, were not at all the mania of Hitler alone (and of his engineer Todt); in the Soviet Union too, through

---

[142] [Fritz Todt (1891-1942) was the engineer responsible for the development of the Autobahnen (highways) during the Reich and was appointed Minister for Armaments and Munition in 1940.]

popular novels like those of Ilf and Petrov.[143] The creation of ultra-fast railways connecting Russia to the Far East was envisioned.

The Tragic Fate of Professor Otto Hoetzsch[144]

The purely scientific part of this enthusiasm for the Great East was incarnated in Berlin from 1913 to 1946 by a professor as brilliant as he was modest: Otto Hoetzsch. He suffered a particularly tragic fate. After having accumulated in his personal institute a mass of documents and works on Russia, over decades, the bombing of Berlin in 1945, on the eve of the entry of the Soviet troops into the German capital, reduced his colossal library to nothing. This tragedy partially explains the pathetic fate of the knowledge of Russia and the Soviet Union in the west. The major part of the most interesting documents had been accumulated in Berlin. The misery of western Sovietology is partially the distressing result of the destruction of the library of Prof. Hoetzsch. In 1945 and in 1946, the latter, at the age of 70, wandered alone in Berlin, deprived of his documentation; this man, broken, nevertheless found the ultimate courage to write a paper, the last that he would give, where he bequeathed to us a veritable political testament (the title of the paper: "*Die Eingliederung der Osteuropäischen Geschichte in die Gesamtgeschichte*" [*The Inclusion of East European History in General History*]).

Slavist and historian of Russia, Otto Hoetzsch, perceived very early that the Europeans of the west, the westerners in general, did not understand anything of the dynamic of Russian history and its territory – which the Russians notice immediately, and which distresses and annoys them. This ignorance, combined with an ill-

---

[143] [Ilya Ilf (1897-1937) and Evgeny Petrov (1903-42) were Soviet authors of satirical novels in the twenties and thirties.]

[144] [Otto Hoetzsch (1876-1946) was appointed professor for Eastern European History at the University of Berlin in 1913 and was a member of parliament in the twenties. He served as an interpreter during the negotiations for the 1922 Treaty of Rapallo.]

placed ambition and an irrepressible and irritating propensity to teach lessons, is true equally of the Balkan space (except in Austria, where the institutions specialised in the European south-east have produced remarkable works which the western chancelleries have never taken into consideration). Hoetzsch declared, right from the beginning of his brilliant career, that the press produced only lamentable articles when it came to comment on or describe the existing situations in Russia or in Siberia. He wished to remedy this gap. From 1913, he began gathering documents, studying and reading the great classics of Russian political thought, reading Russian historians, which led him to found in 1925, some months after the publication of the first issue of Haushofer's ZfG, a journal specialising in Russian and Central Asian, and East European questions. He was captivated by the figure of Tsar Alexander II, on whom he produced a master-work, whose manuscript was saved in extremis from the destruction of Berlin in 1945; Hoetzsch transported it in his suitcase while fleeing from burning Berlin. Why Alexander II? This tsar was a social reformer, he set Russia on the path of industrialisation and modernisation, which the thalassocracies could not tolerate. He died of an assassination, besides. In spite of the losses of Russia under Nicholas II, its heavy defeat suffered in 1905 against Japan, armed by England and the United States, in spite of the terrible loss constituted by the seizure of power by the Bolsheviks, the work of Alexander II must, in Hoetzsch's eyes, remain the model for every Russian statesman worthy of the name.

A Friend of the White Russians and "Republican of Reason"

Hoetzsch was a left liberal, close to Social Democracy, but he detested the Bolsheviks, for him, these were agents of English capitalism, insofar as they destroyed the work of the emancipating and modernising tsars; they plotted against the latter and against excellent statesmen like Witte and Stolypin[145] (who was similarly assassinated). Hoetzsch visited the White *emigrés* in Berlin, consolidated his institute thanks to the collaboration of scholars expelled by the Bolsheviks, but remained what was called at the time, in Weimar Germany, a "republican of reason" (*Vernunftrepublikaner*), which obviously differentiated him from Oskar von Niedermayer. His institute and journal met with a well deserved success during the twenties; these were havens of knowledge and intelligence where Russians and Germans cooperated in full friendship. In 1933, with the accession to power of the National Socialists, Hoetzsch underwent a series of misfortunes. For the new power the *Vernunftrepublikaner* were emanations of "the Centrist swamp" or, worse, "November traitors" (*Novemberverräter*) or "salon Bolsheviks" (*Salonbolschewisten*). Hoetzsch's institute was dissolved. Hoetzsch was "invited" to take an early retirement. The closure of this institute is a tragedy of the first order. Hoetzsch's fate was worse than that of the political activist and editor of revolutionary nationalist journals, Ernst Niekisch.[146] For one can obviously, looking back, reproach Niekisch for having been a passionate and outrageous polemicist. This was obviously not the case of Hoetzsch, who remained a punctilious scientist.

For a Greater European Approach to History

In the paper that he prepared in August 1945 and which he would read a little before his death in 1946, in his dear city of Berlin in ruins. Otto Hoetzsch has left us a message that remains perfectly topical. The objective of this testament-paper is to make one understand the imperative necessity, after two disastrous world wars, of developing a vision of history that is valuable for all of Europe,

---

[145] [Peter Stolypin (1862-1911) was one of the major statesmen of Tsarist Russia and was appointed Prime Minister in 1906 by Tsar Nicholas II.]

[146] [Ernst Niekisch (1889-1967) was a German socialist who developed a movement that he called "National Bolshevism".]

that of the west, that of the east and Russia (*gesamteuropäische Geschichte*). Personally we consider that the practical premises of such a Greater European vision of history is found already in a seminal way in the political and military work of Prince Eugene of Savoy, which succeeded in mobilising and uniting the European powers in the face of the Ottoman danger and in making the Sublime Porte[147] to retreat on all fronts, to the point that it would lose control of 400,000 square kilometres of European and Russian lands. Prince Eugene definitively removed the Turkish danger from Central Europe and prepared the reconquest of the Crimea by Catherine the Great. Never again, after the blows dealt by Eugene of Savoy, were the Ottomans victorious in Europe, and their French allies were no longer able to encroach on the imperial territory of the Spanish and then Austrian Netherlands; the Ottomans were no longer even capable of serving as auxiliaries of that other anti-imperial and anti-European power that France had been before Louis XVI.[148]

Hoetzsch's Testament Calls Out to Us

But Hoetzsch's aim in his last conference was not to evoke the figure of Prince Eugene but to lay the foundations of a historical and sociological methodology for the future; it was to rest on the theoretical knowledge of Karl Lamprecht,[149] of Gustav Schmoller[150] (inspirer of Gaullism in the sixties of the 20th century) and of

---

[147] [The Sublime Porte was the French translation of the "High Gate" (*Bab-i Ali*) that served as the entrance to the offices of the Ottoman government in Istanbul. It was named so by the French diplomats in 1536 when Sultan Suleiman the Magnificent entered into an alliance with King François I of France.]

[148] [Louis XVI (1754-93) was King of France from 1774. He was deposed during the French Revolution, in 1792, and guillotined the following year.]

[149] [Karl Lamprecht (1856-1915) was a German social and cultural historian.]

[150] [Gustav von Schmoller (1838-1917) was a leading member of the Prussian "historical school" of economics that focused on the achievements and ambitions of Prussia and the Hohenzollerns.]

Otto Hintze.[151] Hoetzsch said that it was necessary to develop an integral and comparative history for the decades to come. In affirming that he had no chance of seeing his wishes fulfilled in 1946, much less in 1948, when, after the Prague Coup,[152] the Iron Curtain fell on Europe for four decades. In 1989, immediately after the destruction of the Berlin Wall and the opening of the Austro-Hungarian and inter-German borders, Europe and Russia would have been interested in placing Hoetzsch's proposals again on the table. On the scientific level remarkable studies have in fact been made, but nothing seems to appear in the press, due to the lack of professional journalists capable of applying the pedagogical lessons of Haushofer and Radó. Journalists are no longer men and women in search of innovating, interesting subjects but for the most part those whom Serge Halimi[153] calls very pertinently the "watchdogs" of the system. The newspapers and journals constituted the path of penetration to the public which formerly the social science institutes and the universities had at their disposal. Regarding all that is truly innovative, everything that opposes common places repeated *ad nauseam*, this path is henceforth closed off since journalists are no longer free men animated by a will to consolidate the commonwealth but ignoble and contemptible mercenaries in the pay of the system and the dominant powers. However, the challenge that Brzezinski posed to us in 1996 in publishing his famous book, The Grand Chessboard, in which all the thalassocratic formulae are shamelessly presented for neutralising Europe and Russia with the help of the instrument constituted by the Turkish military-mafia complex – potentially extended to the entire Turkophone region of Central Asia – shows again that

[151] [Otto Hintze (1861-1940) was a German economic and political historian who worked for a while with Schmoller at the Prussian Academy of Sciences before becoming professor at the University of Berlin in 1902.]

[152] [The Prague Coup was the coup through which the Czechoslovak Communist Party, aided by the Soviet Union, seized power from the Third Czechoslovak Republic in February 1948.]

[153] [Serge Halimi (1995-) is a journalist who is now director of the left-wing monthly newspaper *Le monde diplomatique*.]

a European and Russian counter-attack must necessarily include a clear view of history that may be popularised for the masses. The tragic destiny of Hoetzsch, the admirable courage of his opinions, his modesty as a great scholar appeals to us directly: our friendly pan-European historiography has as its duty to work humbly, in its mind, for the coming of the Greater European one that Hoetzsch desired. To work!

VARIATIONS AROUND THE THEME OF "RUSSIA"[154]

*R*ussia – you hear and read it every day in the media of the system – is the object of an unrelenting propaganda, always denigrating and negative, a permanent intellectual harassment which portrays it as an immense hotbed where horrors and breaches of "good governance" succeed each other ceaselessly; this propaganda has indeed been reactivated since the "August war" in the Caucasus two months ago. This negative propaganda, this *Greuelpropaganda* (atrocity propaganda) is not new for, as historians know, it was already deployed in the history of the last two centuries, essentially for two groups of reasons:

First Group of Reasons:

First, because of the autocratism of the tsars: Paul I,[155] who wished to march with Napoleon against British and democratic India and demonstrated, through this desire, that the control of the Black Sea and the Caspian allowed eventually an entry into India, a civil arsenal and source of profit for the dominant English power; and

---

[154] Speech delivered at the colloquium of the "Nouvelle alternative solidariste" in Ruddervoorde/Bruges, 11 October 2008. Published in www.voxnr.com, 8 June, 2011.

[155] [Paul I (1754-1801) was the son of Catherine the Great and Tsar of Russia from 1796.]

Nicholas I,[156] who started the march of the Russian armies in the direction of the Caucasus and Central Asia; this tsar wished to solve the Eastern Question by liquidating the Ottoman Empire, which sparked the Crimean War. This reproach of authoritarianism is part of a recurrent propagandist arsenal and it is equally directed against broad minded tsars such as Alexander II,[157] who launched a programme of industrialisation, modernisation and emancipation of the serfs, or Nicholas II,[158] who was sometimes an angel, sometimes a demon, according to the fluctuations of English geopolitics, which intended first to shake Russia in order to seize the petrol of the Caucasus and then ally itself to it within the framework of the Entente[159] in order to contain Germany, which had become the principal enemy taking over – as the prime target of the denigrating propaganda – from the Tsarist Empire, as is excellently demonstrated by the Swedish geopolitician William Engdahl in his work on the petrol war.[160] Nicholas II shares with the Mexicans Zapata[161] and Pancho Villa[162] the sad honour of having been at the same time, within the space of just a few years, a bloody tyrant and a brave ally. The two Mexicans, we may recall, wanted to nationalise the petrol of their country, seize them from the British and Yankee administration. Last year, we had to lament the passing

[156] [Nicholas I (1796-1855) was Tsar from 1825 and seized the lands of Armenia and Azerbaijan from Persia at the end of the Russo-Persian War of 1826-8.]

[157] [Alexander II (1818-81) was Tsar from 1855 and noted for his reforms including the emancipation of the serfs in 1861.]

[158] [Nicholas II (1868-1918) was the last Tsar of Russia.]

[159] [The Anglo-Russian Entente was signed in August 1907, followed immediately by the Triple Entente between the Russian Empire, the French Third Republic and the United Kingdom.]

[160] William Engdahl, *Pétrole – une Guerre d'un Siècle – L'ordre Mondial Anglo-Américain*, Paris: Ed. Jean-Cyrille Godefroy, 2007. [*A Century of War: Anglo-American Oil Politics and the New World Order*. London: Pluto, 2004.]

[161] [Emiliano Zapata (1879-1919) was a peasant leader of the Mexican Revolution that took place between 1910 and 1920.]

[162] [Pancho Villa (1878-1923) was a general who commanded the Northern Division during the Mexican Revolution.]

of Henri Troyat,[163] of the Académie Française, a writer of Russian and Armenian origin, who has left us biographies of all the tsars; they explain to us in great detail the great axes of their politics in a clear and limpid language accessible to all, without jargon.

Second Group of Reasons:

Later, on account of Bolshevism and the Bolsevisation of Russia, after 1917, the propagandist demonstration focused on the ideology and practice of Communism. It had a much easier task because tsarism was less demonisable than Sovietism. The Belgian and Flemish Catholic world especially depicted Sovietised Russia as the hotbed of absolute evil, particularly to prevent any progress of Communism in Belgium itself, the publication of Hergé's[164] comic book Tintin *au pays des Soviets* derives, to give but a single example, from this Catholic and militant anti-Communism of the twenties and thirties. This anti-Soviet propaganda left traces: in spite of the definitive collapse of the Soviet Union and the de-Bolsevisation of Russia, the anti-Russian reflexes mobilised to combat Sovietism, especially the propaganda in favour of NATO, remained anchored in the same mentality, incapable of integrating the new geopolitical facts after 1989. This anti-Communism – muted after 1941 for reasons of the sacred union against Nazism and in order to cover the actions of the Communist resistance (as an instrument of guerrilla warfare) – was succeeded by an anti-Stalinism shared by certain Communists elsewhere in the world; this anti-Stalinism attributed all the idiosyncracies of Communism solely to the Stalinian administration of the Soviet Union. Like Nicholas II, first bloody tyrant and then "good father of the peoples of all the Russias" according to the London propaganda, Stalin was

---

[163] [Henri Troyat (1911-2007) was a prolific Russian-French author of biographies and novels of Russia.]

[164] [Georges Remi (pseudonym Hergé) (1907-83) was a Belgian cartoonist who is famous for his comic-book series called *Les Aventures de Tintin*, which first appeared in 1929.]

a monster, then a good "Uncle Joe", then the "little father of the peoples", and then again a dictator whom one could not associate with.

In my article entitled "Stalin's diplomacy"[165] for whose tenor I have often been reproached I underlined the originality, after 1945, of the Soviet diplomacy, which counted on bilateral relations between powers and not on a system of blocs, at least at the beginning. In fact, the Warsaw Pact was born in 1955 only after the death of the Georgian leader. This pact consolidated the system of blocs and is the work of the post-Stalinism that Dugin[166] denounces today in Moscow as an emanation of a certain "Atlanto-Trotskyism". In spite of atrocities like the elimination of the kulaks in the black and very fertile lands of the Ukraine which deprived the Soviet Union of a peasantry capable of guaranteeing it a total autonomy in food production, and the purges of the party and the army during the great purges of 1937, it is necessary to objectively place on the positive side of the late Stalinian period the notes of 1952 proposing the neutralisation of Germany along the lines of the model provided for Austria in accord with the Austro-Marxist stratagem of Austrian Social Democracy.

De-Stalinisation and the System of Blocs

The desire to rehabilitate bilateral relations between powers according to the old proven criteria of classical diplomacy, and the project of neutralisation of a large part of the centre of Europe between the Atlantic and the Soviet border, whose German industrial arsenal was called on to rise from the ashes ("Hitlers may come and go, Germany remains"), are two positions which displeased Washington deeply and brought about ipso facto an anti-Stalinist propaganda and then, immediately after, de-

---

[165] See http://euro-synergies.hautetfort.com

[166] [Aleksandr Dugin (1962-) is a Russian political scientist who first belonged to the National Bolshevik Party and later founded the Eurasia Party.]

Stalinisation in favour of a perfectly schematic system of blocs which doomed Europe to partition and stagnation, to a permanent geopolitical blockade. The de-Stalinisation, in spite of the "good face" that it gave itself, forbade a return to the extreme message of the end of the Stalinist era: classical diplomacy and the neutralisation of Germany.

Present-day China, partially heir to this Communism of the end of the forties and the beginning of the fifties, advocates international relations based on bilateral relations respecting the political identities of the actors on the international scene, outside all formation of blocs and all "interfering" ideologies (Wilsonianism, the Carter and Reagan strategies of "human rights", etc.).[167]

The Return of Anti-Autocratic Themes

With Putin and Medvedev the habitual propaganda recomposes the anti-autocratic themes, of hostility to any power not only strong but just solid, to the residues of Communism, in the sense that any reorganisation of the ancient lands of the Russian Empire and any inclination to control the economy and the market of raw materials are equated with a return to Communism. These are the traps into which one should not fall, by taking into consideration the following:

- Russia needs a more controlling power than the lands situated in the west of the European sub-continent, the coordination of resources of its immense territory demanding more direction.

- In a European and Russian perspective the peaceful control of Central Asia, the Caucasus, the Caspian and the Black Seas

---

[167] Cf. Our articles on the question: Robert Steuckers, "Les Amendements Chinois au 'Nouvel Ordre Mondial'" & "Modernité Extrême-Orientale et Modèle Juridique 'Confucéen'"; these two articles are reprinted in Robert Steuckers, "Le Défi Asiatique et 'Confucéen' au 'Nouvel Ordre Mondial'", *Synergies Européennes*, Forest, 1998; the two texts appear now on: http://euro-synergies.hautetfort.com

is an important geopolitical and geostrategic advantage that cannot be undone lightly at the risk of seeing the triumph of the dearest wish of the Anglo-Saxon geopolitics whose foundations were theorised by Halford John Mackinder and Homer Lea[168] in the first decade of the 20th century.

- A demonisation of Russia has a strong smell of hydrocarbon; each historical stage of this demonisation is marked by one or another petroleum stake, yesterday as today, in the Caucasus.

- Communism, as a messianism that was exported and shook the political balance of neighbouring nations, has ceased to exist and the defensive reflexes that its existence dictated no longer have a place to exist and, if they are still active, vitiate the perception of present reality.

- The anti-Russian propaganda of yesterday and today share in the interventionist and internationalist strategy applied yesterday in London, today in Washington since the presidency of Teddy Roosevelt and the Wilsonian system; it had as its result the torpedoing of all attempts at a continental unification and the transformation of Europe into a political dwarf in spite of its economic giganticism.

The ruling historiography thus makes Russia a bogeyman and this historiography is dictated to the media agencies, the international press, by back rooms based in London or in Washington. It is a matter of henceforth countering, in the spaces of freedom like ours, the ever recurrent common places if this propaganda and of referring to another interpretation of history, an alternative historiography, different also from the Soviet/Communist historiography (connected to the Anglo-Saxon historiography of the events of the Second World War).

---

[168] [Homer Lea (1876-1912) was an American geopolitical strategist who was involved in Chinese revolutionary movements in the early twentieth century and served as adviser to Dr. Sun Yat Sen during the Chinese Republican Revolution that overthrew the Qing (or Manchu) dynasty in 1911/12.]

The Memory of "Pietje Kozak"

Within the restricted framework of the Flemish movement, we should remember that, without the Cossacks of Alexander I, the southern Dutch provinces would never have been liberated from the Napoleonic yoke and that their cultural and linguistic identity would have disappeared forever if they had remained French districts. If a quarter is called "Moscow" in Ghent, it is in memory of the Cossack liberators led by Pietje Kozak, whose horses had galloped from Aix-la-Chapelle to the banks of the Escaut passing through Brussels where they camped at Porte de Louvain, the present-day Place Madou. The Cossacks did not leave behind any bad memories. They did not stay long: they rushed towards Paris while the volunteers of Ghent were incorporated into the Prussian army, a poor army, an army raised from the masses according to the orders of Clausewitz, who wished to keep the Republican, then Napoleonic conscription in check. This army had to live off the population, especially on the eastern bank of the Meuse which Prussia coveted, making the English anxious, who saw a great power approaching from Anvers and occupying a valley of the Meuse leading directly to the Delta and to Hoek van Holland, one's night's voyage from London, as at the time of Admiral De Ruyter.[169] The Prussian requisitions left behind bad memories, especially in Liège, in Ardennes and the Condroz. The English paid for everything that they took and created for themselves a good reputation: it is there that one should see the origin of Belgian Anglophilia.

After the collapse of the Napoleonic system, which had perhaps the advantage of unifying Europe but the disadvantage of doing so in the name of the modernist philosophers of the French Revolution, Europe acquired in Vienna, in 1814-15 a sort of restorative unity. This was the Pentarchy, the concert of five powers (Prussia, Russia, England, Austria, France) whose territory extended from the Atlantic to the Pacific. We have thus for the first

---

[169] [Michiel de Ruyter (1607-76) was a Dutch admiral famous for his successes in the Anglo-Dutch wars of the 17th century.]

time in history a European and Eurasian space between the two great oceans of the globe. The coherence of this space remains an ideal and a nostalgia in spite of the weakness of this Pentarchy, about which we shall speak later. Let us recall that it survived almost intact up to 1830 and that the first cracks of its edifice date just from this fateful year 1830, from the Belgian revolt in Brussels, where the French and British accepted the demands of the rebels, the former in the hope of absorbing the country little by little, the latter to break the unity of the Netherlands, which brought considerable advantages in the dawn of the industrial revolution: a metal industry in Liège, coal mines from Mons to Maastricht, a good textile industry in Flanders and in the Vallée de la Vesdre an impressive Dutch navy and colonies in the process of development in Indonesia, and a continental and littoral Germanic hub as attractive as, if not more, for the populations of North Germany as Prussia and Brandenburg.[170] While the French and British favoured Belgian secession, the other European powers saw in it a first breach of the "Pentarchic" cohesion and the triumph of a sterile particularism.

The Monroe Doctrine Against the Pentarchy

Proof of the immense potential of the "Pentarchy": it was at the time of its strongest cohesion that the Puritans of North America became worried about it when they were divining the potentialities of their own continental and bi-oceanic vocation in the New World. The proclamation of the Monroe Doctrine in 1823 constitutes an American challenge to this formidable European cohesion which was imposed on the Eurasian continental mass.[171] It required some audacity to dare in this way to challenge the five powers of the Pentarchy. With an unheard-of nerve, without having at that

---

[170] See. L. Simmons, "*Van Duinkerke tot Königsberg – Geschiedenis van de Aldietsche Beweging*", Nijmegen: Uitgeverij B. Gottmer, 1980. Cf. Also Alan Spanjaers, "Constant Hansen", in *Branding*, n°2, 2008.

[171] Dexter Perkins, *Storia Della Dottrina di Monroe*, Bologna: Il Mulino, 1960.

time the means to defend its policy on land, James Monroe dared to declare this programme of exclusion of the European powers, beginning with weakened Spain, for, if the Pentarchy wanted, it could have shared out the New World in zones of influence and the thirteen rebel colonies would not have been able to cross the Appalachians nor reach the basin of the Mississippi if Bonaparte had not had the disastrous idea of selling Louisiana to them in 1803.

The Crimean War[172] definitively broke the cohesion of the Pentarchy, inaugurated the era of compositions and re-compositions of alliances which led to the explosion of 1914, to the First World War and to the implosion of European culture. Tsar Nicholas I intended to complete the work of liquidating the Ottoman Empire begun in 1828 when the English, French and Russian navies had together forced the Sultan to concede independence to Greece, which would have a Bavarian king. The objective of the tsar was to progressively liquidate the Ottoman Empire, a foreign body to the Pentarchy on the European sub-continent, by protecting and then granting independence to the Christian (Orthodox) subjects of the Sublime Porte. The logic of the tsar was continentalist: he wanted an enlargement of the *ager pentarchicus*[173] and the reoccupation of key strategic positions that the European empires, Roman and Byzantine, had held before the Arab and Ottoman tidal waves. The enlargement of the ager pentarchicus implied, after the interval of the Greek independence supported by all, the encirclement of the entire Pontic maritime territory and the hurtling, partially or by means of new small interposed Orthodox powers, into the eastern basin of the Mediterranean, with Crete and Cyprus, close to Egypt. England's strategy was maritime, thalassocratic. For the imperial English reasoning the Tsarist Empire, with its immense territorial depths and its enormous resources, could not advance so far towards the south and weigh with all its weight on the Malta-Egypt maritime line with the risk of cutting off the route to India

---

[172] Alain Gouttman, *La Guerre de Crimée 1853-1856, la Première Guerre Moderne*, Perrin, 1995; cf. Also *The Collins Atlas of Military History*, London: Collins, 2004.

[173] Pentarchic field.

for, in London, they were already counting on cutting through the isthmus of Suez.

The Nerve-Centre of the British Empire is no Longer in Europe

The English preoccupations at the time of the Crimean War (1853-56) remain topical, with the difference that it is henceforth the Americans who assert them. For London yesterday and for Washington today neither Russia, nor any other European power besides, could have the complete control of the Black Sea nor have at its disposal a good window on the eastern Mediterranean. In 1853 London took up the cause of Turkey dragging France in its wake, and the two western powers ruined in this way, definitively, the fertile and pacifying notion of the Pentarchy: they are responsible before history for all the catastrophes that bled Europe dry ever since the Crimean War. The unity and cohesion of Europe did not count for London and Paris, excentric powers in relation to the heart of the sub-continent. The west would ally itself to any power or any people whatsoever external to Europe in order to destroy any cohesive force emanating from the Rhineland, Danubian or Alpine centre of our sub-continent. This strategy of betrayal and of anti-Europeanism had begun with François I, the Sultan and Barbarossa[174] in the 16th century.[175] England rushed to the aid of the morbid Ottoman Empire, prolonged the servitude of the Balkan peoples by not showing any solidarity with Europeans mouldering under a Muslim yoke because the nerve-centre of the British power was no longer situated in Europe, nor even in England, but in India. England thus possessed an empire whose centre, on the globe, was the Indian sub-continent; even though a hegemon, it was situated on the periphery of the initial springboard space of

---

[174] [Friedrich I ("Barbarossa") (1122-90) was the German Holy Roman Emperor from 1155. He was a Hohenstaufen (Ghibelline) through his father and a Guelph through his mother.]

[175] Jacques Heers, *Les Barbaresques – La Course et la Guerre en Méditerranée – XIV°-XVI° siècle*, Paris: Perrin, 2001-2008.

the heart itself of its own empire and combated everything around India that could, in the short – or medium term, in reality or in the imagination, threaten its territorial integrity. The French and English strategies of the second half of the 19th century were thus no longer Eurocentric but exotic. This slide sealed the end of the Pentarchic cohesion.

It was following the Crimean War that the term "the west" became pejorative in Russia. None other than Dostoyevsky explained it most clearly in his *A Writer's Diary*. In 1856, when Russia had to accept the humiliating clauses of the peace, the first crack went through Pentarchic Europe, a crack which constituted the first step towards the frightful cataclysm of August 1914. In fact, the crack henceforth separated a western Europe (France and England) from a central and eastern Europe (Prussia, Russia, Austro-Hungary). In spite of the Austrian mistrust before and during the Crimean War, of Russia, which was attempting to install itself in the delta of the Danube by taking under its protection all the Romanian principalities (Wallachia and Moldavia) of Orthodox faith, under the direction of Bismarck the three imperial powers sought to reproduce by themselves the cohesion of the Holy Alliance. After the German unification of 1871, people spoke of "the Three Emperors' League" (*Dreikaiserbund*). Bismarck exhorted the Austrians not to succumb to the western temptations, which was quite easy since Austria never had extra-European colonies.

The Fear of Seeing a Russo-Byzantine Empire Reborn on the Bosphorus

The theoretician most pertinent to the Pentarchy was incontestably Constantin Frantz:[176] it was he who demonstrated that the exotic "ex-centricism" of England principally in the direction of India and of France in the direction of Africa (Algeria, Saint-Louis/Dakar, the Ivory Coast, Gabon before 1860) broke the cohesion of Europe and

[176] Robert Steuckers, "Constantin Frantz", in: *Encyclopédie des Oeuvres philosophiques*, Paris: PUF, 1992.

could produce on its territories conflicts generated elsewhere. The Crimean War was the first international conflagration after 1815 whose motivations derived from extra-European preoccupations: England did not want a Russian fleet in the Mediterranean because it threatened Egypt and contained the risk of seeing Russian posts and bases installed on the Red Sea with access to the Indian Ocean; France did not want it any more because a Russian fleet in the formerly Ottoman bases risked threatening recently conquered Algeria, which, we may recall, was indeed the most advanced base of the Ottomans in the western Mediterranean in the 16th century. The fear shared by Paris and London in 1853 was to see a re-Christianised Russo-Byzantine Empire reconstituted on the debris of the Ottoman Empire capable, with the Russian reserves, of controlling the principal strategic points in the hinge between the Asiatic and African continental masses and replacing in this way the Ottoman Empire. This fear did not exist twenty five years before that, at the time of Greece's acquisition of independence: France had not yet disembarked its troops in Algeria and England counted simply on making Greece a more solid satellite than just the small cordon of Ionian islands which it had made a republic under English protection in 1815.

Let us return to the present anti-Russian propaganda: it goes back to the time of the Crimean War. Even today, the lineaments of this propaganda and the geopolitical motifs that it conceals or travesties still remain and are still used – and show more virulence in the Anglo-Saxon sphere and in France than elsewhere in Europe, apart from the countries of the east recently liberated from Communism. The inner circles, newspapers, publications of the milieus called "nationalist" or "national-conservative" of the French and English west evoke much less often an European alliance than their counterparts of Germanic Central Europe (Germany, Austria). In Flanders, we witness an English contagion, a veritable "Anglo-Saxon *aigüe*" totally contrary to the European interests of this region connected to the Rhineland-Westphalia and unproductive of any metapolitical fight confronted with the French danger where the conquest is no longer military or cultural but economic.

The "New Philosophers" as Instruments of Russophobia

The anti-Russian propaganda, today hostile to Putin, functions marvellously in the Anglo-Saxon linguistic sphere. It is from back rooms that are increasingly less British and increasingly more American that it is deployed over the entire globe. In France this propaganda is disseminated under a different disguise, at first not from conservative or national conservative circles but from Trotskyist networks of admitted adherence or infiltrated into the syndicalist or socialist circles and above all, at first from the media and journalism sectors where the sect of "New Philosophers" is installed which straddles the new left (the famous second and third lefts) and an Atlantist soft, liberal and "orléanist" right which seeks to turns its back on Gaullism. This bastion, well positioned at the crossroads between the centrist right and centrist left, allows this propaganda to insinuate itself everywhere and prevent the development of an alternative geopolitical thought that is non-Atlantist, that could emerge in several potential political fringes today chastised into the margins of the dominant politics and often decried as "extremist", Communist, Gaullist (in the sense of Couve de Murville),[177] nationalist, sovereignist or neo-Maurrasian.[178]

The Crimean War thus definitively smashed the Pentarchy, the only European cohesion of the modern and contemporary era. Nevertheless the dominant conflict – the one whose stakes had the greatest territorial curve because it concerned both the (Siberian and Central Asian) Central Land and the Central Ocean (the Indian Ocean with the Indian sub-continent) – remained the Russo-British one. The Franco-Prussian conflict of 1870-71, perceived as essential in France or in Germany because it was a local one, remains marginal in spite of everything, in spite of its

---

[177] [Maurice Couve de Murville (1907-1999) was a French politician who served as Minister of Foreign Affairs from 1958 to 1968 under de Gaulle and Prime Minister from 1968-69.]

[178] [Charles Maurras (1868-1952) was a French nationalist and monarchist thinker who led the "Action Française" movement founded in 1899 to combat the left-wing supporters of the accused Jewish officer Alfred Dreyfus.]

importance, in spite of the fact that it is one of the major sources of the two world conflicts of the 20th century.

Versailles and the Return to the Politics of Richelieu

However, the permanence of the Anglo-Russian conflict on the confines of the Hindu Kush, the rivalry between London and St. Petersburg in Central Asia and the French desire for revenge and the reconquest of Germanic Alsace and Lorraine would weigh sufficiently to modify the order between 1871 and 1914. France invested in Russia in order to have an "ally in the back", just as François I had allied himself to the Sultan and to the Barbary pirates to hold the Holy Empire and Spain in check and to cause the Spanish and Venetian offensive in North Africa and in the direction of the eastern Mediterranean to fail. The disastrous effect of this policy has not yet been completely measured. The French policy of investments in Russia, better known under the name of "Russian borrowings", would contribute to the progressive disintegration of the league of "Three Emperors",[179] the final residue of the spirit of the Pentarchy of 1814. To this project of joining the "Russian steamroller" was added a Masonic desire to break up the space of the Austro-Hungarian "Danubian monarchy", to fraction Central and Eastern Europe into as many small states as possible, all doomed to economic dependence or unviability: this would be a revival of the politics of Richelieu bestowing *Kleinstaaterei*[180] on Germany which found a new culmination in the Treaty of Versailles.

Bismarck would doubtlessly have succeeded in maintaining the cohesion of the League of the Three Emperors. His successors did not have this political intelligence and this geopolitical "feeling". Without reacting in an opportune manner, they gave free rein to

---

[179] [The Three Emperors' League was an alliance between the German, Russian and Austro-Hungarian Empires that lasted from 1873 to 1887.]

[180] [The status of a small state.]

this French policy of satellisation of Russia. When the latter swung definitively into the French camp, the alternative policy of Germany was to search in moribund Ottoman Empire a space to sell the export goods of its new industry and to obtain raw materials from. This policy would collide with the Russian desire to find an outlet beyond the Dardanelles in the direction of the eastern Mediterranean, Suez and Egypt and the British desire to maintain or to create a blockade starting from Cairo and ending in Calcutta in Bengal in order to complete, with the English possessions in Africa and Australia, an absolute dominance over all the coastlines of the Indian Ocean.

Twenty Years to Perfect the Entente

However, it took twenty years to consolidate the alliance that the Entente would be between London, Paris and St. Petersburg. The sources of potential conflicts remained latent between England and France in Indo-China, where England accepted whether it liked it or not that the French would control the Pacific façade of Indo-China but did not accept any extension of this control in the direction of Siam and the Bay of Bengal. Similarly, England took a dim view of the violent conquest and then the pacification of Madagascar by General Gallieni[181] (whom they would detest even more after the battle of the Marne in 1914 when this battle decided the fate of the war in favour of the Allies). Later, the affair of the seizure by the British of the Suez Canal was not appeased quickly, underwent some unexpected developments, especially when the expedition of Capt. Marchand[182] in the direction of Fashoda in the Sudan suggested a French installation on the banks of the Nile, the axis connecting Egypt to South Africa.

---

[181] [Joseph Gallieni (1849-1916) was a French military commander and administrator of colonies who abolished the monarchy of Madagascar and exiled its queen in 1897.]

[182] [Jean-Baptiste Marchand (1863-1934) was a French military officer who, in 1890, commanded a French expedition that intended to take control of Fashoda, where it was met by Sir Herbert Kitchener of the Anglo-Egyptian army. After intense diplomatic discussions, the French withdrew from Fashoda.]

A French presence on the Nile would have been able to break the territorial cohesion of the British Empire in Africa through an alliance either with Somalia under Italian domination or to Christian Abyssinia or to Belgian Congo. There would have been a continental European presence on an important portion of the African littoral of the Indian Ocean with, on the one hand, a great territorial depth connecting the Atlantic to the Central Ocean and, on the other hand, a Madagascan naval base (and, later, an aircraft carrier) opposite Portuguese Mozambique, Tanganyika, at that time German, and above all the mines of South Africa, where there lived a rebellious Boer population, partially of French origin. Can we imagine today what power a European colonial bloc could have had that gathered together the French, Belgian, German and Portuguese colonies and the independent Boer states? The Red Sea would have been controlled at the level of Aden and Djibouti by a Germano-Turkish, Italian and French European constellation. For London one of the most interesting results of the First World War was the control of the Red Sea from Suez to Aden, eliminating there all Germano-Turkish and, indirectly, French presence, France having emerged worn out from the Great War.

Ratzel, Tirpitz and the Awakening of Germany

In the nineties of the 19th century, the Russians made themselves masters of present-day Tajikistan and exercised a preponderating influence on "Chinese Turkestan" north of Tibet, while, in order to counter this gain of power, the English annexed to the Empire of India the Afghan regions that are today Pakistani and that are called the Pashtun "ethnic zone" – today in full rebellion and sanctuary of the Taliban rebels against the occupation of Afghanistan. Between 1890 and 1900 it was impossible to predict an Anglo-Russian alliance as so many potential conflicts accumulated along the Afghan frontiers. The very fine film Kim, based on a novel of Rudyard Kipling, depicts a local Muslim Indian loyal to the British crown and some Russian explorers suspected of espionage and of having come to raise hostile tribes against the English presence. The film's scenario takes place precisely in the nineties of the 19th century.

After the Boer War and the ruthless elimination of their two free republics of southern Africa, a period when Victorian England had been despised all over Europe, Germany became enemy number one because it developed efficient commercial strategies and competed with the British industrial products everywhere in the world, began to construct a navy under the inspiration of the geopolitician Friedrich Ratzel[183] and Admiral von Tirpitz,[184] exercised a preponderant influence in the Low Countries, proposed a Central Africa Union to Belgium and Portugal capable of ruining the projects of Cecil Rhodes,[185] and above all reorganised the Ottoman Empire to make it a supplementary space for its industry (Ergänzungsraum) cutting the route of the Russians towards Constantinople and occupying strategic positions in the eastern Mediterranean by taking over, with Austria-Hungary and its Dalmatian marines, the place of Venice, the Serenissima, in this maritime space opposite Suez and on an important segment of the maritime route to India.

Mackinder and the "Central Land"

Despite the emergence of a "German danger" for London, Russia remained implicitly the principal enemy in the speech that Halford John Mackinder gave in 1904 to explain through geography the Land/Sea dynamic of history where England held the Sea and India and Russia the Land and Central Asia, rechristened the

---

[183] [Friedrich Ratzel (1844-1904) was a German cultural geographer who contributed to the foundation of geopolitical science.]

[184] [Alfred von Tirpitz (1849-1930) was a German admiral who served as Secretary of State of the German Imperial Navy from 1897 to 1916.]

[185] [Cecil Rhodes (1853-1902) was a British mining magnate and colonialist politician who founded the southern African state called Rhodesia (now Zimbabwe) and championed Anglo-Saxon supremacy.]

"Central Land" and posited as inaccessible to the naval instrument of the English power. In a way Mackinder sounded the alarm in 1904 because, contrary to the era of the Crimean War, Russia was beginning, under the impetus of Sergei Witte, to equip itself with a network of railways and a trans-Siberian rail line which would henceforth procure for it the military capacity to quickly transport troops towards the Black Sea, the Caucasus, Central Asia and the Far East. At a technological level, the order had thus changed. Russia, handicapped by the vastness of its territories and the logistic problems that they raise, had just acquired a not negligible supplement of land mobility. It weighed with a more considerable weight on the "rimlands", including Persia and India, which gave access to the Indian Ocean, the "Central Ocean".

De facto, Russia became the protector of China after the Sino-Japanese War of 1895, which allowed it to make the trans-Siberian railway pass through the rich Chinese province of Manchuria. This more mobile Russia, thanks to the railway, and therefore more "dangerous", worried England: it had henceforth to be held in check by a policy of containment and by the constitution of a *cordon sanitaire*[186] of small powers dependent on the principal thalassocracy of the globe. Better: the Far Eastern policy of Russia, in the face of the old and new Asiatic powers of the region, received the full support of Wilhelm II of Germany, who in this way turned Russia away from the Danube and defused the potential conflicts with Austro-Hungary; faced with these German encouragements, England, which saw in them another danger to its interests, intended to bring Russia back eventually into Europe so that it might act against Austria, the principal ally of rising Germany.

---

[186] [Sanitary barrier, a term used by French Prime Minister Georges Clemenceau in 1919 when he sought to form a buffer zone constituted of the small states that had seceded from the Soviet Union in order to prevent the westward spread of Communism.]

Russia Moves its Pawns Towards the Pacific

The Entente was being sketched: France financed Russia, but tied it in this way to itself and England had at its disposal two "continental assassins" to slaughter the power that it judged to be most dangerous to itself using the blood of their millions of conscripts. Sergei Witte advocated a policy of small steps in the Far East: Germany's acquisition of the Chinese base of Tsingtao precipitated matters, obliged the Russians to abandon their initial moderation and to claim and occupy Port Arthur; at the same time the English seized Weihaiwei. The powers slashed each other on China, eroded its plurisecular sovereignty, sparked a xenophobic revolt, that of the Boxers, supported in petto[187] by the Dowager Empress.[188] To subdue this revolt the powers organised a punitive expedition in the course of which the Russians seized the entirety of Manchuria. Through Kharbin and Moukden, the trans-Siberian railway was prolonged upto Port Arthur: at the same time, Russia was present in the warm waters of the Pacific.[189] Admiral Alexeyev,[190] the governor of the region, undertook the exploitation of the port and the new naval base more ambitiously up to the Korean peninsula, which was likely to provide a territorial bridge between Vladivostok and Port Arthur. On the course of the river Yalu the Russians discovered gold. Alexeyev's policy collided with Japan, which coveted Korea. The scenario was ready for a full war. This time against Japan, with the disadvantage that this war was very unpopular and did not correspond to the customary political myths of the Russian people, who still wanted a surge towards Constantinople, the Balkans and the Aegean.

---

[187] [In secret.]

[188] [Empress Dowager Cixi (1835-1908) was the Manchu (Qing) regent who ruled China from 1861 until her death.]

[189] Richard Moeller, *Russland – Wesen und Werden*, Leipzig: Goldmann, 1941.

[190] [Evgeny Alexeyev (1843-1917) was an admiral in the Imperial Russian Navy, viceroy of the Russian Far East and commander-in-chief of Russian forces at Port Arthur and Manchuria for a brief period at the start of the Russo-Japanese War of 1904-5.]

In 1905, during the Russo-Japanese War, England and already the United States supported Japan, the archipelago on the border of the Sino-Korean "rimland". Japan thus became the little Asiatic soldier of the first policy of containment just after the speech of Mackinder. The propaganda against Nicholas II, depicted as the "butcher" of his people, was in full swing. Some revolutionary circles received mysterious financing. The Russian fleet in the Baltic, which departed from the Gulf of Finland to bring aid to that of the Pacific, could not get a supply of coal along its itinerary in the British bases, which were the most numerous. Result: the disaster of Tsushima.[191]

Let us note, in this context, the ignoble hypocrisy of France, which had promised marvels to its "ally" Russia but had coldly let it fall in its confrontation with Japan so as not to offend England. A dangerous game, for, at one point, this betrayal almost brought Russia into a system of alliance including Germany without excluding France. The Paris/Berlin/St. Petersburg axis was almost born in October 1904. France refused and the Tsar, dependent on French funds, did not sign. In July 1905, there was a second attempt to establish a European unity with Germany, France and Russia during the interview between Wilhelm II and Nicholas II in the Swedish island of Björko. These interviews were due to the goodwill of the two monarchs, who did not have the benefit of any ministerial countersignature. Once again France refused, banking on its English alliance and on the immediate advantages that Morocco had procured for it. As for the English, the weakening of Russia, after its defeat by Japan, no longer allowed any dangerous manoeuvre in the direction of India. It was thus no longer the principal enemy.

---

[191] [The Battle of Tsushima was a decisive battle fought in May 1905 during the Russo-Japanese War and ended in the destruction of the Russian navy by the Japanese.]

The Terrible Year 1905

Russia, defeated by Japan, and weakened by the revolutionary schemes, softened its positions; it was ripe to enter into the Franco-British Entente[192] signed in 1904. Worse, the military humiliation was succeeded by a civil dissent of a revolutionary nature: in July 1904, the Nihilists assassinated the Minister of the Interior, Plehve;[193] in January 1905, a demonstration directed by Father Gapon[194] turned into a carnage; in February 1905, it was the turn of the Grand-Duke Sergei to be assassinated; troubles surged in Manchuria behind the troops; in June, mutineers burst onto the ships of the navy of the Black Sea including the famous battleship Potemkin; in October 1905, Lenin organised a first revolutionary movement in St. Petersburg which began with a general strike; the peasant revolts proceeded to "illuminations", that is, conflagrations of castles or public buildings in the provinces; the Baltic people attacked the German aristocracy and set fire to their estates; in December 1905, Lenin struck at Moscow but the troops had returned from Manchuria and the Bolshevik revolution was subdued. Witte, recalled to government, launched the "October Manifesto" promising the creation of a duly elected Duma as well as reforms. In 1906, when Russia gave up its policy of Far Eastern expansion, when it accepted new French loans, the internal troubles ceased "miraculously"; the Tsar, once again turned from a "monster" into a "good man".

In 1907, the British and the Russians signed an accord behind the back of the Persia of the decadent Qajars[195] sharing the country

---

[192] [The Entente Cordiale.]

[193] [Vyacheslav von Plehve (1846-1904) was appointed Minister of the Interior in 1902 and was assassinated by members of the Socialist Revolutionary Combat Organisation founded by the Lithuanian Jew Grigory Gershuni, whose parents were killed in a pogrom.]

[194] [Georgy Gapon (1870-1906) was a Russian Orthodox priest and working class leader who organised the workers' procession that turned into the Bloody Sunday incident of 1905.]

[195] [The Qajars were a Turkic royal dynasty that ruled Iran from 1794 after the Zand dynasty.]

into zones of influence. The next year, 1908, was marked by two major events: the annexation by Austria of Bosnia-Herzegovina and the revolution of the "Young Turks". In spite of the Franco-British schemes to create discord between Vienna and St. Petersburg, the Austro-Russian relations continued to be good. In June, Austria planned to construct a railway through the Sandžak of Novi Pazar[196] in order to organise the Balkan peninsula according to their interests. This intention immediately provoked a reinforcement of relations between Russia and Great Britain, in the aftermath of the interview between Nicholas II and Edward VII at Reval. In July, the "Young Turks" triumphed, demanded a constitution and elections, to which the inhabitants of Bosnia-Herzegovina – administered by the Austrians but still Ottoman citizens – were invited. Russia feared that the "Young Turks" would give a new vitality to Turkey, ally themselves to the French and British as during the Crimean War and would resume the old policy of blocking the Straits. The revolution of the "Young Turks" brought the Austrians and Russians closer. Ährental[197] and Izvolsky,[198] ministers of foreign affairs, during the secret accords of Buchlov in Moravia were agreed on the following policy:

1. Austria-Hungary would abandon its railway projects in the Sanjak of Novi Pazar,

2. Vienna would promise to support all the Russian efforts to unblock the Straits.

On the basis of these accords the Austrians annexed Bosnia-Herzegovina in October 1908 without referring to the Italians or Germans, their real or theoretical allies within the Triple Alliance, about it. The Bulgarians profited from it to declare themselves totally independent of Turkey. The Montenegrin wives of the two

---

[196] [Novi Pazar is a city in south-western Serbia in the region of Sandžak.]

[197] [Count Alois von Ährental (1854-1912) was an Austrian diplomat who was appointed Minister of Foreign Affairs in 1906.]

[198] [Count Alexander Izvolsky (1856-1919) was a Russian diplomat who was appointed Minister of Foreign Affairs in 1907.]

Russian Grand-Dukes and of the king of Italy, hostile to Vienna, incited the warmongering and interventionist parties to combat all the Austrian policies in the Balkans. Stolypin did not want war, obliged the warmongers to moderation but Russia no longer had any support in Europe to support its ambitions in the Straits. The British diplomats, such as Ambassador Nicolson[199] and Sir Eyre Crowe[200] spread the rumour that the Austrians and, behind them, the Germans were the only ones responsible for the blockade of the Straits. In 1909, England supported the French ambitions in Morocco in exchange for a definitive recognition of the English predominance in Egypt.

From the Assassination of Stolypin to the Assassination of Sarajevo

In 1911, with the assassination of Stolypin by a fanatic revolutionary,[201] all the chances of avoiding a Germano-Russian and Austro-Russian conflict disappeared. Sazonov,[202] Stolypin's brother-in-law and successor to Izvolsky, however opted for a pacifist policy and organised a last interview between Wilhelm II and Nicholas II at Potsdam, where Bethmann-Hollweg[203] and Kiderlen-Wächter[204] tried for the last time to save the peace by proposing to the Russians that they join the Berlin-Baghdad railway

[199] [Sir Arthur Nicolson (1849-1928) was a British diplomat who served as British ambassador at St. Petersburg from 1906 to 1910.]

[200] [Sir Eyre Crowe (1864-1925) was a British diplomat who, in January 1907, produced for the Foreign Office a Memorandum on the Present State of British Relations with France and Germany in which he warned of the German danger to the balance of power in Europe.]

[201] [Stolypin was assassinated at the Kiev Opera House in September 1911 by the Jewish anarchist, and informer, Dmitry Bogrov.]

[202] [Sergei Sazanov (1860-1927) served as Russian Minister for Foreign Affairs from 1910 to 1916.]

[203] [Theobald von Bethmann-Hollweg (1856-1921) was Chancellor of the German Empire from 1909 to 1917.]

[204] [Alfred von Kiderlen-Wächter (1852-1912) was German Foreign Secretary from 1910 to 1912.]

plan and collaborate in a future railway line in the north of Persia. But the warmongers did not disarm: the Russian ambassador in Belgrade, Hartwig,[205] supported the Greater Serbia movement against Austria, Delcassé[206] ordered the march of French troops on Fez in Morocco clinching in this way the definitive conquest of the Sharifian kingdom,[207] where Germany lost all its interests; Lloyd George[208] threatened Germany directly. The latter ceded Morocco, accepting in compensation a territorial strip that it would join to its colony of Cameroon. In Europe it was fully encircled. The scenario was ready: only a spark was necessary; and that would be the assassination at Sarajevo on 28 June 1914.[209]

In 1918, when Germany definitively lost the war and Russia became Bolshevik, many voices were raised, on the left and the right of the political ideological chessboard, to demand a new Germano-Russian alliance. These negotiations would lead to the Rapallo accords between Chicherin and Rathenau (1922). Germany and Russia maintained privileged relations especially at the level of military cooperation until 1935, when Hitler decided to reintroduce obligatory military service, occupy the Rhineland and launch a programme of rearmament.

In 1936, with the Rome/Berlin Axis and the creation of the Anti-Comintern Pact, relations were broken with Soviet Russia.

---

[205] [Baron Nicholas Hartwig (1857-1914) was the Russian ambassador to Serbia from 1909 to 1914.]

[206] [Théophile Delcassé (1852-1923) was a vigorous French colonialist who served as Foreign Minister from 1898 and adopted a firm anti-German stance during the First Moroccan Crisis of 1905-6 relating to the status of Morocco.]

[207] [The Sherif dynasties of Morocco include the Idrisids, Saadians and Alawites, the last ruling from 1659.]

[208] [David Lloyd George (1863-1945) was a Liberal British statesman who served as Chancellor of the Exchequer from 1908 and Prime Minister from 1916 to 1922. His Mansion House speech warning Germany was made during the Moroccan Agadir Crisis of 1911 involving France (Britain's ally) and Germany.]

[209] [On this date Archduke Ferdinand of Austria and his wife Sophie were assassinated by the Bosnian Serb, Gavrilo Princip, recruited by another Bosnian Serb, Danilo Ilić, who belonged to the Black Hand secret society and 'Mlada Bosna' (Young Bosnia)].

When the Spanish Civil War broke out, Germany supported the nationalists of the "Alzamiento nacional"[210] and the USSR the Republicans of the "Frente Popular",[211] which counted Communists within its ranks. The support to Franco brought Germany and Italy together definitively, but the Spanish Communists and their Soviet allies broke with the bloc of the "Frente Popular", which was at first united and collided with the other anarchist and Trotskyist militant factions of the left (POUM)[212] in the territories controlled by the Spanish Republicans, especially in Barcelona, contributing to the definitive ruin of the "Frente Popular" and the collapse of its armed forces. After the victory of the Francoist camp and the crumbling of the camp of the leftists, everything was in place for bringing together the Axis, and particularly Germany, and the USSR. In August,[213] the famous Germano-Soviet pact, or the Ribbentrop-Molotov Pact, was signed in Moscow. Germany was free to turn all its forces towards the west while receiving Soviet petrol and cereals. The idyll lasted until 1941, when Molotov, already worried about the Balkan policy of the Germans, could not admit their definitive control of Yugoslavia and Greece. These disagreements, reinforced by the real threats that the English caused to be applied on the Caucasus with visible aeroplanes of the RAF, constituted the prelude to Operation Barbarossa, initiated on 22 June 1941. The Germano-Russian relations between 1918 and 1945 are worthy of having an entire seminar devoted to them. It is not our subject today. That is why I shall remain brief on this theme, which is however of capital importance in order to understand the dynamic of the century.[214]

---

[210] [The name given to the rebels who carried out the nationalist coup in July 1936 against the Second Spanish Republic that led to the Spanish Civil War.]

[211] [The Republican forces.]

[212] ["Partido Obrero de Unificación Marxista" (Workers' Party of Marxist Unification) was a Trotskyist Communist party in Spain during the Spanish Second Republic and the Spanish Civil War.]

[213] [1939.]

[214] The most complete work to approach this very complex subject is: *Gerd Koenen, Der Russland-Komplex – Die Deutschen und der Osten 1900-1945*, Munich: C. H. Beck, 2005.

No Free Europe if the East/West Bi-Polarity Persists

After 1945, the Cold War was established with the blockade of Berlin and the Prague coup. It would last more than forty years, impregnate all minds, because all imagined that this situation would persist for long centuries. In this bi-polar context, where ideology seemed to dominate, Europe was cut into two, Germany was crossed by an Iron Curtain and divided into two antagonistic republics; the Danube, the central artery of Europe, was blocked close to Vienna; the Elbe, the principal river of the North European plain, which runs from Prague to Hamburg, was cut off from the immediate hinterland of this big port. Such a Europe was no longer anything but an Atlantic trading post. In the fifties, it still possessed its colonial external lung. From the decolonisations of the first years of the "Golden Sixties" this lung was no longer guaranteed, and the palliative of the multinationals, which created employment and replaced the colonial vocations, plunged Europe into a dangerous dependence. This is the international political context in which the political conscience of my generation emerged. For me, this conscience emerged slowly around my fourteenth year; after five or six years of tentative steps, around 1975-76, our informal groups, or rather groups of buddies, inspired by the descendants of the "Jeune Europe" school,[215] excited by new reading materials and stimulated by the new political orders, arrived at the general conclusion that it is impossible to grant a free future to the western portion of Europe if the east-west bipolarity persisted.

In the Belgian context, Pierre Harmel[216] had attempted an opening to the east by multiplying the bilateral relations between Belgium and the small powers of the Communist bloc such as Poland, Romania and Hungary. It was a matter of pragmatism, without aligning itself with the France of De Gaulle insofar as France still remained a danger for the psychological and

---

[215] ["Jeune Europe" was the name of the anti-American and anti-Soviet Europeist movement founded by Jean Thiriart in Belgium.]

[216] [Count Pierre Harmel (1911-2009) was a Christian Democrat who served as Prime Minister of Belgium from 1965 to 1966.]

territorial integrity of our country (which is, with Grand Duchy of Luxembourg and its completely dismembered borders in the south, the last independent shred of the Grand Lothier[217] of mediaeval memory). However, Harmel did not imitate the Ostpolitik of Willy Brandt,[218] with his discourse marked by the German sense of guilt, which was evidently not enforced in Belgium. Harmel intended to restore a "Total Europe" and detach the sub-continent from its rigid system of blocs. Unfortunately, these efforts were of short duration and, within his own party, he was hardly followed. After the Harmel era, Vanden Boeynants[219] arrived with an Atlantist, pro-NATO and philo-American politics. More tragic though less visible: the failure of diplomatic "Harmelism" meant also the end of coherent political Catholicism in Belgium, heir to the Burgundian and Hispano-Austrian imperial tradition. Belgium then forgot that it had embodied that tradition in history during the last five centuries with an unchanging brio and it accepted, with "Polle Pansj" ("Pol Boudin",[220] alias Vanden Boeynants) and his successors, the miserable status of a subordinate little pawn on the Atlantist chessboard.

Kissinger Makes Advances to Mao's China

In this context, posterior to the agitations of 1968, the general order on the international chessboard was in the process of changing so that the Eurasian Communist bloc based on the Chinese pillar

---

[217] [Lothier refers to the territory within the Duchy of Lower Lotharingia ruled by the dukes of Brabant from 1190 to 1796.]

[218] [Willy Brandt (1913-92) was a German Social Democrat who was Chancellor of West Germany from 1969 to 1974. He sought to improve relations with Eastern European countries through his "Neue Ostpolitik" (New Eastern policy). This policy was reflected in the "détente" initiated in the USA by Nixon and Kissinger from 1969.]

[219] [Paul van den Boeynants (1919-2001) was Prime Minister of Belgium from 1966-68 and from1978-79.]

[220] [Boeynants was nicknamed "blood sausage" since he was born in a butcher's family.]

and the Soviet pillar would be disintegrated through a very real conflict that had just emerged within this red bloc, or the hot Sino-Soviet war along the rive Amur; the American diplomacy of Kissinger positing as its principle that Moscow remained and would remain the principal enemy, "made advances" to Mao's China and established with it, from 1971-72, normal diplomatic relations even while supporting it in eastern Asia against the USSR. This diplomacy was based, once again, on the geopolitical theories of Mackinder and his disciples: according to these theories, it was necessary, if need be, to support a power of the "rimland" (or "inner crescent"), or an alliance of smaller powers of the rimland, against the ruling power of the "Central Land". The Maoists of May '68 would partially swing to the American camp against the "Moscowteers". Washington had already deployed its own "Communists", mostly of Trotskyist faith or emerging from the old POUM of the Spanish Civil War; these were soon joined by Maoists deriving from the Washington/Peking alliance.

With the disappearance from the foreground of Harmel and his policy of bilateral relations between small powers of the western bloc and small powers of the eastern bloc, and with the disappearance from the military margins of the politics of Thiriart's "Jeune Europe", which aimed at the liberation of our sub-continent from the American and Soviet tutelage, no real and concrete political field of action was still open to us. We lived in the premises of the "Great Confusion", with fracture lines that henceforth divided all the camps that had been present on the field before the Sino-American reconciliation. This great confusion essentially struck the activist groups of the left but did not allow more clarity in the little Europeist and revolutionary national phalanxes.

A Euro-Russian Rapprochement is the Only Solution

According to the "Jeune Europe" movement of the sixties, the two superpowers were posited and viewed as equally harmful to the development of a free Europe. When Washington came closer to

China and the red bloc was divided into two antagonistic powers, "Jeune Europe" could no longer advocate either limited and partial alliances between small powers of the two blocs (as during Thiriart's travel to Romania) or a reverse alliance with China to oblige the USSR to back off from Danubian Europe. The Sino-American bloc became a threat to Europe and, ipso facto, a Euro-Russian rapprochement seemed like the only viable solution in the long term, for followers of Realpolitik. This step the Italian general Guido Giannettini,[221] Jean Thiriart and the Franco-Romanian writer Jean Parvulesco[222] would take, supporting their positions with solid arguments.

In the meantime, in 1975, the United States, worn out, abandoned South Vietnam to victorious and pro-Soviet North Vietnam and initiated immediately with their new Chinese allies a war on the Sino-Tonkin and armed, through China, the Cambodia of Pol Pot to harass the new reunified Vietnam in Cochinchina. Vietnam was thus neutralised and ceased to be a "pocket or resistance" on the rimland of the Asiatic south-east now extended to China, as it was, besides, foreseen on all the maps drawn by the Anglo-Saxon school of geopolitics from Mackinder to Lea to Spykman.[223] Nobody any more, especially among the young generation, can imagine what the state of mental confusion was among the militant leftists where there were harsh disputes between "Moscowteers", Trotskyists, pro-Albanian Maoists, self-management Titoists,[224] anti-Soviet Maoists,

---

[221] [Guido Giannettini (1930-2003) was an agent in the pay of the Italian secret services.]

[222] [Jean Parvulesco (1929-2010) was a Romanian French journalist who was influenced by the Traditionalism of René Guénon and Julius Evola. His geopolitical essays continue the project - suggested earlier by Gabriel Hanotaux (see above p. 73) – of a "Paris/Berlin/Moscow axis" to counter the Anglo-Saxon hegemony.]

[223] [Nicholas Spykman (1893-1943) was an American geostrategist who largely followed Mackinder's geopolitical theories but laid particular stress on the control of Eurasia for global hegemony.]

[224] [The theory of socialist self-management, or management of organisations by workers, was propounded in Yugoslavia in the fifties by Josip Tito and Edvard Kardelj.]

partisans and adversaries of Pol Pot or Ho Chi Minh. This chaos sealed the end of the classical militant left between 1975 and 1978-79, when the fragmentation into antagonistic schools of thought no longer allowed the emergence of an offensive viable bloc. The hard, youthful and revolutionary leftist sects are dead for lack of a coherent geopolitical argument. Worse, because they had earlier accepted geopolitical arguments foreign to their own nation or continental nation.

Carter and "Human Rights", Reagan and "the Empire of Evil"

With the accession to power of Jimmy Carter in Washington in 1976 we enter fully into the gestation period of the mental universe that prevails today and which is increasingly felt to be suffocating. The fetish terms of "political correctness" were set up along with the introduction of the diplomacy of so-called "human rights" and a Republican opposition that was aligned with the theses of neoliberalism propagated by Margaret Thatcher in Great Britain. In 1979, the latter inaugurated the neoliberal era which came to an end with the crisis of Autumn 2008. In 1980, when Reagan took up the American presidency, his version of neoliberalism, Reaganomics, would support and not efface the Carterian diplomacy of "human rights" and serve it with an apocalyptic sauce by evoking an "empire of evil", the prelude to Bush Jr.'s "axis of evil".

In Europe, the talk of "human rights" obliterated everything and one part of the disintegrated, orphaned, militant left marched in the direction of this well publicised new "subjectivism", the first philosophical basis of the hyper-individualist philosophy of the neoliberalism of Hayek,[225] Friedman,[226] etc. The engine of this new synthesis in a France marked by Gaullist and Communist statism

---

[225] [Friedrich Hayek (1899-1992) was an Austrian economist who championed classical liberalism.]

[226] [Milton Friedman (1912-2006) was an American economist who advocated the free market economic system and served as adviser to Ronald Reagan and Margaret Thatcher.]

was the discourse of the "New Philosophers", borne essentially in these transitional years by two writings of Bernard-Henry Lévy,[227] "*Le Testament de Dieu*" and "*L'idéologie française*". The latter constituted a veritable diabolisation of all the French political forces because all, indifferently, bore in themselves the germs of Fascism or a propensity leading to a world of concentration camps.

The ideological ingredients of the two manifestos of Lévy, whose philosophical foundations were well maintained, chastised the more militant discourse of May '68 into the political and media margins and – what is more serious because more sterilising – this entire set of thoughts, theories and reflections which Ferry and Renaud would call the "68er thought". The latter constituted a seductive intellectual surpassing of the simple student and workers' militantism of the time, which had been imbibed from the (typically French) Rousseausist and Communist vulgates and had received the benediction of the aged Sartre ("one should not make Billancourt despair").[228]

Potentialities of "French Theory", the Skulduggery of the "New Philosophers"

This "68er thought", which the American scholars then called "French Theory", had included Deleuze, Guattari,[229] Lyotard[230] and

---

[227] [Bernard-Henri Lévy (1948-) is a Jewish French intellectual who founded the group of "New Philosophers". Lévy criticises Marxist socialism and projects a more blatantly Jewish ideology that resembles the American Neoconservative.]

[228] [Sartre, who was a supporter of the French Communist Party in the fifties, confided to his friends that "il ne faut pas désespérer Billancourt" by telling workers (the Renault workers at Boulogne-Billancourt were taken as a symbol of the proletariat) the truth about Communist society and thereby disillusioning them.]

[229] [Pierre-Félix Guattari (1930-92) was a French psychoanalyst who collaborated with Gilles Deleuze on the books *L'Anti-Oedipe* (1972) and *Mille Plateaux* (1980), which were combined together in one work, *Capitalism and Schizophrenia*.]

[230] [Jean-François Lyotard (1924-98) was a relativist, anti-universalist philosopher.]

Foucault;[231] it was accused – mostly by its Parisian New Philosophers in the manner of Lévy or neo-Quietist in the manner of Comte-Sponville,[232] by thundering inquisitors or honeyed apologists of the consumerist humdrum – of dangerously privileging "life" against the "law", of equally dangerously opting for genealogising and archaelogising ideologies in the manner of Nietzsche, etc. For the rather informal network of the "New Philosophers", the German "master thinkers" of the 19th century (Glucksmann)[233] and beacons of "French Theory" should give way to a "literary and philosophical marketing" (to use the stinging critique that Deleuze made of their media pandemonium), or a well circumscribed "ready made thought" which posed as the unsurpassed intellectual attitude that would put a definitive end to the horrors of history, which would inevitably lead to the world of concentration camps described by Solzhenitsyn in The Gulag Archipelago.[234] The "New Philosophers" and their like were the "vigilants" who would ensure that the end of history (Fukuyama) occurs and that humanity finally ends in the great anti-totalitarian peace. The Parisian clique of the "New Philosophers" and their like intended to represent "the radical hope of the end of evil". This antithesis of the attitude of the "master thinkers" – who would generate a world of concentration camps – is found fully focussed in the discourse on human rights inaugurated by Carter and constitutes the main instrument to combat the "empire of evil" and all its incarnations – as Reagan and, later, the father of Bush Jr. wished to do. The discourse of the "New Philosophers" thus corresponds fully to the general objectives of the American imperialism, and its appearance in the "French intellectual landscape" is certainly not an accident: one can consider it without any hesitation as a clever and subtle creation

---

[231] [Michel Foucault (1926-84) was a French thinker who wrote on mainly psychological subjects.]

[232] [André Comte-Sponville (1952-) is an atheist but spiritualist philosopher.]

[233] [André Glucksmann (1937-2015) was a Jewish French thinker whose ideology is similar to Lévy's.]

[234] [The Gulag Archipelago is a work by Aleksandr Solzhenitsyn, written between 1958 and 1968, about the Soviet labour camps.]

of the media agencies of America, the vanguard of American "soft power".

This ideological slide beyond the disturbing questioning of the "French Theory" was systematically supported by the media, which have destroyed all the nuances and subtleties of the politico-ideological discourse and, worse, do not tolerate them any longer in the name of any concocted tolerance; it was in operation from the accession to power of Thatcher in London and was considerably re-enforced when Reagan took over the American presidency. The Maoist militant past of certain major or minor exponents of the "New Philosophy" of Glucksmann, Lévy and their counterparts allowed Guy Hocquenghem[235] to satirise them in an "Open letter to those who moved from the Mao collar to the Rotary Club". The image is as pertinent as it is striking: Maoists who were in the past stark rabid admirers of the excesses of the "Cultural Revolution" effectively became *salonfähig*[236] from the time of the Sino-American rapprochement of the first half of the seventies. The common denominator: anti-Sovietism. This Sovietism which their Trotskyist comrades called "Panzercommunism". So, one can easily conclude that our old Trotskyist or Maoist revolutionaries of the Parisian barricades had much more than a few points in common with Zbigniew Brzezenski.[237] The latter, we may recall, was the advocate, within the American diplomacy, of a new alliance with China and the major partisan of a destruction of the USSR by a dismantlement of its Caucasian and Central Asian buffer zones. Later, in Afghanistan, he would advocate an alliance with the mujahideens and, finally, with the Talibans.

---

[235] [Guy Hocquenghem (1946-88) was a French thinker who drew on the work of Deleuze and Guattari in studying homosexuality.]

[236] [Socially acceptable.]

[237] [Zbigniew Brzezinski (1928-) is an American political and geopolitical scientist. Brzezinski, who adheres to the tradition of Mackinder and Spykman, was adviser to presidents Lyndon Johnson and Jimmy Carter.]

The Great Return of Slavophile Thought

In the Soviet Union, the period that runs from 1978 to 1982 (the year of Brezhnev's death) is marked by an entirely different intellectual development. One witnessed a veritable "conservative revolution", a return to the sources of "Russianness", to the lineaments of the Slavophilia of the 19th century, a return to Dostoyevsky. The emblematic figure of this "völkisch" and Slavophile renewal was incontestably the writer Valentin Rasputin.[238] For this writer with a pastoralist character the notions of memory, remembrance, continuity are cardinal and primordial. For Rasputin consciousness is as it is only because it remembers and inscribes itself in the continuities imposed by the vital flux (and thus by the particular history of the people of which the individual is a part). A human action is morally justifiable only if it is intertwined in a continuity, if it fights against the schemes of those who wish, through particular or selfish interest, to provoke discontinuities. The literary theme of deracination and alienation (in relation to one's origins) implies that of the simultaneous loss of moral integrity. This was already encountered in the Norwegian Knut Hamsun.[239] The forgetting of his own past plunges man into moral depravity, ugliness of the soul.

This fundamental philosophical position collided head on with the modern ideologies of the "*tabula rasa*", of which Communism was the most caricatural incarnation. From the French Jacobinism or Babouvism[240] of the end of the 18th century to Communism, there is, without any discontinuity, a red thread that does not produce any good, nothing but germs and bacilli of decline and

---

[238] [Valentin Rasputin (1937-2015) was a Russian writer from Siberia who sought to preserve traditional Russian culture from the onslaught of modernisation.] Günther Hasenkamp, *Gedächtnis und Leben in der Prosa Valentin Rasputins*, Wiesbaden: Otto Harrassowitz, 1990.

[239] [Knut Hamsun (1859-1952) was a Norwegian novelist who was sympathetic to National Socialism.]

[240] [Babouvism is a movement of egalitarianism and communism first propagated by François-Noël Babeuf (1760-97) during the French Revolutionary period.]

depravity. At the time when the Soviet Union reached its apogee, the apex of its power, and justified its existence and its successes by a "progressivist" ideology that had the intention of leaving behind it all the legacy of the past, there emerged within the Soviet society itself a spectrum of literary subjects whose philosophical tenor was radically different from the official ideology. I still remember, in this context, having bought at the "Librairie de Rome" on Avenue Louise, and at the "Librairie du Monde Entier" directed by the PCB,[241] a copy of *Sciences Sociales*, the journal of the Academy of the Soviet Union, with a long article by Boris Rybakov on Russian paganism before the conversion to Christianity, and a copy of the Lettres soviétiques dedicated to the rehabilitation of Dostoyevsky and edited, at that time, by Alexander Prokhanov,[242] the editor of Dyeïenn and Zavtra, whom I met in Moscow in 1992. The texts of Prokhanov appeared in the nineties from the Presses Universitaires de France.

"Occidentalists" and "Slavophiles" in the Dissidence and in the Establishment

Apart from the articles of Wolfgang Strauss in Germany[243] the most significant work of the time which explained this Slavophile renewal, by criticising it in a very acerbic manner, was from the pen of a dissident exiled in the United States: Alexander Yanov (German: Janow) attached to the Institute of International Studies of Berkeley (University of California). To give here the broad outlines of Yanov's work,[244] let us say that it subdivided in a rather

---

[241] [Parti Communiste de Belgique, Communist Party of Belgium]

[242] [Alexander Prokhanov (1938-) is a Russian novelist who engages in political activism as a Russian nationalist.]

[243] Wolfgang Strauss, "Die Neo-Slawophilen – Russlands Konservative Revolution", in *Criticon*, Munich, n°44, 1977; cf. Robert Steuckers, "Wolfgang Strauss: Les Néo-Slavophiles ou la Révolution Conservatrice dans la Russie d'aujourd'hui", in *Pour une renaissance européenne*, Bruxelles, n°21, 1978.

[244] Alexander Yanov, *The Russian New Right – Right-Wing Ideologies in the Contemporary USSR*, Berkeley: Institute of International Studies, University of California, 1978.

binary manner, the politico-intellectual landscape of the USSR of Brezhnev as the field of confrontation between "Zapadniki" (occidentalists) and "Narodniki" (populists, or the "völkische", or, more exactly, what we call in Flanders the "*volksgezinden*" or in Denmark the "*folkeliger*"). Yanov, emigrated to the United States, presented himself without any doubt as an occidentalist and denounced the new Narodniki or neo-Slavophiles, portraying them as "dangerous". Yanov, however explained to his American readers that the Soviet dissidence included within it "zapadniki' and "narodniki" (whom he mistrusted, of course) exactly as in the high circles of Soviet power, where occidentalists and populists equally rubbed shoulders. Among the great figures who tended towards populism Yanov included Solzhenitsyn. His conclusion? In the USSR, at the end of the seventies, the populists and statists had gained ground, in comparison with the occidentalists and constituted in fine the major metapolitical force in the Soviet Union, a force that was certainly not official and implicit but nevertheless decisive. This implicit domination of the "Narodniki" over minds should, according to Yanov and a good number of occidentalist dissidents, incite the United States and the Atlantists to vigilance for, Communist or not, Russia remained a danger because its essence was intrinsically "dangerous" resistant to the "civilised" forms of government in the occidentalist or Anglo-Saxon manner. This "Russophobic" attitude Solzhenitsyn denounced with all vehemence in his invigorating pamphlet "We pluralists". We hasten to add that the criticism of "narodnism" in all its forms, new or old, and the hateful tirades that Solzhenitsyn himself had to suffer all show that the Russophobia that aimed at the tsars of the nineteenth century or was discernible behind a certain anti-Sovietism was not about to disappear in the occidentalist discourse.

The era of the end of Brezhnevism was thus marked by the new Sino-American alliance, by the deployment of the theses of Brezhnev among the strategists of the Pentagon and the secret services by the establishment in broad outlines of an already post-Soviet Russophobia and later by the alliance between the United States and the Wahhabi fundamentalists and, finally, by the elimination of the Shah with the creation from scratch of a fundamentalist and offensive Shiitism in Iran. The map of the world was thereby clearly modified: the clean and dual break, characteristic of the dual politics of Yalta, gave place to a greater complexity, especially through the coming of the Islamist factor, supported at first by the American strategists. Based on this alliance with the Afghans mujahideens armed with Stinger missiles, the United States attempted to move their pawns in Europe by deploying their Pershing rockets in Germany opposite the Soviet SS-20s. In case of a direct confrontation between NATO and the Warsaw Pact, Germany, Benelux, Austria, Alsace and Lorraine risked being devastated. This eventuality, not in the least reassuring, caused the neutralist movement in Germany, forgotten since the fifties, to be reborn once again. For us the neutralist movement was embodied chiefly in the German journal *Wir selbst* founded in 1979 by Siegfried Bublies[245] with the intention of detaching the national movement from its backward-looking emphasis, its sterile nostalgias and its ridiculous sabre-rattling. Bublies maintained in Flanders friendly relations with the founders of the journal Meervoud, which still exists.

From the Rhetoric of "Human Rights" to Permanent War

The fight against the deployment of missiles in Europe experienced its apogee in the years 1982-83, borne essentially by a pacifist left that was accused of being "crypto-Communist" and consequently of being funded by Moscow. But this hostility to the belligerence of NATO was not the characteristic of just pacifist movements of the left and extreme left. Elsewhere on the political chessboard a good number of people were worried by the new rhetoric of Carter and Reagan which contaminated the liberal and conservative milieus or those of the extreme right and had as an obvious corollary the undermining of the principles of traditional diplomacy. In

---

[245] [Siegfried Bublies (1953-), who runs the Verlag Siegfried Bublies, started *Wir selbst* as a national-revolutionary journal in 1978.]

fact, the rhetoric of "human rights" manipulated in the media by the Carterian democrats and the "New Philosophers" ruined the cardinal principle of non-intervention into the internal affairs of other states characteristic of traditional diplomacy. When the Republican Reagan added to this pernicious "interventionist" rhetoric the apocalyptic language of the American religious fundamentalists, the principles of Metternichian diplomacy, the system of the treaties of Westphalia and Vienna were further pushed back. The process of the decay of classical diplomacy was completed when the neoconservatives of the entourage of Bush Jr. decreed straight away that respecting these principles was a timid archaism unworthy of the Americans, presented as the "virile sons of the god Mars" and the most obvious evidence of the cowardliness of Old Europe governed by the "cowardly sons of the goddess Venus". For us, from 1983-84, it was General Jochen Löser,[246] former commander of the 24th Panzer division of the Bundeswehr, who declared the guidelines of our arguments:[247] the rhetoric of "human rights" made the exercise of classical diplomacy impossible; the internal disputes that it exploited through the media and the agencies that inform them no longer found a balanced solution since they were perpetuated, inaugurating in this way cycles of "long wars"; "human rights", contrary to appearances, were not hoisted to the rank of dominant ideology in order to cause a humanism of good alloy to triumph all over the world but to initiate an indefinite process of wars, revolutions and troubles.

The neutralist movement as we conceived it at the beginning of the eighties was thus based on three cornerstones:

---

[246] [Major general Hans-Joachim (Jochen) Löser (1918-2001) served in the Wehrmacht during the Second World War and in the Bundeswehr after it, until 1974.]

[247] See Robert Steuckers, "Adieu au Général-Major Jochen Löser", in *Nouvelles de Synergies Européennes*, n°50, March-April 2001; cf. also Detlev Kühn, "En Souvenir d'un Soldat Politique de la Bundeswehr: le Général-Major Hans-Joachim Löser", *loc. cit.* These two texts appear on http://euro-synergies. hautetfort.com/

1. The rejection of the deployment of missiles in Europe in order to prevent the definitive transformation of our sub-continent into a "sound and light" show,

2. The rejection of the perpetuation of the system of blocs along with the dissolution of NATO and the Warsaw Pact and the creation of a vast neutral space in Central Europe from the North Sea to Brest-Litovsk and from Lapland to Albania; this neutral space should organise an efficient defence system on the Helvetian model; it thus did not reject either armed forces nor the principle of the soldier-citizen following the pacifists of the left,

3. It intended to return to the principles of classical diplomacy and refused thereby to engage in the discourse imposed by the media (or "soft-power"). Neutralism, by opposing the ready made thought of the media, asserted a space of freedom against the global "newspeak" so well decried by George Orwell in 1984.

We had the Naïveté to Believe in the Coming of a European "Common House"

If the neutralist movement had been able to disseminate its arguments for a longer period and impregnate minds more lastingly, the diffuse political thought in Europe could have generated anti-bodies. But the anti-missile turmoil and the neutralist reflections lasted for only four years. From 1984-85, Gorbachev launched two ideas, one very positive one of a "European Common House" and the other, a dual one, of "*perestroika*" and "*glasnost*", of reform and transparency. This change of discourse in Moscow definitively undermined the traditional Soviet Communism. Between 1989 and 1991, in fact, Communism as a monolithic bloc disappeared from the international political landscape. Our conclusion at that time: if there is no longer any Communism there cannot be any animosity any longer with regard to the peoples beyond the old Iron Curtain.

The motives for an eventual conflict no longer existed. We had the naïveté to believe in the coming of a pacified European Common House, in the beginning of an era marked by a spirit more or less equivalent to that which was discernible behind Kant's idea of perpetual peace.

Quickly the armed universalist idea of Soviet Communism gave place to a Neoconservatism derived from the matrix of American and New York Trotskyism. Joining neoliberalism, the new great universalist ideology, to this Trotskyism loyal to the notion of permanent revolution but cleverly disguised by a conservative and Puritan terminology, Neoconservatism would consolidate itself in two stages: the first, with Reagan, constituted a "mixture" of paleo-conservatism, anti-fiscalism, neoliberalism and, in international politics, a diplomacy apparently more classical than in the case of the human rights of Carter but nevertheless eroded by an apocalyptic terminology (the "empire of evil", etc.). Reagan finally took over the baton from Nixon, the last American president to have applied more or less correctly the rules of classical diplomacy. But, even while taking over the baton from Nixon, he had to take into consideration the acquisitions or advances of the Carterian anti-diplomacy based on the ideology of human rights. Nevertheless the apocalyptic language was attenuated during his second term.

The Crypto-Trotskyist Neoconservatism puts a Definitive End to Classical Diplomacy

With Bush senior began the attempts to force the hand of the international authorities and to move to real offensives on land; Yeltsin's Russia not opposing any credible veto, Clinton renewed, especially during the Balkan War against Serbia, with the ideology of human rights, supposedly mocked by Milošević in Kosovo. With Bush Jr., the crypto-Trotskyist Neoconservatism put a definitive end to classical diplomacy, scorned it as a debilitating "old fashion" typical only of "Old Europe" and Russia (often presented as "Stalianian" or "Neo-Stalinian" since the coming of Vladimir Putin). This rejection of classical diplomacy and of the rules of international decorum is the most patent evidence that allows one to demonstrate – beyond the personal connections and itineraries of the major exponents of Neoconservatism – that Neoconservatism is in reality a Trotskyism insofar as it refines the notion of "permanent revolution" by abolishing all the rules in force, all invasions become a quite natural and acceptable mode of operation. The "big stick" policy of Teddy Roosevelt[248] was henceforth at the service of a Trotskyist group that intended to plunge the whole into a permanent chaos (approximated to "revolution").

It is only by drawing back that one perceives clearly the vicissitudes of this American politics and its game of advances and retreats camouflaged by the alternation of Democrats and Republicans at the rudder of power. The accession of Bush Sr. to the supreme magistracy in the United States constituted also the coming of the Texan petrol magnates who remembered at every moment that the American power derives from the control of hydrocarbons in the world, and in particular in the Arabian peninsula and the Persian Gulf. The fear of the next petrol "peak" entails the desire to control the maximum of wells in this region in order to guarantee the global hegemony of Washington at least until the end of the 21st century. Whence the PNAC (Project for a New American Century) project. The European chancellories know perfectly well that America intends to perpetuate its hegemony by controlling the sources of Middle Eastern hydrocarbon to the detriment of all the other powers of the world and that the rejection of classical diplomacy ends by being a convenient modus operandi to impose its will without discussion or debate or consultation. But these same chancelleries are incapable of opposing, through a lack of will and intellectual consistency, through an imbecile fascination with the American model, a general European metapolitics, a

---

[248] [The expression used by President Theodore Roosevelt, in 1901, was "speak softly, and carry a big stick" and came to characterise his foreign policy.]

European "soft power" capable of distilling into minds, through the media, arguments and "great incontestable ideas" that are contrary to their American counterpart, the "great incontestable ideas" conveyed by the big media agencies of America.

The "White Virtues" of Global Democracy

America is the master of the world not only because it controls its hydrocarbons but also and especially because it forges, spreads and imposes the dominant opinions in the world, especially in Europe. In 1999, when the good "disciple" Clinton, presented as such because he was a Democrat and thus of the "left", launched his bombings on Belgrade, the European countries of NATO fell into step without baulking. Since Franklin Delano Roosevelt, the Democrat who had launched the Crusade against German Europe in 1941, the political "goodness", the white "virtues" of universal democracy were incarnated especially by the American Democrats. Consequently, if one does not follow their injunctions, one plunges into "evil", into "crypto-Nazism" or into some resurgence of Hitlerism. This immense simplification is deeply anchored in the contemporary mentalities and woe to one who attempts to extirpate it like a bad weed! In fact, the pro-American networks were born in Europe in the forties under the direction of the Roosevelt administration, Democratic in its affiliation; militant Atlantism had at first rather a social-democratic basis (with the exception of Schumacher249 in West Germany) than a conservative or even liberal one in the European sense of the term.

The participation of the European countries of NATO, the France of Chirac included, in the bombings of the Serbian cities is

---

249 [Kurt Schumacher (1895-1952) was chairman of the Social Democratic Party of Germany and opposed Konrad Adenauer of the Christian Democratic Union, whom the Americans had chosen for their purposes. He equally opposed the various European organisations that were planned to perpetuate American control over Germany such as the Council of Europe and the European Defence Community.]

the sign of a perfect "political brainlessness": the policy of Clinton and his assistant Madeleine Albright (who had as her student Condoleeza Rice – did we speak of continuity?) reintroduced Turkey indirectly into the Balkans by detaching from Serbia and from Croatia, and in spite of the Serb or Croat populations, the old Ottoman provinces belonging to their common trunk, inducing in this way the emergence of an "Islamic spine" from the Mediterranean to the Aegean to the Black Sea. All the neighbouring states were weakened by it: Macedonia, the part of Greece between Thessaloniki and the Turkish border, Bulgaria which has ten to fifteen percent of Muslims, often ethnically Turkish, without counting the secession of Kosovo, foreseeable since 1998. Further, the non-Muslim minorities within the new majority Muslim states are eventually threatened in Albania, Kosovo, Macedonia.

The deliberate creation of chaos in the Balkans is not a Democratic policy that opposed an earlier Republican policy. It is, on the contrary, part of a perfect continuity: Bush Sr., Republican, installed his troops on the border of Saddam Hussein's Iraq, controlled the Iraqi airspace and prepared in this way the second half, or the total invasion of Iraq, which took place under the reign of his son, in 2003. Clinton, a Democrat, used the springboard of Europe in the direction of the Near and Middle East for the first time since the time of Alexander the Great. The control of the Balkans and of Mesopotamia are part of one and the same large-regional strategy . The Macedonian Hellenistic empire of Alexander the Great; the Ottoman Empire always controlled, at the apex of their power, the Balkans and Mesopotamia simultaneously. This is a law of history. The American strategists bore this in mind.

The Pro-American Networks were at the Beginning Socialist

The war against the remnant Yugoslavia of Milošević in 1999, the first conflict of a large scope in Europe since 1945,was thus the work of a president and a team originating from the American Democratic party. This is the reason why the European powers, large and small, followed as one man, contrary to that which happened in 2003 during the invasion of Iraq. This unanimity is explained quite simply because Europe always placed its trust in a Democratic America, mistrusting Republican America. Why? Because, I repeat, the pro-American networks emerged, during the Second World War, under the double impetus of the American president and of his wife Eleanor and militant Altantism, "Spaakism" Prof. Coolsaet[250] of the University of Ghent calls it, had a socialist basis rather than a conservative (Pierre Harmel, on the contrary, strove to disassociate himself from the system of blocs which Spaak[251] had emphasised).

In transforming the Balkan springboard into a zone controlled by the United States, the Clinton/Albright partnership neutralised the region to its own benefit: the latter could no longer constitute an advantage for the Germanocentric Central European bloc nor for a regenerated Russia which would have asserted its old interests in the Balkans. In 1999, Europe lost all the potential advantages that it had gained from 1989. It lost them because it did not cultivate any sense of unity, because it did not have a clear vision of its geopolitical destiny. In 2001, following the "attacks" in New York, America completed its "Alexandrian" project in quickly seizing the eastern zone of the ancient empire of the Macedonian leader. In 2003, when Bush Jr. intended to finish the work of his father in Mesopotamia, Europe seemed to awaken and create around Paris, Berlin and Moscow a front of opposition which the American services weakened immediately sowing discord between this new dissident "axis" and small powers like the Netherlands, Poland, the Czech Republic and the Baltic countries, by benefiting from the support of Great Britain and the pusillanimity of Spain and Italy. We may recall the distinction effected between "Old Europe", with reflexes dictated by the classical diplomacy, and "New Europe", in line with the system of the Neoconservatives' *fait accompli*.

---

[250] [Rik Coolsaet is a professor of International Relations at the University of Ghent who has held important positions in the Belgian government as well.]

[251] [Paul-Henri Spaak (1899-1972) was a socialist politician who was Prime Minister of Belgium three times between 1938 and 1949.]

"Colour Revolutions" and Petrol

The American services and the "soft power" of Washington were activated to devoid the Paris/Berlin/Moscow axis of its contents: de Villepin[252] was eliminated in France from the presidential race following a corruption file no doubt fabricated in favour of Sarkozy, who conducted, as we know, a pro-Atlantist politics. The German Social Democrat Schröder[253] had to yield his place to Angela Merkel, more sceptical of the continental European bloc, more ready to take the demands of the United States into consideration. Schröder however remained in place by managing with a masterly hand the energy relations between Germany and Russia. The orange revolutions which broke out in Ukraine, Georgia and Serbia (with "Otpor")[254] or in Kyrgystan were thus not the only interventions of the services and the "soft power": in western Europe too politics was manipulated in an underhand way, with national and/or European independence undermined at its base as soon as it tries to assert itself through manipulation of elections and factions. In the future, an independent European bloc should refrain from recognising the governments deriving from "colour revolutions".

In Georgia, the power put in place by the "pink revolution" has as its objective the guarantee of the good progress of American petrol policy in the Caucasus and on the border of the Caspian Sea. For the American strategists Georgia should be a transit space for the oil and gas pipelines bringing hydrocarbons from the Caucasus and the Caspian towards the Black Sea and the Mediterranean via Turkey. From there they will reach Europe under American control. The misfortune of Europe is not having any petrol. We have to buy

---

[252] [Dominique de Villepin (1953-) served as Prime Minister of France from 2005 to 2007. As Jacques Chirac's Foreign Minister he opposed the 2003 invasion of Iraq.]

[253] [Gerhard Schröder (1944-) was a Social Democratic politician who served as Chancellor of Germany from 1998 to 2005. Like Jacques Chirac, Schröder opposed the 2003 war against Iraq.]

[254] [Otpor was a Serbian political organisation that existed from 1998 to 2004 and opposed the Yugoslav president Slobodan Milošević.]

the major part of our hydrocarbons from Saudi Arabia or in the Emirates through the intermediary of American consortiums. The Russo-Georgian conflict of summer 2008, regarding Abkhazia and South Ossetia, had energy as its real stake. To avoid energy dependence Europe must try, with all possible technological means, first of all to reduce this petrol dependence by counting on its own sources like nuclear energy and all the other imaginable and realisable sources, following a policy of diversification adopted but not completed in his time by Gaullist France. Solar panels constitute a first alternative that is perfectly popularisable in our country; in fact, why cannot the households that constitute our nation generate their own domestic electricity, or a good part of it, without passing through suppliers controlled by foreigners like "Electrabel" entirely in the hands of France's hereditary enemy which has occupied for three and a half centuries almost three quarters of the territory of the Grand Lothier? Some people tell us: per annum the number of days of sunshine is too limited in Belgium, compared to the Mediterranean zone, to constitute an alternative to petrol. Perhaps. But take a country like Norway, which however has its own petrol: the technology of solar panels generates 50% of the domestic energy of its households in a country where the average sunshine is much more reduced than in ours. Our first objective is the gradual reduction of the dependence, not the immediate acquisition of a total autarky.

Shanghai Pact and Ibero-American Initiatives

We have just seen that the American control over our foreign policy is complete. It determines also our energy policy. America seduces minds (or rather, the brainless masses) through the means of its omnipresent "soft power". The chief danger that awaits us now in Europe is the gradual and silent disappearance of spaces that are still neutral. The countries that maintained their status of neutrality increasingly tend towards NATO. I recall that our initial position based on that of General Jochen Löser in the Federal Republic of

Germany in the eighties aimed on the contrary at the enlargement of the neutral space in Europe. We are just the opposite! Löser intended to extend the status of Switzerland, Austria, Yugoslavia, Finland and Sweden to the Germanies, the Benelux states, Poland, Czechoslovakia and Hungary. Today, these last three countries are part of NATO and have indeed become its model pupils: proud representatives of the "New Europe" as defined by Bush Jr. Europe, totally stultified by the propaganda disseminated by the "soft power" cannot constitute at the moment, in the present conditions, a space of political revival that would be exemplary for the entire world. The only consistent defence barriers are situated today in Asia and in Latin America. In Asia, the resistance is embodied in the "Shanghai Pact"[255] and in Latin America in the initiatives of the Venezuelan president Hugo Chavez combining, along with the other Ibero-American dissenters, the Peronist, Castroist and continentalist doctrines, which fused together, allow the Ibero-American states to create unitary structures capable of driving back the traditional interference of the United States in their political and economic affairs in the name of a so-called pan-Americanist ideology forged during the era of the "big stick" policy of Teddy Roosevelt.

Without the "Shanghai Pact" and without the separatist and continentalist desires of the Ibero-Americans, the American domination of the world would be total, as it is almost total in Europe since the liquidation of Gaullism by Sarkozy and the systematic "mobbing" of Switzerland and Austria (the Waldheim[256]

---

[255] [The Shanghai Cooperation Organisation is a Eurasian political, economic and military organisation founded in 2001 that includes China, Russia, Kazakhstan, Kyrgyzstan, Uzbekistan and Tajikistan. India and Pakistan are expected to join in 2016.]

[256] [Kurt Waldheim (1918-2007) was President of Austria from 1986 to 1992 and Secretary-General of the UN from 1972 to 1981. Even during his campaign for the presidency the World Jewish Congress accused him of hiding his activities during the Second World War, though an international committee that later investigated his past was not able to discover any incriminating evidence.]

and Haider[257] affairs). The potential spaces of resistance are becoming increasingly rare: there remain scraps of Gaullism in France, some good neutralist reactions in Austria, a desire to conserve the status of neutrality in Austria, Switzerland and Sweden; public opinion in Belgium, according to a recent poll, fears the belligerent American initiatives more than those of the Russia of Putin (in spite of the Russophobic propaganda of Le Soir),[258] while in Germany, where the Russophilia of a good number of well established circles is more solidly anchored, Washington and Moscow are placed on equal footing.

Volksgezindheid and Solidarism

In order to cause a barrier of resistance to develop in Flanders it seems to me opportune to say today that it should be based on two cornerstones: *Volksgezindheid* (populism in the sense defined by the Herderian tradition or the Russian Slavophile tradition) and solidarism. Volksgezinheid is a more profound feeling than "nationalism" because it does not derive solely from a political principle but also and especially from a love of the past and of the culture of the people from whom one originates. The term "nationalism", moreover, covers very different interpretations in different countries.[259] Its use can sow confusion, while the term Volksgezinheid indicates well the content of our tradition. Solidarism is a term that is deliberately chosen to replace "socialism", now burdened with too many ambiguities or equated with deviances of all sorts which make the official socialists out to

---

[257] [See above p. 20]

[258] [*Le Soir* is a liberal Belgian newspaper.]

[259] See our two studies on nationalism: Robert Steuckers, "Pour une Typologie Opératoire des Nationalismes", in *Vouloir,* n°73/74/75, Spring 1991, Robert Steuckers, "Pour une Nouvelle Définition du Nationalisme", in *Nouvelles de Synergies Européennes,* n°32, January-February 1998 (text of a talk held at Brussels on16 April 1997). These two texts are available on http://euro-synergies. hautetfort.com/

be everything but socialist. Solidarism should in future express a socialism without Atlantism (in the manner of Spaak or Claes),[260] a socialism without the "consolidations" in the manner of Di Rupo[261] (when it was a question of privatising the RTT[262] so that it would become Belgacom), a socialism that defends the solidarity of all the direct producers of goods and services against the administrative and parasitical bonds. Such a solidarism derives also, for those who still have a classical culture, from the famous "fable of the stomach"[263] of Roman tradition: "all the organs of the popular community serve the others and form together a harmony".

A desire for general political renewal based on Volksgezindheid and solidarism will immediately cause implacable enemies to be raised against it. The affirmation of popular and united values automatically implies the designation of their enemies, according to the formula of Carl Schmitt. Let us identify three of them today:

1. The media programmed by the American "soft power",

2. The neoliberal ideology, the new universalism that levels all popular specific features and social policies permitting the revival of elites (in the sense used by Gaetano Mosca[264] and Vilfredo Pareto,[265]

3. The carnival ideology which drowns the nations in insolence.

---

[260] [Wilhelm Claes (1938-) was Belgian Minister of Foreign Affairs from 1992 to 1994 and Secretary General of NATO from 1994 to 1995.]

[261] [Elio di Rupo (1951-) was Prime Minister of Belgium from 2011 to 2014.]

[262] [The Belgian telecommunications agency Régie des Télégraphes et Téléphones, established in 1930, became Belgacom in 1991.]

[263] [The fable of the stomach is mentioned by both Livy and Plutarch in relation to civil unrest.]

[264] [Gaetano Mosca (1858-1941) was an Italian political scientist who developed his theory of elitism in *Elementi di Scienza Politica*, 1896.]

[265] [Vilfredo Pareto (1848-1923) was an Italian economist, sociologist and political scientist who studied elites and their political fortunes in his major work *Trattato di Sociologia Generale* (4 vols.), 1916.]

The Verstrepen Case

Volksgezindheid and solidarism imply the fight against all the cultural phenomena which do not derive naturally from a popular matrix (ours or that of another real people) but are imposed on us by the internationalist and cosmopolitan "soft power". One example: you all recall that cool journalist, Jurgen Verstrepen,[266] who wandered, we do not know why, into the Flemish nationalist movement, where he got himself elected. In a recent interview given to the variety weekly *Dag Allemal*, this Verstrepen complained of the "backward looking nature" of his fellow candidates, who sang traditional songs, which he presented generally as old-fashioned or obsolete, an old-fashionedness and an obsolescence that aroused in him a form of the fright felt by devotees before the works, real or supposed, of the Devil. Thus every expression of the vernacular culture arouses in him, as he says, the disgust of the progressivist for whom nothing older than, or different from, the media mishmash has the right to exist. And, rather than retreat into a fine Burgundian abbey, as his party had suggested to him, he would prefer to stroll through a "mall" to choose cool clothes marked with a logo in the company of another gadget member of parliament allergic to roots. Unintentionally Verstrepen revealed in his interview to *Dag Allemal* a very contemporary state of affairs: the fight between the vernacular matrix, roots and traditional culture, on the one hand, and the media cool, on the other. There remains one question: how would this Verstrepen reconcile in his mind – subjected to the postmodern homogeneisation, this devout cult of media cool – to his aspiration to fight against "political correctness"? One cannot adulate one and fight against the other; one can only, in our point of view, reject both. One cannot be an Atlanto-Hollywooder, succumb to the seduction of the Californiacentric attitude of the '68ers and claim at the same time that one adheres to a "nationalism" fighting against the freedom-killing ideology of "political correctness".

---

[266] [Jurgen Verstrepen (1966-) was a member of the Flemish parliament and member of Vlaams Belang, the Flemish nationalist party.]

Verstrepen indeed embodies the inconsistency of a good number of our contemporaries in the Flanders of today. Let us hope that the crisis will open their eyes. For "soft power" has promoted neoliberalism, the cause of the crisis, at the same time as it has the media manipulations, the fashions (which catch people's attention) and the carnival spirit.

Volksgezindheid and solidarism imply therefore the fight against all the forms of neoliberalism that have been imposed on us since Thatcher and Reagan, since the beginning of the eighties. Our admonitions up to now, especially those at the beginning of our adventure of Georges Robert and Ange Sampieru[267] have changed nothing. G. Robert and A. Sampieru paid much attention to the productions of the La Découverte publishing house which began the critique of the outrageous liberalism looming in the horizon. Today, in the western world, in the Americanosphere, in the Euro-Atlantic space, in the European Commission completely subjected to the neoliberal attitude, the dominance of this ideology is total. And the crisis of the beginning of this autumn 2008 allows us to glimpse what its catastrophic consequences will be, with the sole consolation that the system has learnt to restrain the effects of crises and recessions, to delay them over time. The crisis proves that the neoliberal formula does not work – quite simply. In the meantime, the outsourcing perpetrated for more than thirty years leaves Europe deprived of a layer of small and medium industries, providers of work, and afflicted by an unproductive service sector which only offers employment detached from the reality of production and injects into mentalities a deleterious ideology of "non-work". This ideology of non-work is also that of the carnival spirit: it has served as an intellectual sweetener to justify the process of dismantlement of our local industrial layers through the intervention of outsourcing to the Far East, North Africa or Turkey (especially textiles) and to exalt the non-productive work of the service sector that has become dangerously inflationary.

---

[267] [Ange Sampieru was a founding editor, along with Steuckers and Louis Sorel, of the journal *Vouloir* which appeared between 1983 and 1999.]

Neoliberalism and Anti-Globalism

The coming of neoliberalism was rendered possible by a metapolitical battle. You will recall the enthusiasm for Hayek who was exhumed from oblivion at the same time as the "think tanks" of Mrs. Thatcher at the end of the seventies. People insisted chiefly on his pamphlet, "The Road to Serfdom" and not so much on the organic (and sometimes interesting) dimensions of his economic theory based on the notion of "catallaxy" (letting things happen naturally without voluntarist statist interventions). The neoliberal infiltration of the dominant discourse was especially the work of the "New Philosophers", whose role we have just explained and of ultra-publicised figures like Jacques Attali,[268] the biographer of bankers, and Alain Minc,[269] the principal propagator of the new vulgate in the conservative journals. Nobody has defined the contemporary ideology better than François Brune,[270] collaborator of the Monde diplomatique, in his work *De l'idéologie Aujourd'hui* (Paris: Ed. Parangon/L'Aventurine, 2003): "Ideology is omnipresent: in the sophisms of the image, in the events hype of the media, the rhetoric of the politically correct, the clamour of merchandise. A machine to produce consent, it demoralises the citizen by dedicating him to the ardent obligation to consume, to find his identity in mimetic exhibition,[271] his freedom in an adherence to the market, and his salvation in "growth" ... That is the ideology of today: a vast falsely consensual mental grid which orders everybody to be quiet in his conformist misfortune and which blinds our societies to the global catastrophe, where its socio-economic models involve other nations".

---

[268] [Jacques Attali (1943-) is a Jewish French economist who wrote an economic history of the Jews, *Les Juifs, le Monde et l'argent: Histoire Économique des Peuples Juifs*, Paris: Fayard, 2002.]

[269] [Alain Minc (1949-) is a Jewish French businessman who served as adviser to Nicolas Sarkozy.]

[270] [François Brune (pseudonym of Bruno Hongre) (1940-) is a French writer who criticises the propagandistic methods of advertising.]

[271] Isn't that so, Mr. Verstrepen?

The system, in launching the operation of neoliberalism from the end of the seventies, guessed that this ideology would finally come up, rather quickly, against diverse resistances. It would then have two objectives:

1. To prevent the fusion of these resistances such as the ex-Communist theoretician Roger Garaudy[272] had advocated (or prevent the "red-brown" plots such as Plenel's newspaper *Le Monde* made use of in Paris and certain circles or personalities around the PTB/PvdA in Belgium),[273]

2. To create an artificial resistance (antiglobalism) in such a way as to neutralise all real resistance. Antiglobalism announces a heap of interesting and seductive ideas. But it announces them without a precise political statist and geographical base, without a territorial foundation, the condition sine qua non for granting it a real substantiality. Every empire, and every challenger of an empire, fortifies itself on a territory: the American hegemon of today is no exception. It has at its disposal a territory of continental dimensions. It practises protectionism and a good dose of autarky, even while preaching to others that they should not adopt the same attitudes and keeping them in this way in a state of weakness. If the hegemon develops a "network", it does so on the basis of a vast logistic basis, or on the basis of its own bi-oceanic territory from the Atlantic to the Pacific, and its Pacifico-Arctic extension, Alaska. To create the illusion of a global resistance the entertainment services have forged the concept of "network".

---

[272] [Roger Garaudy (1913-2012) was a Jewish French resistance fighter who joined the Communist Party, which expelled him for his criticism of the Soviet invasion of Czechoslovakia in 1968. He later converted to Islam and decried the Israeli "founding myth" of the Holocaust.]

[273] [The "Parti du travail du Belgique" or "Partij van de Arbeid van Belgie" is a Marxist-Leninist workers' party in Belgium.]

It is not the "network" that is anti-establishment but the old statist and imperial structures

Militant antiglobalism intends to be the only large anti-establishment network against the global establishment. But, ever since the well publicised disturbances of Gênes or Nice, one does not see very clearly what damage to the system in place this famous "network" has been able to cause. The thesis of Michael Hardt and Toni Negri[274] about the "empire" whose bases will "one day" be definitively sapped by the "antiglobalist network" proves to be an illusion. During the Cold War, the American services were able to cause "Washington Communists" (to repeat Jean Thiriart's expression) to emerge; they now recycle, in the figure of Toni Negri, old "terrorists" for an entertainment operation of global scope that absorbs and neutralises the challenge by publicising it by transforming it into a mere "show" (Guy Debord),[275] for our contemporaries, programmed like the citizens of Oceania in Orwell's 1984, believe (televised) images more than (lived) facts, the show more than reality. The resistance to the Americanocentric globalist system is not to be found, in fact, in a global "network" of hippy dissidents or thugs stoned on cocaine but derives much more from classical statist and imperialist structures deeply anchored in the past: the Shanghai Group with a China of thousand year old political traditions, Putin's Russia which is recovering its memory, an Ibero-American independence movement in the spirit of the Mercosul[276] and of the Venezuelan president Chavez.

---

[274] [Antonio Negri (1933-) is an Italian Marxist sociologist and political philosopher. His major work *Empire* (2000) was co-authored by the American political philosopher Michael Hardt (1960-).]

[275] [Guy Debord (1931-94) was French Marxist whose best known work is *La Société du Spectacle* (*The Show-Business society*) (1967).]

[276] [Mercosur or Mercosul (Common Market of the South) is a free-trade union in South America that was established in 1991.]

Combating the Carnival Spirit

Finally, after "soft power" and "neoliberalism", the third aspect of the general system of stultifaction and deracination of the masses which should be combated fully is represented by the "carnival" ambience which the French philosopher Philippe Muray,[277] who died recently and prematurely, denounced vigorously. In his very last work *Festivus Festivus* (Fayard, 2006) Muray pronounced an indictment that is as vehement as it is invigorating against what he calls the carnival spirit, the mode of operation of advanced western societies. In the long interview with the truly non-conformist journalist and philosopher Elisabeth Lévy that this book records, Muray, in his swansong, denounces a society that operates solely in the style of the media fiction, a style that aims at total dis-inhibition, the flaunting of everything that was in the past "private", "intimate", "secret" (including obviously sexual attributes and practices). Power, Muray explains, will be exercised with a maximal sharpness when the last enclaves of that which was "secret" will be divulged and exhibited, when the last limits and the last distances (and social distances make civilisation, promiscuity abolishes it) will have been crossed and suppressed. Television, with its exhibitionist broadcasts ("Love Story", etc.), is the instrument of this power which declares a permanent carnival and universal shamelessness with the intention of eliminating the "pockets" of seriousness, established or alternative, in order to prevent any return to a less trivial past or any preparation for a coherent future. The universal shamelessness blurs all borders and announces a global amalgam of promiscuity and absence of differentiation in the form of a "let's play doctor" infantilism and "adultophobia".

In an earlier work entitled Désaccord parfait Muray qualified every society "where the masters are masters of shows and the slaves spectators of the latter" as a "Disneyland society". "Soft power" will therefore imagine and prefabricate "shows" to nip all free thought in the bud, all creative spontaneity based in the popular spirit

---

[277] [Philippe Muray (1945-2006) was an anti-modernist essayist and novelist.]

by substituting for the free and spontaneous creator originating from the people (such as Rabelais and the dissident carnivals) the official or subsidised host, and subsidised only after having passed through the yoke of the imposed ideology, after having learnt his single lesson, which he will repeat for centuries. Neoliberalism will prosper on the margins of this large artificial carnival – totally fabricated and, in spite of its apparent disorder, well framed by little cops with apostolic faces – which will straight away stifle all true revolt. Through the action of the old dissidents who have come to power the *mixtum compositum*[278] of May '68 will thus be reduced progressively to just its festive, libidinous and playful dimensions drawn, by the agents of the OSS,[279] from the book *Eros and Civilisation* by Herbert Marcuse[280] or from caricaturist vulgates originating from the pseudo-Marxism of Reich,[281] with which they will fabricate a "ready-made thought" in the direction of their designs. In his best work, now a classic, *One-dimensional Man*,[282] Marcuse feared the coming of a programmed humanity reduced to its material needs alone; he was right, but it was he perhaps who, in self-defence, provided the rules of this programming to the system. In his definition of "eros" which has been solicited somewhat for the needs of the cause they have formulated and found the bait. It is not the rigidity of the totalitarian world of Orwell's *1984* but the *Brave New World* of Aldous Huxley, with its artificial paradises, that they attempt to inflict on us.

---

[278] [Composite mixture.]

[279] [Office of Strategic Studies was the US intelligence agency during the Second World War and predecessor of the Central Intelligence Agency.]

[280] [Herbert Marcuse (1898-1979) was a Jewish thinker of the Frankfurt School who attempted a synthesis of Marx and Freud in his Eros and Civilisation: A Philosophical Inquiry into Freud (1955).]

[281] [Wilhelm Reich 1897-1957) was a Jewish Austrian psychoanalyst who, like Marcuse, combined psychoanalytical theory with Marxism.]

[282] [*One-dimensional Man: Studies in the Ideology of Advanced Industrial Society*, was published in 1964.]

ROBERT STEUCKERS

Death of the Zoon Politikon[283] and Death of the Nations

The magistrates (or mayors) of Paris and Berlin, Delanoë and Wowereit, or the deputy magistrate Simons of Brussels, all of present-day French Socialism (especially to the left of Ségolène Royal)[284] have as their real (and hardly concealed) strategic objective the preoccupation of the"citizens" with all sorts of festivities, concerts, "happenings", "gay prides", "Zinneke parades",[285] anti-racist or other demonstrations in order that they may no longer concern themselves directly with politics, in order that they may definitively forget who they are, the trajectory from which they operate. The objective? To eradicate the essence of man, who is, according to Aristotle, a *"zoon politikon"*. It is a question of distracting the human imagination at any cost from all tradition or historical reality. In the west, in the Franco-Anglo-American Atlantist complex, according to the definition given to it by my professor Peymans at the end of the seventies, the dominance of the mercantile castes or of the French bourgeois third estate has smashed, wrecked and destroyed the most intimate springs of the nations (Ireland excepted), to such an extent that Moeller van den Bruck, the translator of Dostoyevsky, stated that a few decades of "liberalism" sufficed to definitively destroy a nation.

The carnival lifestyle, the mode in which the contemporary despotism is expressed, contributes to leading the final assault on the intimate resources of the peoples: it penetrates their deepest core and sows corruption there. Philippe Muray, to return to him, revives in a truly invigorating manner the critique of the "society of the show" expressed in the sixties by Guy Debord and the situationalist school, throwing at the same time a new and very relevant light on the process of dissolution at work in the western sphere.

---

[283] [Political animal.]

[284] [Ségolène Royal (1953-) is a French Socialist politician who was François Hollande's mistress from the late seventies until 2007.]

[285] [Zinneke (nickname for residents of Brussels) Parades, begun in 2000, are supposed to bring the people of Brussels together.]

The Northern League and the FPÖ

To articulate a resistance at the European level, to translate into facts our philosophical options and our historical aspirations, two identitarian parties can serve us as models: the Northern League and the Austrian FPÖ. I do not see much else. Why? Because these are the only two identitarian mass movements that have published or published clearly "non-western" formulae. The Northern League and its daily La Padania had a very courageous attitude in 1999 when NATO bombed Serbia. The daily and the "Senatur" Umberto Bossi[286] did not hesitate to vigorously denounce the Americans and their belligerent accomplices in Europe. Later, through this league, there was a manifesto *"Come Cambiare?"* (*How to Change?*) from the pen of the great lawyer Gianfranco Miglio.[287] This manifesto denounced the characteristics of the Italian party-rule which is so similar to ours. The lessons of Miglio can thus be directly maintained by any political militant among us. The clarity of the arguments and suggestions of Miglio, whom I had the honour to meet in 1995 in his magnificent private library at Como, would allow us to develop rapidly the sketch of a counter-power.[288]

---

[286] [Umberto Bossi (1941-) was leader of the Italian Lega Nord (Northern League) party from 1991 until 2012.]

[287] [Gianfranco Miglio (1918-2001) was an Italian jurist and political scientist who belonged to the Lega Nord. He was the author of numerous political theoretical works.]

[288] cf.: "L'Italie toute chamboulée...", Interview with Gianfranco Miglio, edited by Andreas K. Winterberger, in; *Vouloir*, n°109-113, Oct.-Dec. 1993; Alessandro Campi, "Au-delà de l'Etat, au-delà des Partis: la Théorie Politique de Gianfranco Miglio", in: *Vouloir*, n°109-113, Oct.-Dec. 1993; Luciano Pignatelli, "Les Idées Pratiques de Gianfranco Miglio: Comment Changer le Système Politique Italien", in *Vouloir*, n°109-113, Oct.-Dec. 1993; "Quelques Questions à Gianfranco Miglio", edited by Francesco Bergomi, in: *Vouloir*, n°109-113, Oct.-Dec. 1993; Robert Steuckers, "La Ligue Lombarde", in: *Le Crapouillot, Nouvelle Série*, n°119, May-June 1994; "L'Etat Moderne est Dépassé!", Interview with Prof. Gianfranco Miglio, edited by Carlo Stagnaro, in *Nouvelles de Synergies Européennes*, n°46, June-July 2000; "Pour une Europe Impériale et Fédéraliste, Appuyée sur ses Peuples", Interview with Prof. Gianfranco Miglio, edited by Gianluca Savoini, in *Nouvelles de Synergies Européennes*, n°48, October-Decembre 2000.

In the orbit of the FPÖ, the weekly Zur Zeit edited by Andreas Mölzer in Vienna, contains every week pages of international affairs without any concession to the ambient Americanism. Jörg Haider died this morning in an car accident but, in spite of his recent rupture with the FPÖ and his personal option in favour of the Turkish membership, he will remain for me the unmatched author of the manifesto *Die Freiheit, die ich Meine* (*The Freedom that I have in Mind*). The Austrian party-rule offered, before its cudgelling of the FPÖ, surprising similarities to ours. The general critique of the Austrian political system as Haider formulated it is very technical, just as Miglio's is. But it does not resort to any abstruse language. And it suggests paths to get out of the political impasse. The clarity of these manifestos gave to the Northern League and the FPÖ a formidable driving force in the public debates and, consequently, in the electoral battles.[289]

The constant successes of these parties, their undeniable impact on political debate and on the reforms under way prove that the two manifestos that I refer to here indeed contain good suggestions. If they are valid for Austria and Italy, they should be valid for us, given that the political systems of these two countries and their malfunctions are similar and comparable to ours. And, what is more, the geographic vision of these two manuals is Europeist and anti-Atlanticist, essential qualities for a solid and positive critique of the system in place that no party or movement has repeated in our country, precluding thereby any concrete effectiveness.

The men of the left who operated the good *aggiornamenti*[290] ... To serve as further inspiration to us we would add the corpus established by the men of the left who became non-conformist

---

[289] cf. Robert Steuckers, "Autriche: Haider, le Capitaine du Pays", in *Le Crapouillot, nouvelle série*, n°119, May-June 1994; "Nous Sommes en Avance sur notre temps!", Interview with Jörg Haider, edited by Andreas Mölzer, in *Au fil de l'épée*, n°8, February 2000; "Rafraîchir la Mémoire des Coalisés anti-Haider!", in *Au fil de l'épée*, n°8, February 2000; Mauro Bottarelli, "Haider Contre Chirac: non à l'UE Centraliste et Parisienne – la Bonne Santé de l'économie Autrichienne", in *Au fil de l'épée*, n°12, August 2000, translated in La Padania, 11 July 2000.

[290] [Updates.]

in the course of time, like the family of Rudi Dutschke[291] or his companion Bernd Rabehl,[292] who write regularly in the Berlin weekly Junge Freiheit; or like Günther Rehak[293] in Austria, former secretary of the Socialist chancellor Bruno Kreiski. In French Switzerland, still within the Alpine curve, the "Unité populaire" movement manages to give us every week on the Internet analyses or reflections worthy of interest for all those who dream of a future of solidarism that is capable of overcoming the contradictions and stagnations of established Socialism. In Italy, the Roman daily Rinascita, deriving from classical nationalism, presents itself at the moment as the newspaper of the sinistra nazionale[294] and opts for a Europeist and Eurasianist, anti-imperialist and anti-capitalist perspective. Our sources of inspiration should not be limited to just the movements that, rightly or wrongly, give themselves labels of "national", "regionalist" or "identitarian". Some circles, formerly or recently classified on the left on the political chessboards of Europe have proceeded intelligently to good *aggiornamenti*: they have refused all involvement in the direction of the paths suggested by the "New Philosophy" and its satellites and rejected the attitude of those who, in spite of their vibrant militantism of some decades ago, remain, through intellectual laziness, "journeymen" of the Social Democratic parties everywhere in Europe. The attitude of a "journeyman" is the surest way to get stuck, to come to a standstill, to enter into the infernal spiral of the decline, a decline engendered by "mimetism" which no longer produces any difference (or "differEnce", with a wink at Derrida) but repeats the same thing unceasingly in a dismal tone. It is the surest way to become the yes-men of the system, its Pavlov dogs.

---

[291] [Rudi Dutschke (1940-79) was a leading Communist spokesman for the German student movement of the sixties.]

[292] [Bernd Rabehl (1938-) is a German political activist who began as a socialist and then, from 1998, began to represent a more nationalist political position.]

[293] [Günter Rehak (1939-) is an Austrian politician who began as a socialist but now heads the nationalist 'Nationale Volkspartei' of Austria.]

[294] [Nationalist left.]

The creation of a Euro-Siberian strategic space is inseparable from a complete reorganisation of our national institutions in the sense of Volksgezindheid and solidarism, in the sense of the anti-party critique of Miglio and Haider in order to immunise these institutions totally against the bacilli of Jacobin or American "soft power".

EUROPE AND THE CHALLENGE OF GLOBALISATION[295]

My talk today will obviously have a geopolitical dimension, but also a geo-economic one, for the broad routes and networks of communication, on land as well as on sea, and the range of the most modern systems of armaments play a considerable role in the present competition which opposes Europe to the United States. The extent of these routes, these networks, determines the categories in which it is necessary to think: whether in terms of peoples or in terms of empire.

If one talks of peoples, one should know what this is about. In the era of popular revolutions in the 19th century, the peoples rose against the multi-ethnic empires which they considered as enforced straitjackets. From 1848, the Polish and Finns in Russia, the Czechs and Italians on the territory where Imperial and Royal Austro-Hungarian sovereignty was exercised, the South Slavs and the Greeks within the Ottoman Empire, the Irish in the United Kingdom rebelled and developed an identitarian movement that was peculiar to them. In France, the Breton or Provençal cultural movements (the Félibriges) developed within a anti-centralist and anti-Jacobin context.

[295] Talk delivered at the congress of the "Gesellschaft für freie Publizistik", April 2004. Published in www.voxnr.com, 22 October, 2005. German original: R. Steuckers, "Europa der Völker statt US-Globalisierung", in *Veröffentlichungen der Gesellschaft für Freie Publizistik*, XX. Kongress-Protokoll 2004, Die Neue Achse. Europas Chancen gegen Amerika, Gesellschaft für Freie Publizistik e. V., Oberboihingen, 2004. Dr. Rolf Kosiek, Dr. Dr. Volkmar Weiss, Dr. Walter Post, Prof. Dr. Wjatscheslaw Daschitschew [Viatcheslav Dachitchev], Harald Neubauer, Dr. Pierre Krebs, Dr. Gert Sudholt also participated in the congress.

Whence comes this general revolt of a cultural sort? It originates, *grosso modo*,[296] from the philosophy of history of Johann Gottfried Herder, for whom language, literature and historical memory constitute, among each people, a bundle of forces that can be considered as being its active identity. Identity is consequently specific to the people, which means that each people has the right to possess its own political form and to constitute a state according to its specific character, tailored to its dimensions and modifiable at any moment. The advantage of this perspective is that each people can freely deploy its own forces and its own characteristics. But this perspective equally contains a danger: within a community of peoples or a civilisational space Balkanisation threatens. Herder was well aware of that: that is why he attempted, under the reign of Empress Catherine II, to sketch a synthesis, especially a new political, ideological and philosophical form which should be applied to the intermediary space between Russia and Germany. Herder dreamed of causing to emerge a new Greece of Homeric workmanship between the Baltic states and the Crimea. The Germanic, Baltic and Slavic elements would have all agreed on a return to the most ancient and heroic Greece, which would have been at the same time a return to the most ancient and sublime sources of Europe. This notion of Herder's may seem to us today somewhat ethereal and utopian. But from this sketch and from the totality of Herder's work one can retain a fundamental element for our era: a synthesis of Europe is only possible if one goes back to the most ancient sources, that is, to the first bases of European humanity, to the core of our human specificity which one will take care to activate permanently. Archetypes are in fact engines, moving forces that no progressivism can extinguish for, with the latter, culture ossifies, becomes a desert of dryness and aridity.

---

[296] [Roughly.]

The "Nation" According to Herder

The nation, as a concept, was, for Herder, a more or less homogeneous unity, in itself an inalienable unity, made up of a composite of ethnicity, language, literature, history and customs. For the French revolutionaries the nation, on the contrary, was not at all such a bundle of objective and tangible facts but was only the people in arms, no matter what the language was that this mass spoke or, to be more precise, was always only the demos in arms, or the *tiers état*[297] mobilised in order to extend indefinitely the space of the universalist republic. Tilo Meyer has given us an excellent definition of the nation. According to him, the term *ethnos*, or the people, according to Herder's definition, cannot be put purely and simply granted to the demos. Only the political systems that are based on the definition that Herder gives of the nation are democratic and popular, in the proper sense. The other systems which derive from the notions of the French Revolution are, on the contrary, egalitarian (in the sense that they reduce everything to a single one) and, for that reason, totalitarian. The present project of developing a "multiculture" is related to this mixture of brutal egalitarianism and totalitarianism.

The mobilisation of the masses at the time of the French Revolution had of course a military motivation: the armies of the Revolution acquired in this way a considerable and decisive punching force to fight the professional armies of Prussia and Austria, which were well trained but inferior in numbers. The battles of Jemmapes and Valmy in 1792[298] proved this. The Revolution introduced a new method of conducting war which obtained for it decisive victories. Clausewitz studied the reasons of the Prussian defeats and ascertained that the total mobilisation of

---

[297] [Under the *ancien régime* the land was divided into three estates, the clergy (first estate), the nobility (second estate) and the commoners (third estate), comprising the bourgeoisie and peasantry.]

[298] [The Battle of Jemappes (in Belgium), which took place during the French Revolutionary Wars, ended in the victory of the French forces against those of the Austrian Netherlands.]

all the masculine forces within a state constituted the only possible response to the Revolution in order to outflank the masses of armed citizens of Revolutionary France and not be outflanked by them. The example that the rural Spanish populations gave in their war against the Napoleonic troops, where all the people rose to defend Tradition against the Revolution, proved that masses orientated according the principles of Tradition could defeat or battle for a long time mass armies inspired by the Revolution. The thought of Jahn,[299] the "Father of gymnastics" as he was called in Germany, constituted a Germanic synthesis of Clausewitz's theory and the practice of the insurgent peasants of Europe. The mobilisation of the people was first effected in Spain before being effected in Germany and in this way rendered possible the European victory against Napoleon, that is, against the mechanistic principle of the French Revolution.

After the Congress of Vienna of 1815, the reactionary forces wished to disarm the peoples. The Europe of Metternich wanted to, retrospectively, render null and void the political freedom that was nevertheless promised. Now, if the peasant or the artisan should become a soldier and pay, if necessary, the toll of blood, he should receive in exchange the right to vote and to take part in politics. When each citizen receives the right and the possibility to study, he receives simultaneously the right to participate, in one way or another, in the political debates of his country; such were the demands of the nationalist and democratic student bodies of the time. These students revolted against a restoration that preserved obligatory military service without wishing to grant political freedom as a corollary. They supported their rebellion intellectually with an astonishing mixture derived from the Herderian concept of the nation and pseudo-nationalist mechanistic ideals originating from the ideological corpus of the French Revolution. During this period between revolution and restoration, political thought oscillated between a rebellious view that argued in terms of peoples

---

[299] [The Battle of Valmy marked the first victory of the Revolutionary French forces, against the invading Prussian troops under the Duke of Braunschweig-Wolfenbüttel.]

and a traditional view that argued in terms of empires, which blurred the very fluid ideological boundaries. A necessarily organic synthesis became imperative. Such a synthesis never emerged, which forces us today to reflect on the concepts born in this period.

The Peoples/Empire Dialectic

Let us return to the dialectic of peoples/empire or peoples/ civilisational spaces at the end of the 18th century and the beginning of the 19th century; we have, on the one hand, vast political units that the majority of men were incapable of conceiving or imagining, but, besides, these political units of vast dimension, badly understood and rejected, proved to be necessary to confront the competition which was inevitably going to be imposed by the great transatlantic power that had begun to assert itself. The Spanish colonies had "become free", at least in appearance, only to fall rapidly into a dependence on the United States in rapid rise. The Austrian minister of the time, Hülsemann,[300] after the declaration of the "Monroe Doctrine", as well as the French philosopher Alexis de Tocqueville, who had just finished a long travel in North America, launched a warning to the Europeans to tell them that, beyond the Atlantic, a power was in the process of emerging which was fundamentally different from everything that had been known in Europe before. International politics had just obtained truly continental or global dimensions. Henceforth the future would belong only to those powers having at their disposal sufficient extent and raw materials in the territory on which they exercised their sovereignty, a territory that had to be compact with well defined and "rounded" borders and not colonial empires dispersed to the four winds.

Hülsemann and, after him, Constantin Frantz pleaded for an alliance of colonial powers deprived of colonies, which led especially to the signing of treaties like that which instituted the

---

[300] [Johann, Ritter von Hülsemann was the Austrian Chargé d'affaires in Washington in the middle of the 19th century.]

"League of the Three Emperors" (Russia, Germany, Austria-Hungary) or the application of principles like that of the "Prusso-Russian mutual guarantee". At the beginning of the 20th century, the alliance that united Germany and Austro-Hungary wanted to revive the "sick man" of the Bosphorus, that is, the Ottoman Empire, which they wanted to make a "complementary territory", source of raw materials and outlet spaces. This desire implied a construction of a network of modern communications, at that time a railway line between Hamburg and Baghdad (and eventually to continue the railway line up to the coast of the Persian Gulf). This project contained one of the principal causes of the First World War. In fact, England could not tolerate a non-English presence in this region of the world; Russia could not accept that the Germans and the Austrians would determine politics in Constantinople, which the Russians sometimes called "Tsarigrad".

The Lesson of Spengler and Huntington

In Europe, the structures of imperial type are thus a necessity in order to maintain the coherence of the European civilisational space whose culture has sprung from European soil, in order that all the peoples within this civilisational space organised according to imperial principles might have a future. Today the American professor Samuel Huntington[301] postulates that one should begin to think of politics from the point of view of civilisational spaces. He speaks of "civilisations". The German language made a difference, with Oswald Spengler, between the notion of Kultur which represents an organic force and that of Zivilisation which includes in itself all the purely mechanical and technical acquisitions of a civilisational or cultural space. These acquisitions attain their apex when the force emerging from cultural roots is almost

---

[301] [Samuel Huntington (1927-2008) was an American conservative political scientist whose most famous book is The Clash of Civilizations and the Remaking of World Order (1996) in which he predicted a major confrontation between the Western and Islamic civilisations.]

THE EUROPEAN ENTERPRISE: GEOPOLITICAL ESSAYS

exhausted. Samuel Huntington, who could be considered as a sort of contemporary disciple of Spengler, thinks that this radical force can be reactivated, if one wished, as the fundamentalist Islamists or the revivalists of Hinduism do today. Samuel Huntington evokes an "occidental" civilisational space which groups Europe and Asia within an "Atlantic" unit. But for us, as previously for Hülsemann and Tocqueville, Europe – as the dormant fount of primordial European humanity – and America – as a novelty without a past on the international scene and whose essence is revolutionary and mechanistic – constitute two fundamentally different poles even if, on the surface of conservative or Neoconservative American political discourse we observe the presence of virtually "classical" fragments, but these are only fragments of a culture that is fabricated, sold as "classical" but their sole function is to serve as mere respectability. This "classical" respectability is the object of interesting ideological and philosophical discussions in the United States today. Such questions as the following are posed: should these elements of "classicism" be considered as the mere relics of a common European past, more or less forgotten, or should they be removed definitively from the philosophical horizon, thrown overboard, or should they be used as intellectual elements to perfect the conjuring tricks of the world of the media to have people believe that they are still attached to classical European values? We should follow this debate attentively without ever being duped.

Present-day Europe, which has taken the form of the Brussels Eurocracy, is obviously not an empire but, on the contrary, a developing super-state. The notion of the "state" has nothing to do with the notion of an "empire", for a "state" is static and does not move while, by definition, an empire encompasses within itself all the organic forms of the civilisational space that it organises, transforms and adapts on the spiritual and political levels, which implies that it is permanently in ferment and in movement. The Brussels Eurocracy will lead, if it persists in these errors, to a total ossification. The present Brussels Eurocracy does not have a memory, refuses to have one, has lost all historical foundation, poses as if it does not have any roots. The ideology of this construction of a "mechanistic" type is associated with mere ideological cobblery, a cobblery that refuses to draw any lessons of the experiences of the past. That implies that economic practice of the Brussels Eurocracy poses as being "open to the world" and neoliberal, which constitutes a negation of the historical dimension of the really extant economic systems that really emerged and developed from the European soil. What is worse, neoliberalism does not permit any positive evolution in the sense of a continental autarky. The Brussels Eurocracy is thus no longer a European authority in the real and historical sense of the term, but a western authority, for all doctrinaire neoliberalism, as a modernisation of the old Anglo-Saxon Manchesterian liberalism, is the ideological mark par excellence of the West, as has been remarked and demonstrated in a convincing and sufficient manner, through the decades, by authors as diverse as Ernst Niekisch, Arthur Moeller van den Bruck, Guillaume Faye and Claudio Finzi.[302]

Peoples Die of an Excess of Liberalism

But all the plans to unify and concentrate the forces of Europe which followed one another in the course of these decades did not at all pose as an *a priori* condition a Europe "open to the world" but, on the contrary, all wished an autarkic Europe, even if this autarky accepted the principles of a market economy but in the sense of ordoliberalism, that is a liberalism that took non-economic factors into consideration. In fact, an economy cannot, without danger, refuse on principle to take into consideration other fields of human activity. The cultural heritage, the medical and educational organisation should always receive a priority in relation to other purely economic factors because they achieve order and stability within a given society or a civilisational space guaranteeing at the same time the future of the peoples who live in this civilisational

---

[302] [Claudio Finzi is a professor of political philosophy in the University of Perugia, and has written on Italian Humanism as well as on contemporary technocracy.]

space. Without such a stability the peoples literally die of an excess of liberalism (or of economism or "commercialism"), as Arthur Moeller van den Bruck very rightly stated at the beginning of the twenties of the 20th century.

As regards the destiny of Europe itself, Austrian industrialists and economists had suggested a coherent European politics from the end of the 19th century. For example, Alexander Peez[303] had very early remarked that the United States aimed at the elimination of Europe not only in the New World in the name of pan-Americanism but also everywhere else, including in Europe itself. The question of survival, for all the European peoples, was thus posed; either one was going to witness a Greater European unification within an autarkic economic system similar to the German Zollverein[304] or else one was going to witness a general colonisation of the European continent by the new pan-American power which was in the process of rising. Alexander von Peez warned the Europeans of the danger of a "universal Americanisation". The economic theoretician Gustav Schmoller, a figurehead of the "German historical school", pleaded, for his part, for an "European economic bloc" capable of offering a response to the dynamism of the United States. For Schmoller such a bloc would be "autarkic" and would protect itself with customs barriers, exactly the opposite of what the Brussels Eurocracy recommends today.

Julius Wolf,[305] another German economic theoretician, foresaw that the gigantic pan-American market would one day be closed to European merchandise and products and a reinforced competition between European and American products would be instituted on a global level. Arthur Dix[306] and Walther Rathenau made this

---

[303] [Alexander von Peez (1829-1912) was a German-Austrian industrialist and politician who wrote several works on American, British and European political strategy.]

[304] [The Zollverein was a German Customs Union which united most of the German states economically before their political unification in 1871.]

[305] [Julius Wolf (1862-1937) was an economist who taught at the Universities of Zurich and Breslau and the Technische Hochschule in Berlin.]

[306] [See above p. 54]

vision theirs. Jäckh[307] and Rohrbach,[308] for their part, became advocates of an economic bloc that would extend from the North Sea to the Persian Gulf. It is in this way that the "Eastern Question" was born along the Hamburg/Kuwait axis. The German emperor, Wilhelm II, wanted the Balkans, Anatolia and Mesopotamia to become a "supplementary space" (*Ergänzungsraum*) for the fast expanding German industry but he invited all the other European powers including France to participate in this big project in a knightly spirit of conciliation. Gabriel Hanotaux[309] was the only French statesman who wanted to continue this rational project. In Russia, Sergei Witte, statesman of the first rank, equally viewed this plan positively. Unfortunately these clairvoyant statesmen were led to a dead end by short-sighted obscurantists of all ideological complexions.

Constantinople, the Apple of Discord

The apple of discord, which led to the outbreak of the First World War was in fact the city of Constantinople. The object of this very murderous war was the domination of the Straits and the eastern basin of the Mediterranean. The English had always wanted to leave the Straits to the Turks, whose power had considerably declined (the "sick man" of the Bosphorus, said Bismarck). But, in return, they could not accept a Turkey that had become the complementary space (Ergänzungsraum) of a Central Europe whose economy would be organised in a coherent and uniform manner under German direction. Consequently, in order to avoid this nightmare of their strategists, they conceived the plan to "Balkanise" and divide still more the rest of the Ottoman Empire in such a way that

[307] [Ernst Jäckh (1875-1959) was a German political scientist who promoted the German-Turkish Alliance of 1908-14.]

[308] [Paul Rohrbach (1869-1956) was a colonial commissioner in south-western Africa who wrote on the condition of German colonies and international politics before the First World War.]

[309] [See above p. 73]

no territorial continuity might exist, especially in the space situated between the Mediterranean Sea and the Persian Gulf. Turkey, Russia and Germany had to be excluded from this highly strategic region of the globe, which implied the implementation a policy of "containment" before the term was used. The Russians dreamed before 1914 of reconquering Constantinople and of making this magnificent city their "Tsarigrad", the city of the (Byzantine) emperors, of whom their tsars were the successors. The Russians saw themselves as the principal bearers of the "Third Rome" and intended to make ancient Byzantium the central convergence point of Christian Orthodox cultural space. The French had interests in the Near East, in Syria and Lebanon, where they were supposed to protect the Christian communities. The telescoping of these divergent and contradictory interests led to the catastrophe of 1914.

In 1918, France and England were almost in a state of bankruptcy. These two western powers had contracted staggering debts to the United States, where they had bought enormous quantities of military materials in order to be able to maintain the front. The United States, which, before 1914, had debts everywhere in the world, found itself in the twinkling of an eye in the position of creditor. France had not only lost 1.5 million men, that is, its biological substance, but was constrained to repay debts *ad infinitum*: the Treaty of Versailles chose to make the Germans pay in the name of reparation.

This unhealthy game of debts and repayments ruined Europe and plunged it into a frightful spiral of inflations and economic catastrophes. During the twenties, the United States wanted to obtain Germany as a principal client and outlet in order to be able to "penetrate", as they said in those days, the European markets protected by customs barriers. The economy of the Weimar Republic, regulated by the Dawes- and the Young Plan,[310] was considered in the highest American economic spheres as a "penetrated" economy. This situation forced on Germany at that

---

[310] [The Dawes Plan of 1924 and the Young Plan of 1929 were attempts to restructure the reparations programme that Germany was bound to under the Treaty of Versailles of 1919.]

time was to be extended to all of western Europe after the Second World War. It is in this way that the "universal Americanisation" was, step by step, imposed through the ideology of Roosevelt's "One World" or through the notion of globalisation in the manner of Soros today. The terms to designate it vary but the strategy remains the same.

The Plan to Unify the Continent from Within

The Second World War had as its principal objective, according to Roosevelt and Churchill, the prevention of European unification under the rule of the Axis powers in order to prevent the emergence of an "unpenetrated" and "impenetrable" economy capable of asserting itself on the international scene. The Second World War thus did not have its goal the "liberation" of Europe but the indefinite precipitation of the economy of our continent into a state of dependence and its continuance in this state. I therefore do not proclaim a "moral" judgement on the responsibilities of the war but I judge its outbreak on the basis of objective material and economic criteria. Our media fail to mention some further war-aims, though clearly affirmed at that time, which should certainly not lead us to think that they were insignificant. On the contrary! In the journal *Géopolitique*, which is published today in Paris, and is distributed in the most official circles, an article reminded us of the British wish in 1942 to prevent river navigation on the Danube and the digging of the canal connection between the Rhine, the Main and the Danube. The *Géopolitique* journal, in order to illustrate this point, republished a map that appeared in the London press in 1942 in the middle of articles that explained that Germany was "dangerous" not because it possessed such or other form of government that would have been "anti-democratic" but because this government, independently of its form, showed itself capable of realising an old plan of Charlemagne as well as the political testament of the king of Prussia, Friedrich II, that is, the optimal river navigation in the interior of the entire continent or a network of communications controlled by the powers that constituted this continent physically, a control that they would exercise in total independence and without the instrument of an important fleet, which would have as an immediate corollary the total relativisation of the British maritime control in the Mediterranean and the ruin, ipso facto, of the strategy that had been deployed there by the United Kingdom since the Spanish War of Succession and the operations of Nelson in the Napoleonic era. Thus, in order to reach the Atlantic coasts, the wheat zones of the Crimea and the basins of the Dniester, the Dnieper and the Don or to reach Egypt, Europe would no longer have needed cargo ships of shipowners financed by England. The Black Sea would have been connected directly to Central Europe and the Rhine basin.

Such a geopolitical, geostrategic and geoeconomic harmony the thalassocratic powers always refused, for it would have meant for them an irremediable decline. The geopolitical visions of the French geopolitician André Chéradame,[311] very probably remote-controlled by British services, implied the division of "Mitteleuropa" and the Danube basin that he had theorised for the dictate of Versailles. His visions aimed equally at creating the maximum of artificial states, hardly viable and antagonistic to one another, in the Danube basin in order that, from Vienna to the Black Sea, there would be neither economic coherence nor dynamism, nor any space structured by an imperial (*reichisch*) principle.

The objective, which was to prevent all communication by fluvial routes, would be further reinforced by the events of the Cold War. The Elbe, or the Paris/Hamburg axis, and the Danube, as the fluvial artery of Europe, were both blocked by the Iron Curtain. The Cold War had as its objective the perpetuation of this gap. The bombing of the bridges on the Danube close to Belgrade in 1999 did not follow other aims.

---

[311] [See above p. 19]

Gold Standard and Work Standard

The Cold War aimed also at maintaining Russia far from the Mediterranean in order not to grant to the Soviet Union an access to warm seas, to keep Germany in a state of division, to grant France a relative autonomy. Officially, France belonged to the victors' camp and this policy of division and Balkanisation was spared to it. The Americans tolerated this relative autonomy because the big French rivers like the Seine, the Loire and the Garonne are Atlantic rivers and did not, at that time, possess important connections with the Danubian space and also because the French industry of consumer goods was rather weak in the aftermath of the Second World War. It was only in the fifties and sixties that such an industry took off in France with the production of cheap automobiles (like the legendary "2CV" of Citroën which the Germans called the "ugly duck", the "Dauphine" or the "R8" models of Renault) or the household electrical appliances of Moulinex, etc., a group of products that remained very far below the German standards. The strength of France had been its reserves of gold, that of Germany the production of excellent products of fine precision and mechanism that could be exchanged for gold or currency.

Anton Zischka[312] wrote once that the American return of French gold reserves – during the reign of de Gaulle, in the course of the sixties, and at the instigation of the economist Rueff[313] – was a good measure but nevertheless insufficient because certain branches of the consumer industry did not yet exist in France: this country did not produce photographic equipment, typewriters, optical products like Zeiss-Ikon, or strong automobiles intended for export.

---

[312] [Anton Zischka (1904-97) was an Austrian writer whose several books commented on the economic and political situation of Europe and the world before, during and after the Second World War.]

[313] [Jacques Rueff (1896-1979) was a French economist who served as adviser to De Gaulle. Rueff criticised Keynesian economics and the use of the dollar as the unit of reserve and advocated a return to the gold standard.]

As Zischka had theorised in his famous work *Sieg der Arbeiter* (*The Victory of the Workers*), gold is certainly a source of national wealth and power but this source remains static while the work standard constitutes a perpetually productive factor corresponding to the dynamism of the contemporary era. The American strategists had seen this well. They allowed the economic miracle of Germany be realised, for this was a quantitative development, certainly spectacular but deceptive. At a certain moment, at the end of some decades, this miracle had to end, for every complementary development of German industry could be achieved only in the direction of the Balkan space, from the basin of the Black Sea to the Near East.

In this context, so rich in real or potential conflicts, whose roots are located in the end of the 19th century, the instruments that served, for several decades, to colonise Germany and consequently Europe and put them out of action are the following:

The Mafia and Drugs

To succeed in controlling Europe the American secret services have always remote controlled diverse Mafia organisations. According to the present specialist on the Mafias, the Frenchman Xavier Raufer,[314] the "Mafia tropism" of American politics already has a long history: everything began in 1943, when the American authorities looked for the Mafia boss Lucky Luciano, originating from Sicily in prison so that he would help in preparing the Allied landing in his native island and the conquest of southern Italy. Since then one can clearly confirm a close connection between the Mafia and the special services of the United States. In 1949, when Mao made China a "people's republic" the Chinese nationalist army of Kuo-Min-Tang withdrew into the "Golden Triangle", a region astride the Burmese-Laotian border. The Americans wanted this army to be held in reserve to eventually conduct operations in Communist

---

[314] [Xavier Raufer (pseudonym of Christian de Bongain) (1946-) is a right-wing thinker who has written several works on criminality and terrorism.]

China. The Congress was however opposed to financing such an army with the money of the American taxpayer and further, would never have supported an operation of this sort. Consequently, the only solution that remained was to ensure its self-financing by the production and trafficking of drugs. During the Vietnam war certain mountain tribes like the Hmongs obtained military materials paid for by drug money. Before Mao's seizure of power in China and before the Vietnam war, the number of drug addicts was very limited, only some avant-garde artists, film actors or members of the so-called "jet society" consumed heroin or cocaine: that amounted to at most 5,000 people in the whole of North America. The media remote-controlled by the services spurred on the consumption of drugs and, at the end of the Vietnam war, America had 560,000 drug addicts. The Chinese and Italian Mafias took charge of the supply and since then have played an important role in the financing of unpopular wars.

The alliance between Turkey and the United States allowed the participation of a third mafia network in this general strategy, that formed by the Turkish organisations who work in close collaboration with para-religious sects and with the army. They have contacts with similar criminal organisations in Uzbekistan or in other Turkophone countries of Central Asia and especially in Albania. The Albanian mafia organisations were able to extend their activities all over Europe following the Kosovo conflict, which allowed them to finance the units of the UCK. The latter played the same role in the Balkans as the Hmong tribes in Vietnam in the sixties. They prepared the country before the offensive of the NATO troops.

Besides, the insidious media support lent to the drug addiction spread among the young follows another strategic objective, that of undermining education in such a way that Europe would lose another of its advantages: that which obtained the best establishments of instruction and education in the world which, in the past, had always aided our continent to save itself from the worst situations.

THE EUROPEAN ENTERPRISE: GEOPOLITICAL ESSAYS

In all of Europe the healthy political forces should fight against the Mafia organisations not only because they are criminal organisations but also because they are the instruments of a state alien to the European space which cultivates a visceral hatred for European identity. The fight against the Mafia organisations implies especially the control and regulation of immigrant flows originating from countries where the presence and influence of mafias are strongly felt (Turkey, Albania, Uzbekistan, etc.)

The Multinationals

Since the sixties the multinationals have been an instrument of American capitalism destined to force the other states to open their borders. On the strictly economic level the principle that consists in favoring the expansion of multinationals leads to strategies of "outsourcing", as it is called in the neoliberal jargon. These strategies of "outsourcing" are responsible for high rates of unemployment. Even in the case of products that are apparently of little importance or harmless, such as toys and sweets, the multinationals have destroyed hundreds of thousands of jobs. For example: miniature cars were in the past, during my childhood, manufactured generally in England such as Dinky Toys, Matchbox and Corgi Toys. Today, the new generation of multinationals, sometimes bearing the same label, like Matchbox, come to us from Thailand, China or Macao. During the period of his enthusiasm for the National Revolutionary political space, the German sociologist Henning Eichberg,[315] today exiled in Denmark, wrote very pertinently in the Berlin journal *Neue Zeit*, that we are undergoing a "total subversion through sweets" (*"Eine totale Subversion durch Bonbons"*). In fact, the sweets and confections for children are no longer products at the local level or confected by a grandmother full of love but sold in mass in drug stores or petrol stations, supermarkets or automatic

---

[315] [Henning Eichberg (1942-) is a German sociologist who focuses on ethnology as the basis of nationalism. His political orientation shifted from right-wing to left-wing over the course of the years.]

vending machines under the names of "Mars", "Milky Way" or "Snickers". It is no longer grandmothers or mothers who confect them but heartless multinationals concerned only with figures and balances managed by vile technocrats who sell them in every nook and corner of the globe. How many people have these infamous strategies deprived of a job, deprived of a meaningful life?

In all of Europe the healthy political forces, if they really wish to fight against mass unemployment, must reject all the systems of outsourcing and effectively protect local productions.

Neoliberalism as an Ideology

Neoliberalism is the economic ideology of globalisation. The French writer and economist Michel Albert[316] declared, at the beginning of the nineties, that neoliberalism, the heirs of the governments of Thatcher and Reagan, corresponds in practice to an almost complete negation of all investment that is local (regional, national, trans-national within a semi-autarkic and self-centred continental framework, etc.). Michel Albert reacted against this new political pathology which consisted in wishing to imitate the Thatcherist administration and "Reaganomics" and recommended that "ordoliberal" politics be made the order of the day. "Ordoliberalism" or the "Rhineland model" (in Michel Albert's terminology) is not only German or "Rhineland" but also Japanese, Swedish, partially Belgian (the patrimonial structures of the old industries of Flanders or of Wallonie) or French (the large family enterprises around the cities of Lyon or Lille or in Lorraine).

This "Rhineland" model privileges investment rather than stock-exchange speculation. The investment is not only made in capital equipment in the industry but also, for Albert, in the research departments of the universities, in the professional colleges or, more generally, in education. Along with the deleterious ideas of the '68 movement, the neoliberal ideology has undermined

---

[316] [Michel Albert (1930-2015) was a French economist who developed the notion of "Rhineland capitalism" in his 1991 book *Capitalisme contre capitalisme*.]

the educational systems all over Europe. In Germany today the situation is serious. In France, it is worse, if not catastrophic. In England, a citizens' initiative called "Campaign for real education" demands at the moment from teachers and parents' associations the revaluation of the school discipline in order to improve the level of studies and the linguistic capacities (in their mother-tongue) of children. The geopolitician Robert Strausz-Hupé[317] who worked in the inner intellectual circles moving at that time around Roosevelt had planned the destruction the implicit strengths of the old European continent in a programme intended for Germany and Europe at the same time that Morgenthau[318] fabricated his plans for a general and definitive de-industrialisation of the Germanic space. According to this Strauss-Hupé, it was necessary to destroy forever the ethnic homogeneity of the European countries and their educational systems. In the attempt to realise this plan at the end of some decades the anti-authoritarian speculations of drugged instructors, the consumption of drugs and the ideology of '68 played a key role. In recalling these events some voices whisper that the philosopher Herbert Marcuse, the idol of the '68ers, worked for the "Office of Strategic Studies" (OSS), the American information agency that preceded the famous CIA.

All over Europe the healthy political forces should militate today to reaffirm the existence of an ordoliberal system of "Rhineland" manufacture (according to Albert), that is, an economic system that invests instead of speculating and which lends its support to schools and universities without neglecting the other non-commercial sectors like the hospital and cultural sectors, for the non-commercial foundation stones of every society cannot be placed at the disposal of or be sacrificed to economics alone. These non-commercial sectors weld the communities, create

---

[317] [Robert Strausz-Hupé (1903-2002) was an Austrian-American political scientist who wrote a work called *Geopolitics; The struggle for space and power*, 1942.]

[318] [Henry Morgenthau Jr. (1891-1967) was the Secretary of the Treasury in Franklin Roosevelt's administration. He proposed his so-called Morgenthau Plan for postwar Germany in 1944.]

a loyalty to the state in all the social categories. Neoliberalism does not weld, it divides, it does not generate any loyalty and causes the law of the jungle to prevail.

The Media

Europe is equally held under the heel of a media system which is, in fine, remote-controlled by certain foreign services which take care to arouse "good" emotions at the right moments. These media fashion the contemporary mentality and aim at excluding from the debate any independent and critical mind, especially if these critical minds are effectively critical because they think in terms of history and tradition. In fact, the minds detached from time and space, without a hearth nor a locality (Jacques Ellul)[319] represent what is called in Germany "*die schwebende Intelligenz*",[320] which is precisely that form of intelligentsia that Americanisation and globalisation need. The domination of Europe through the media instruments began immediately after the Second World War, especially when a journal, apparently harmless in its form and presentation, *Reader's Digest*, was distributed throughout Europe and in all languages, when the France of 1948 was forced to show in all the cinema halls "made in the USA" films, if not they would not receive the Marshall Plan funds. The Blum[321] government accepted this dictate, which signified the death warrant of the French cinema.

When the former cinematographic creator Claude Autant-Lara,[322] classified as a leftist in the time of his glory, was elected to the European Parliament on the ticket of the French nationalist Jean-Marie le Pen, he received the right to deliver the inaugural

[319] [Jacques Ellul (1912-94) was a French philosopher and sociologist who wrote several works on the effects of technology and propaganda on modern societies.]

[320] [Floating intelligentsia.]

[321] [Léon Blum (1872-1950) was the Jewish Prime Minister of France three times between 1936 and 1947.]

[322] [Claude Autant-Lara (1901-2000)was a French film director who became member of the European Parliament in 1989.]

address of the assembly, given that he was its oldest member. He seized this opportunity to condemn, from the Strasbourg tribune, the American policy that had always consisted in imposing Hollywood films to torpedo the national productions of the European countries. The songs, fashions, drugs, television (with CNN), the Internet are so many channels that the American propaganda uses to efface the historical memory of the Europeans and to influence public opinion in such a way that no other world view than the "American way of life" could ever again emerge.

In all of Europe, the healthy political forces should aim at financing independent media, local and connected to the land, which would be capable of supplying to the public ideologically and politically different messages. In order to prevent our peoples from being stultified and influenced by the media systems hyper-centralised and remote-controlled by a superpower foreign to our space. Such a media control is proven to be necessary in the perspective of the wars of the future, which will be "cognitive wars" whose object will be to influence the peoples and render "enemy/ alien audiences" (in the jargon of the CIA or NSA) susceptible to the discourse desired by the special services of Washington in order that no other solution to a problem of international politics might be considered "moral" or "acceptable".

The Military Means

One generally states that the power of the United States is essentially a maritime power. The world powers who are at the same time maritime powers (thalassocracies) are generally "bi-oceanic": one means thereby that they have "windows" on two seas. The objective of the war that the United States imposed on Mexico in 1848 was to make for itself a large window looking out on the Pacific Ocean in order to be able to gain access, in the short or medium term, to the markets of China and the Far East and to make them markets exclusively reserved to American productions. When the

American admiral Alfred Thayer Mahan[323] tried at the end of the 19th century to make the "Navy League" an instrument to promote American imperialism in minds and deeds, he was following simultaneously the objective of making the American fleet, which was then in the process of being developed, an exclusively military monopoly; only this fleet would have the right to impose itself on the globe without experiencing the presence of rivals. His political and strategic goal was to give to the Anglo-Saxon powers a global and ubiquitous "interventional arm" suited to giving to Great Britain and the United States an instrument capable of developing a speed of movement superior to all the other instruments possible at that time in order to ensure the success of their interventions everywhere in the world. The other powers not being able to possess instruments that were as rapid or with a greater speed. Consequently, the objective also aimed at removing from the other powers of the globe in the future the possession of a similar or comparable naval instrument. The conquest of the maritime space of the Pacific thus took place after that of the Californian coasts in 1848, or to be more precise, fifty years later, during the war against Spain which ended in the elimination of this European power in the Caribbean and in the Philippines. Germany, at that time, regained for its part its sovereignty over Micronesia and defended, within this framework, the island of Samoa with its navy against the American ambitions. Between 1900 and 1917, the United States did not venture any decisive act, but the First World War gave it the opportunity to intervene and sell war materials in such quantities to its western allies that in the aftermath of the war it was no longer a debtor to the world but its top creditor.

In 1922, the Americans and the British imposed on Germany and on their own allies the Treaty of Washington. One does not speak enough of this important treaty that was decisive and significant for all of Europe. It imposed on every maritime power of the world a specific tonnage for its navy: 550,000 tons for the

---

[323] [Alfred Thayer Mahan (1840-1914) was an admiral of the US Navy and geostrategist whose principal work focussed on *The Influence of Sea Power on History, 1660-1783* (1890).]

United States and as much for England, 375,000 tons for Japan, 175,000 tons for Italy and as much for France. Versailles had already sounded the death knell of the German navy. France, even though considered as a victor state, could no longer, after the Treaty of Washington, give itself the means to become a strong maritime power. The reduction to almost nothing of the tonnage authorised to the German navy was in fact, in the view of Washington, a vengeance for Samoa and a preventive measure to eliminate the presence of the Reich in the Pacific. Why is it important today to recall all the clauses of the Treaty of Washington? Because, with this Treaty, we are dealing with a textbook example of the American *modus operandi*.

1. This process was later systematised.
2. The wounded nations tried in vain to offer responses to these measures which considerably restricted the exercise of their sovereignty. It suffices to remember the development of French civil aviation in the heroic times when distinguished pilots like Jean Mermoz and Antoine de Saint-Exupéry distinguished themselves or the development of the Zeppelin dirigibles in Germany, which met with a tragic end in 1937 in New York when the "Hindenburg"crashed to the ground engulfed in flames.

From the "Mistral" to the "Mirages"

The two powers France and Germany were not able to replace their navies, lost as a result of the clauses of the Treaty of Washington of 1922, with an adequate and sufficient "aerial fleet".The general objective pursued by the Americans was to not tolerate any autonomous high technology armament industry among their former allies. After the Second World War, France and the small European powers were forced to buy the old American war materials for their armies. The French army was in this way exclusively equipped with American materials. But, with the help of

German prisoner of war engineers, France was soon in a position to manufacture ultra-modern fighter planes as, for example, jets of the "Mistral" type.

After 1945, Germany did not possess any aeronautical industry worth the name. Fokker, in the Netherlands, could not do more than try to survive and finally remained a business too modest for its real capacities. Under De Gaulle, French engineers developed, in cooperation with German colleagues, the famous fighter aircraft "Mirage", serious competition to their American equivalents on the world market. The Mirage III fighters constituted a development of the German "*Volksjäger*" (people's hunter) of the Second World War, the Heinkel 162. In 1975, the Americans forced the governments of the Scandinavian and Benelux countries of NATO to obtain F-16 fighters after having convinced a group of corrupt politicians. The effect of this decision was that the French of Bloch-Dessault and the Swedes of SAAB could no longer conduct major technological innovations because the loss of this internal European market did not allow them to finance advanced research. The same scenario was played out more recently with the sale of F-16s to the Polish and Hungarian air forces. Ever since this "deal of the century" the French and Swedish aircraft manufacturers lagged behind and, lacking in financial means, never succeeded in hauling themselves up to the highest levels of aviation technology. If, at the level of armament technologies, the Germans obtained the authorisation to construct their Leopard cars, it is because America is above all a maritime power and is not a priori interested in armaments intended for land forces. The Americans place a stress more on warships, submarines, missiles, satellites and air forces.

In an article that appeared in the Berlin weekly *Junge Freiheit*,. we are informed that the American consortiums buy the firms that produce advanced technologies like Fiat-Avio in Italy, a branch of the gigantic consortium that Fiat represents and that produces aircraft engines, and then a North German enterprise that produces submarines and the Spanish consortium Santa Barbara Blindados which manufactures the German Leopard cars for the Spanish army. In this way the owners of the American war industry will have access to all the secrets of the German armoured vehicle industry. These financial manoeuvres aim at forcing Europe into dependence so that it will not attain any possibilities of asserting its military independence.

The military organisations that are, or were, under American tutelage, like NATO, CENTO or SEATO served only one purpose: to create a market for downgraded American armaments, especially planes, in order to prevent, in the allied countries, any development or resurrection of independent armament industries capable of competing with their American equivalents. The technological progress which could have resulted from the independence of the armament industries in Europe or elsewhere would doubtless have permitted the production of more efficient armament systems for "alien armies", foreign armies – which would have had as its result a restraint, if the need arose, of the dominant superpower – which has in the meantime become the only superpower of the world – or its reduction to the dimension of a power of second or third rank.

The ECHELON Network

The fear of seeing potentially hostile powers developing efficient military technologies is deeply embedded in the heads of the directing political personnel of the United States. It is this that explains the need to spy on the "allies". As Michael Wiesberg[324] has explained to us very well in the columns of the Berlin weekly *Junge Freiheit*, the ECHELON satellite system was conceived during the Cold War as a military observation system intended to complement the communication methods existing at the time such as undersea cables or the other satellites used for military purposes. But under Clinton the ECHELON system ceased to be a purely military instrument; officially it now pursues civil missions. And when civil objectives become objects of high technological espionage systems that means that the "allies" of the hyper-armed superpower also

[324] [Michael Wiesberg (1959-) is a German journalist who contributes to the right-wing weekly *Junge Freiheit*.]

become, in their turn, the targets of this permanent wire tapping. In such a context these "allies" are no longer "allies" in the conventional sense of the term. The purely political perspective such as it was defined for us in the past by Carl Schmitt changes completely. There exist then no more enemies in the "Schmittian" sense of the term but then no more "allies" either, in the sense in which the latter would be theoretically and legally perceived and treated as equals. The language used henceforth in the high American circles and in the US secret services betrays this semantic and practical slide: one does not speak there any longer of "enemies" and "allies" but of "alien audiences", literally "foreign audiences" or "foreign recipients [of messages]" who should be the target of the American propaganda services whose mission it is to render them "receptive" and docile.

What does this apparently harmless semantic slide, this modification mean? It means that, after the collapse of the Soviet Union, the European "allies" have become superfluous and henceforth constitute only a group of vestigial residues from a past that is fully past so much so that one can without shame go and pump information into them, that one can place them under perpetual surveillance especially in the fields that are connected to high technology. The Europeans were already able to confirm, at their expense, that the French and German firms have been spied upon electronically or through the satellites of the ECHELON system. Some of these enterprises had developed a system of water purification. As the information that they sent by electronic mail had been copied, the competing American enterprises could manufacture the products more cheaply, quite simply because they had not invested a cent in the research.

The American state apparatus favors in this way its own national firms and at the same time plunders the enterprises of its "allies". This form of industrial espionage contains a mortal danger for our civil societies for it generates an unemployment among a highly qualified personnel. Duncan Campbell,[325] a courageous

---

[325] [Duncan Campbell (1952-) is a British investigative journalist who published an article in the *New Statesman* in 1988 entitled "Somebody's listening" which exposed the ECHELON network.]

British journalist who denounced the ECHELON scandal, gives in his report dozens of examples of similar looting in all the domains of advanced technology. The United States, however, is not the only one participating in the ECHELON espionage satellite network; Great Britain, Canada, Australia and New Zealand participate in it too, so much so that an important question arises: does the United Kingdom constitute a loyal European power? Was General de Gaulle not right when he said that the "special relationship" between the United States and Great Britain was from the start hostile to the European continent and would remain so forever?

When we evoke a "Europe of peoples" we should bear in mind two groups of facts each playing an important role.

1. The first group of facts is of a cultural nature. Culture is what should be maintained intact as far as possible, in the incessant turbulence of divergent models that modernity poses to us. We are evidently aware of this, we more than many others. But this awareness of ours contains a great danger characteristic of every cultural struggle: that of transforming all cultural heritage into a "museum-like" jumble or of viewing every cultural activity as a simple pastime. The defence of our cultural heritage cannot in any case be "static", devoid of dynamism. Every living culture possesses a political, economic and geopolitical dimension.

2. The second group of facts: the people, as the ethnic substrate that is the bearer and creator/founder of culture, can never be placed at the disposal of the dominant political class. The popular substrate causes, in the course of time, a specific and inalienable culture and literature to emerge, the products of a particular history. It equally generates a specific economic system which is such and not otherwise. Every economic form is born and is incorporated into a particular space, is the emanation of a particular era. Consequently, any viable economics cannot be absorbed into a conceptual scheme that wants to be straightaway "international" or "universal".

Perroux,[326] Albertini[327] and Silem,[328] the great French theoreticians of economics and economic history, rightly insist on the historical dimension of economic systems, not to mention the great theoreticians of the autarkic systems. To clarify their very pertinent remarks they classified the totality of systems into two didactic categories: the "orthodox" on the one hand and the "heterodox" on the other.

"Orthodox" and "Heterdox" Economic Theories

The "orthodox" are the liberal ones of the school of Adam Smith (the Manchester liberals) and the Marxists, who think on the basis of universal concepts and wish to implant the same models and categories everywhere in the world. They are in fact the philosophical ancestors of the globalist levellers of today. The "heterodox", on the contrary, place an emphasis on the particularities of each economic system. They are the heirs of the German "historical school" and of economists such as Rodbertus, Schmoller and Laveleye.[329] Under the Weimar Republic, the Tat-Kreis[330] and the journal *Die Tat*,[331] with the heirs of this school such as Ferdinand Fried[332] and Ernst Wagemann,[333] pursued this quest and deepened this intellectual

[326] [François Perroux (1903-87) was a French economist and professor at the Collège de France.]

[327] Jean-Paul Albertini is a French economist who has served as advisor to the ministries of the environment and of ecology.]

[328] [Ahmed Silem is a French economist who teaches at the Jean-Moulin University in Lyon.]

[329] [Émile de Laveleye (1822-92) was a Belgian economist who wrote several works on political economy and Belgian and foreign politics.]

[330] [The Tat-Kreis (Action Circle) was a *völkisch* and revolutionary conservative movement during the Weimar Republic.]

[331] [The monthly journal *Die Tat* was founded by the Freemason Ernst Horneffer and published from 1909 to 1939. It was edited from 1929 by Hans Zehrer (1899-1966).]

[332] [Ferdinand Zimmerman (pseudonym Fried) (1898-1867) was an editor of *Die Tat* and joined the National Socialist party in 1936.]

[333] [Ernst Wagemann (1884-1956) was a German economist and demographer who joined the NSDAP in 1933. Between 1948 and 1953 he worked as an academic in Chile.]

vein. As we just said, for the "heterodox" and the adherents of the historical school, each economic space is connected to a place and is the fruit of a particular history that cannot be quite simply put into parenthesis and ignored. History and economics fashion institutions that are connected to an ethnic substrate, to a place and an era, institutions that cause an economy to function in this manner and no other. We see very clearly here why the EU has up to now made a mistake and will continue to do so in the future: it has never utilised this heterdox way. We, obviously, opt for this heterodox approach of economics in the sense in which it was meant by Perroux, Silem and Albertini. Economics is the *nomos*[334] of the *oikos*,[335] which signifies that it is the shaping of a specific living space where I live, as a "potential shaper of politics" along with people like me. According to the etymology itself of the word 'economics', there is no economics without a place.[336] A universal economics does not exist.

Let us return to geopolitics. By definition, the discipline that "geopolitics" constitutes deals with the influence of geographical/

---

[334] [Law.]

[335] [House, or household.]

[336] The Greek word "*oikos*" is of the same Indo-European root as the Latin "*vicus*" meaning "village" or a well constructed site. The term "*vicus*" has given the Dutch "*wijk*" (quarter) and the English onomastic suffix "-wich" as in "Greenwich", for example, which would give "Groenwijk" in Dutch. The sound "w" or "v" having disappeared in classical Greek and having been preserved in the Latin and Germanic languages the original form is "[w/v]oikos", where one recognises the two consonants are fixed while the vowels vary. The "k" has become "ch" in English according to the same phonetic rules that gave the change of "*castellum*" (Latin) into "*castel*" (Old French), "*cateau*" or "*casteau*" (Picard) to "*château*" (modern French); or again the change of "*canis*" (Latin) to "*ki*" (Picard of the Borinage) and then to "*chien*" (modern French) and to "*tché*" (Walloon of Liège). From "*tché*" we pass next to the Germanic domain where many Latin "k"s have given an aspirated "h", passing through the intermediate sound written "ch" in Dutch and in German (for example, "canis"/"*Hond*/*Hund*", "*cervus*"/"*cerf*"/"*Hert*"/"*Hirsch*", etc. Gentilics also follow the same rules: the "*Chattes*" of antiquity have become the "*Hessois*" ("*Hessen*") of today, taking into consideration that the "t" is transformed into "ss" according to the rules of consonantal shift peculiar to the continental Germanic languages.

spatial factors on the eternal sources of politics within a given space. The immediate and surrounding spatial factors of course influence the manner in which economics is practised within the limits of the *oikos* itself. It it appears useful and balancing to us to conserve the inherited modes of practising economics and not to replace them with rules that would apparently be easily applicable to all the places of the world, we can then speak of an "autarkic" principle when economics has as its goal to be and to remain self-sufficient. The notion of economic autarky does not necessarily imply that one should constitute in the end a "closed commercial state" (the narrow interpretation of the idea conceived by Fichte). At the present moment, the notion of autarky should aim at a balance between a reasonable opening of the commercial borders and the equally reasonable practice of *ad hoc* closures in order to protect the local products as they should be. A modern notion of autarky aims at a well balanced "self-centredness" of every national or "large space" (*großräumisch/reichisch*) economy, as it had been theorised by André Grjebine,[337] a disciple of François Perroux.

From Friedrich II to Friedrich List

Friedrich List had advocated in the 19th century independent economic systems. It is he who forged, through his ideas and plans, the modern economics of Germany, the United States, France and Belgium, and particularly also of Russia at the time of the Tsarist minister Sergei Witte, the man who, on the eve of the First World War, modernised the Russian Empire. The principal idea of List was to launch the process of industrialisation in every country and to develop good systems and networks of communication. In List's time these systems and networks of communication were the canals and the railways. From his point of view, and from ours, every cultural or civilisational space, every federation of peoples,

---

[337] [André Grjebine (1948-) is a French economist who is currently director of the Centre de Recherches Internationales at the Institut d'études Politiques de Paris.]

has the right to construct its own network of communication in order to consolidate itself economically. In this sense, List intended to realise the concrete wishes contained in the political testament of Friedrich II.

The king of Prussia wrote in 1756 that the major mission of the Prussian state in the space of the great plain of North Germany was to connect the great river basins to one another through canals so much so much so that between the Vistula and the North Sea communications may be greatly facilitated by them. This plan aimed at surpassing the condition of discontinuity and fragmentation of the North German space that had strained the historical destiny of the Holy Empire for centuries. The system of canals envisaged later reduced the dependence of this plain in relation to the sea. In his time List developed equally the plan to connect the Great lakes situated in the centre of the North American continent to the Atlantic. He encouraged the French to construct a canal between the Atlantic and the Mediterranean in order to relativise the position of Gibraltar. He also advised the Belgian king, Leopold I of Saxe-Coburg,[338] to connect the basins of the Escaut and the Meuse to that of the Rhine. In this way, the Belgian state successively had several canals dug including the "Canal du Centre", the Anvers-Charleroi Canal and, much later (in 1928), the Albert Canal, the crown of this Germano-Belgian project of the 19th century. List advised everybody to construct railway lines in order to accelerate communications everywhere. It is especially Germany and the United States which owe to this great engineer and economist the fact of having become great industrial powers.

Of the Inalienable Right to Deploy One's Own Electronic Systems

The thalassocratic powers cannot in any case tolerate such developments in the continental countries. The English feared, in

---

[338] [Leopold I (1790-1865) was a German prince who became the first king of Belgium after it gained independence in 1830. He established the royal house of Saxe-Coburg-Gotha.]

the 19th and 20th centuries, that the constituent element of their power, that, is, their navy, would automatically lose its importance in the case of an improvement of the intra-continental navigable routes and of the railways. The English press revolted against the construction, by the French, of the great canal between the Atlantic and the Mediterranean. In 1942, the same London press published a map to make clear to its public the dangers that the construction of a connection between the Rhine, the Main and the Danube contained. In his very interesting work entitled *Präventivschlag*, Max Klüver[339] reminds us that the British special services had planned and begun implementing sabotage missions against the bridges on the Danube in Hungary and Romania. The Cold War equally had as its objective – it is sufficient to read a physical map of Europe – the cutting of the river communications on the Elbe and the Danube in order to prevent any vigorous communication between Bohemia and North Germany and between the Bavaro-Austrian complex and the Balkan space. The war against Serbia in 1999 served, among other things, to block all traffic on the Danube and to prevent the development of a system of communications with multiple routes between the region of Belgrade and the Aegean Sea. The ideas of List remain completely valid and indeed deserve to be deepened and intensified, especially by including in their reflections on autarky and economic independence the new technology that the satellite systems today represent. Every group of peoples, every federation like the EU for example, must have the inalienable right to deploy its own electronic means and systems in order to reinforce its industrial and economic power.

To observe some actual realisations of the theories of List which, in Europe, have been suppressed, or "forbidden", like almost all the "heterodox" doctrines, we should turn our attention to Latin America. On this continent, disciples of List and of Perroux work and teach. When these Latin American theoreticians and economists speak of freeing themselves from the American

---

[339] [Max Klüver, *Präventivschlag 1941: Zur Vorgeschichte des Rußland-Feldzuges*, Druffel Verlag, 1986.]

tutelage they use the concept of "continentalism". They designate thereby a political movement present on the entire Ibero-American continent and capable of collecting and federating all the forces that desire to disengage themselves from the dependence imposed by Washington. Argentina, for example, has developed well substantiated autarkic ideas and ideals since the time of General Peron. Before the transnational banking forces of the world had ruined the country using all the tricks imaginable and possible, Argentina benefited from a real independence in food, thanks to its surplus production of cereals and meats intended for export. This civil power constituted a thorn in the side of the American politics. Argentina also had, thanks to the help of German engineers, been able to develop a complete and well diversified military industry. In 1982, the Argentine pilots used fighter planes manufactured in Argentina itself, the famous "Pucaras" which destroyed British warships during the Falklands War. This well followed policy of autonomy made the Peronist ideology, which articulated it, the enemy number one of the United States in Iberian America, and more particularly in the "southern cone", for more than sixty years. The numerous crises created of various factors that shook the country of General Peron reduced the autarkic practices, however well conceived, to nothing. A very positive experiment met with a miserable end, which is a disaster for all of humanity.

Those who today wish to pursue a European policy of independence, beyond all the conformisms suggested by the media under control, must articulate the following six points to respond to the policy of globalisation desired by the United States:

1. Abandon Neoliberalism, Recover Ordoliberalism

Economics must again be based on the principles of the "Rhineland model" (Michel Albert) and recover its "patrimonial" dimension. The principal procedure to return to this "Rhineland" and patrimonial model and thus re-establish an ordoliberal market economics consists in investing rather than speculating. When one speaks of investment that is true equally of the educational establishments, the universities and research. Such a policy implies equally the control of the most important strategic fields, as in Japan or in the United States, what President Putin now practices in post-Communist Russia. Putin, in fact, just recently requested the oligarch Khodorkovski to invest his fortunes "patriotically" in projects to be developed in the Russian Federation rather than "placing" them abroad and speculating on them there without risk. The Brussels Eurocracy has always rejected such a policy. Recently, the parliamentary member of the French Front National Bruno Gollnisch,[340] proposed a European policy according to three guidelines:

- Support Airbus in order to develop a European aeronautical industry independent of America,

- Develop Aérospace in order to give Europe its own satellite system,

- Support all research in the field of energy sources in order to free Europe from the tutelage of the petrol consortiums directed by the United States. Such a clear programme undoubtedly constitutes a step in the right direction.

2. Fight to remove Europe from the hold and influence of the big American media agencies

To make ourselves independent of the big American media agencies which interpret the prevailing reality of the international scene according to perspectives which go against our own interests, Europe should develop a space policy, which implies a close cooperation with Russia. Without Russia we will suffer a considerable delay in this field. For decades, Russia has assembled a considerable expertise in space matters. China and India are also

---

[340] [Bruno Gollnisch (1950-) has been executive vice-president of the Front National since 2007.]

ready to participate in a common project in this direction. But, in order to be able to combat most efficiently the media totalitarianism that the United States imposes on us, we need another intellectual and spiritual revolution, a new metapolitics, which would break the dangerous fascination that the American film and leisure industry exercises. If the European productions offer quality and attract the public even while conserving the diversity and plurality of the European cultures in the sense that Herder intended, we would be in a position to win the "cognitive war" as the French strategists today call it. Every intellectual revolution needs imagination, creativity, a redeeming futurism and, above all, a certain insolence in criticism as is demonstrated by the history of a satirical German paper from before 1914, *Simplicissimus*.[341] A spirit of insolence, when it hits the nail on the head, helps to win the "cognitive war".

3. The principles of foreign policy should never be those which America induces and preaches non-stop.

Europe should impose its own concepts in foreign policy, in other words, reject the universalism of Washington, whether the latter is expressed in terms of "multilateralism", as Kerry wishes, or of "unilateralism", as Bush practiced it in Iraq. For a Europe that will no longer be the expression of the Brussels Eurocracy no model should be considered as universally valuable or announced as such. Let two groups of principles be recalled and cited here:

- Armin Mohler,[342] who died in July 2003, spoke of the necessity of giving a German interpretation and practice to Gaullism in such a way that, as he wrote in his work *Von*

---

[341] [*Simplicissimus* was a satirical German weekly magazine begun in 1896 and published until 1944, and then again from 1954 until 1967.]

[342] [Armin Mohler (1920-2003) was a Swiss conservative thinker whose major work is a study of the Conservative Revolution in Germany, *Die Konservative Revolution in Deutschland 1918-1932* (based on his doctoral dissertation of 1949). He was closely associated with the Nouvelle Droite of Alain de Benoist.]

rechts gesehen (Viewed from the right), Europe should always be interested in – and protect – the countries that the Americans call "rogue states". When Armin Mohler wrote his lines about Gaullism, the rogue state par excellence, in the American propagandist terminology, was China. At the same time, in the "European national" camp, Jean Thiriart and the militants of his "Jeune Europe" movement in Brussels said exactly the same thing. In Germany, Werner Georg Haverbeck[343] tried, at Vlotho, in his Collegium Humanum, to spread among the German intellectual circles more objective information on China. The Queen Mother in Belgium, Elisabeth von Wittelsbach, in order to ostensibly oppose the "Hallstein Doctrine" of NATO, undertook at that time to travel to China. All were saddled with the disqualifying epithet of "crypto-Communists". Now, to orient the international politics of Europe according to certain Chinese models is in no way an idiocy or an aberration.

• This Sinophilia of the fifties and sixties brings us quite naturally to reflect on a model that Europe could perfectly imitate instead of blindly following the principles and practices of American universalism. This model is that which China proposes even today, after the paleo-Communist interval:

• No mixture of the Third Estate in the internal affairs of another state. That means that the ideology of human rights cannot be used to arouse conflicts within a third state. General Löser, who, immediately after the fall of the Wall, militated in Germany for a neutralisation of the

---

[343] [Werner Georg Haverbeck (1909-99) was a National Socialist who became a Christian priest in 1950. He travelled to Russia and China in 1958 when he met the Chinese nationalist leader Chiang Kai-shek. In 1963 he founded the Collegium Humanum as an ecological institute (which was however banned in 2008 on account of its association with National Socialism and Holocaust denial).]

Central European zone (Mitteleuropa), defended similar points of view.

- Respect for the sovereignty of existing states.

- Never act to shake the foundations on which the stability of states rests.

- Continue to work for peaceful coexistence.

- Guarantee to each nation the freedom to fashion its own economic system as it wishes.

- This Chinese political philosophy is based on the works of classical authors like Sun Tzu[344] or Han Fei[345] and on the Tao Te Ching.[346] This thought contains clear arguments clear as crystal without having anything to do with that deleterious moralism which characterises the articulation of American universalism in the media.

4. Force Oneself to be Independent on the Military Level

The principal task of continental freedom movement in all of Europe would be to aim at the unfailing protection of the armaments industry and to prevent the existing firms from falling into the hands of American consortia like the Carlyle Corporation. Fiat Avio in Italy, the last firm that manufactured submarines in Germany, and the Spanish consortium Santa Barbara Blindados have just become fully American through the intervention of stock-exchange speculations. Another task: systematically privilege

---

[344] [Sun Tzu, who is tentatively dated to around the 5th century B.C., was a Chinese general and military strategist who is thought to be the author of the text called *The Art of War*.]

[345] [Han Fei (ca.280-33 B.C.) was a Chinese political philosopher whose emphasis on laws had a strong influence on the first imperial, Qin, dynasty of ancient China.]

[346] [*Tao Te Ching* is a text on Taoism attributed to Lao Tzu (ca. 5th century B.C.).]

Eurocorps[347] instead of NATO, by transforming this Eurocorps into a popular type of the Swiss type, or as a militia as Löser wished in Germany, Spannochi[348] in Austria and Brossolet in France. NATO in fact no longer has any reason to exist ever since Germany and Europe were reunified in 1989. In the aftermath of the disappearance of the Iron Curtain, the Europeans have missed a historic chance to fashion a world order according to their interests. That is why the fine idea of a "Paris/Berlin/Moscow Axis" doubtless comes too late. Third task – to construct a European navy endowed with aircraft carriers. Fourth task – to launch a European satellite system in order that Europe might finally have arms at its disposal to conduct military wars and cognitive/cultural wars. Which leads us to state the fifth point:

5. Fight the ECHELON Network

As a system of surveillance and espionage in the service of Great Britain, Australia, Canada, New Zealand and the United States, ECHELON is a weapon directed against Europe, Russia, India, China and Japan. It embodies the dangerous idea of a total surveillance such as Orwell and Foucault had predicted. The American and Anglo-Saxon practice of a similarly ubiquitous surveillance must be countered and combated by all the other powers of the world who are subjected to it. It can be only through the constitution an equivalent system, fruit of a close cooperation between Russia, Europe, India, China and Japan. If ECHELON is no longer the only system of this type, the powers of the great Eurasiatic continental mass could offer their own cultural, military and economic response. In ECHELON, in fact, are merged the cultural, economic and military operations that are conducted everywhere in the world today. The response to offer to it rests in

---

[347] [The European Corps is an intergovernmental European army corps stationed in Strasbourg.]

[348] [Emil Spannochi (1916-92) was an Austrian general who supervised the reorganisation of the Austrian army from 1973 to 1986.]

the constitution of a "Eurospace" in connection with the Russian expertise accumulated since the launching of the first Sputnik at the end of the fifties.

6. For an Independent Energy Policy

As for energy policy, the path to be followed is the maximal diversification of the energy sources, as De Gaulle had begun in France in the sixties when he intended to maintain his distance from America and NATO. The French Planning Bureau wished at that time to exploit all possible sources of energy: air, solar, tidal, hydraulic without however excluding petrol and nuclear energy. Diversification allows the disengagement from a too close dependence on a unique and/or exclusive source of energy. Today this policy of diversification remains valuable. Which does exclude not the participation in a vast project of development of the Eurasian oil and gas pipelines, in cooperation with Russia, China, the Koreas and Japan. The major object is the disengagement from the dependence on Saudi petrol and, indirectly, on the petrol sources controlled by the United States.

These six points can never be realised by the present political personnel. This is not a conclusion that is peculiar to me, the result of a bitterness towards the dominant political establishment. The analysis that comes to this conclusion regarding this general incompetence of the established political personnel already exists diffused in solidly produced reference works. They constitute an inexhaustible source of new political ideas, or realisable programmes. Erwin Scheuch,[349] Hans-Herbert von Arnim,[350] Konrad Adam,[351] the Italian anti-party-political tradition, the

---

[349] [Erwin Scheuch (1928-2003) was a German conservative sociologist.]

[350] [Hans Herbert von Arnim (1939-) is a German political scientist who has specialised in constitutional law.]

[351] [Konrad Adam (1942-) is a German journalist and politician who served as a federal chairman of the 'Alternative für Deutschland' party which opposes any centralisation of the European Union.]

work of Roberto Michels,[352] critic of the oligarchies, the work of the former minister of Franco, Gonzalo Fernandez de la Mora,[353] offer us the necessary counter-concepts to deploy an offensive and general critique of the rule of parties and of the "cliques" (Scheuch) in place. This critique should eventually force the "planless elites" to leave the field to new elites capable of offering true responses to the contemporary problems.

To conclude, it seems to me to be useful to consider an opinion expressed in the past by Arthur Moeller van den Bruck, who said that partisan (party rule) politics was an evil because the parties seize the apparatus of the state when the latter should theoretically belong to all; in this way, says Moeller van den Bruck, a "filter" is instituted between the real people and the world of politics which destroys all *immediacy* between the governed and the governing.

Only this immediacy postulated by Moeller van den Bruck establishes true democracy, which can only be populist and organic. If there is neither populism nor organicism permanently, the state degenerates into a rigid and purely formal institution, inorganic and devitalised.

This great idea of immediacy in pure politics allows us to realise true projects and to unmask the ideological messages that lead us into the wrong paths. It is for the restoration of this immediacy that we intend to work.

---

[352] [Robert Michels (1876-1936) was a German sociologist who joined the Italian Fascist party in 1924 and wrote an influential work in 1911 on the tendency of political parties to become bureaucratic oligarchies (*Zur Soziologie des Parteiwesens in der Modernen Demokratie. Untersuchungen Über die Oligarchischen Tendenzen des Gruppenlebens* (*On the Sociology of Political Parties in Modern Democracy: A Study on Oligarchic Tendencies in Political Aggregations*)].

[353] [Gonzalo Fernandez de la Mora y Mon (1924-2002) was a Spanish conservative and monarchist politician who was a member of the Allianza Popular party constituted of former Francoist ministers.]

GENERAL REFLECTIONS ON THE CONCEPT OF "EURASIA"[354]

When one speaks of Eurasianism today one tends to see in it a sort of substitute for defunct ideologies which continue the latter, as the Eurasianists of the twenties and thirties – whose approaches have been analysed in detail by Prof. Marlène Laruelle[355] – indeed suggested. Prof. Laruelle demonstrates the eminently Russian character of the Eurasian approach of the twenties and thirties. Consequently, if Europe, the Indian sub-continent, China and other powers of Central Asia or East Asia adopt a "Eurasian" or "Eurasianist" strategy; the concept of a new Eurasianism in keeping with the aspirations of Europe or of these other small or big powers must certainly retain its Russian theoretical nucleus given the quality of the arguments developed by the Eurasianists of the Russian emigration in Berlin, Prague, Brussels and Paris between 1920 and 1940. But it should also be enlarged to make it the natural practice of the BRICS powers and give substance to the pragmatic geopolitics suggested to everybody by the Kazakh president Nazarbayev who controls today the fate of the most central state of the Eurasian continental mass, of the "heartland" as it was theorised by Sir Halford John Mackinder in 1904.

---

[354] Speech delivered at the "Rencontres Eurasistes" in Brussels, 18 October 2014 (edited January 2015). Published in www.egaliteetreconciliation.fr, 21 February, 2015.

[355] Marlène Laruelle, *L'idéologie eurasiste russe, ou comment penser l'empire*, Paris: L'Harmattan, 1999.

The Chinese and the Japanese (the Manchu geopolitical system of the so-called Tokyo school inspired by the Great Continental theses of Karl Haushofer) certainly made their contribution to the new edifice and the task of future "Eurasianist conferences" could well be to illustrate and comment on the works produced at the other end of the Eurasian continental mass, since pragmatic reason makes us think quite naturally that the future of the Far East will certainly gain from an appeasement of the recent tensions between China and Japan and from a reactivation of the plans for a large "sphere of mutual East Asian prosperity" (Daitoa Kyoeiken) theorised immediately after the Second World War by Prince Konoe,[356] by the Japanese minister of foreign affairs Matsuoka Yosuke[357] and by the geopolitician Sato Hiroshi (who also spoke of a "sphere of mutual prosperity of the southern seas).[358] Sato Hiroshi derived his inspiration from Haushofer insofar as the latter considered in his writings that Japan had as its historical mission the control of the territories of the "monsoon zone", of which the American geopolitics of today speaks again with great precision formulating a project of strict control of this zone from the bases situated in the Indian Ocean in order that Washington may definitively, or at least lastingly, inherit the advantages that the British Empire possessed until 1947, the year when the two rival powers of the Indian sub-continent gained their independence.[359]

---

[356] [Prince Fumimaro Konoe (1891-1945) who was Prime Minister of Japan three times between 1937 and 1941.]

[357] [Yōtsuke Matsuoka (1880-1946) was Minister of Foreign Affairs between 1940 and 1941.]

[358] Christian W. Spang, Karl *Haushofer und Japan: Die Rezeption Seiner Geopolitischen Theorien in der Deutschen und Japanischen Politik*, Munich, Iudicium Verlag, 2013.

[359] Robert Kaplan, *Monsoon – The Indian Ocean and the Future of American Power*, New York: Random House, 2011.

From Krymski to Beckwith

For us Europeans of the far west of the Eurasian continental mass a Eurasianist theory is only possible on the condition of integrating in every future and "Eurasianist" political and diplomatic process the Indo-European archaeological and linguistic fact – as a pre-Eurasianist but Indo-Europeanising Russian historian of the 19th century, Agafangel Efraimovitch Krymski,[360] also admitted. In fact, before the rush of the Cossacks of the Tsar towards the Pacific from the 16th century on, the European peoples underwent a projection towards the centre of the Eurasian mass only during the time of the conquest of these vast steppe spaces by the horse-riding Proto-Iranian peoples – as is demonstrated with remarkable erudition by Prof. Christopher I. Beckwith,[361] who sees the most symbolic politico-religious ideal of the peoples of Eurasia implicitly formulated already from the axial age of this first migration towards the centre of Asia, towards the Iranian high plateaus and then towards China (beyond Dzungaria),[362] a migration borne by adventurous warriors mounted on chariots, grouped in *comitati*[363] around an energetic prince, the founder of solid political structures, a charismatic figure who should be imitated and reembodied constantly for the glory of the people or the lineage from which one has descended. For Beckwith the Eurasian idea, the only idea capable of giving strength to the "empires of the Silk Road" and of the peripheries that Mackinder named the "rimland", is directly derived from these first waves of the Indo-European diaspora into Central Asia, Iran(as well as into the Middle Eastern kingdom of

[360] [Agafangel Krymski (1871-1942) was a Ukrainian Orientalist who specialised in culture of the Arabs, Iranians and Turks as well as of the Crimean Tartars.]

[361] Christopher I. Beckwith, *Empires of the Silk Road – A History of Central Eurasia from the Bronze Age to the Present*, Princeton: Princeton University Press, 2009.

[362] [Dzungaria is a region in north western China.]

[363] [A comitatus was an ancient Indo-European social system whereby warriors pledged allegiance to a warlord in return for protection and privileges. It is one of the sources of mediaeval feudalism.]

the Mitanni) and beyond the Indus into the Indian sub-continent under the leadership of the caste of kshatriyas.

For Beckwith this model is certainly of European origin, is manifested for the first time among the Proto-Iranians but it was repeated successively by all the founders of empires of this very vast region that they had Europeanised – the Huns, Turks, Mongols, Manchus, etc. Every western European theoretician of a new Eurasianism must therefore integrate this proto-historic fact of the Indo-European (or Proto-Iranian) diaspora into his (geo)political reflections, know that it has a superior claim, on an axiological level, the repercussion from the Hunnish invasions that followed this first Proto-Iranian expansion having forced Europe into the dead end of the European peninsula between the Black Sea and the Atlantic (*res nullius*[364] at the time).

The European Dead End

No valuable geopolitical perspective can want this mediocre status of isolation in a dead end where the Eurocrats seem to be complacent today motivated by lame amnesiac and contemptible ideologies that make the contemporary Russian writer Eduard Limonov say that western Europe has become a "big old-age home". Already in the 12th century, the erudite Englishman William of Malmesbury[365] justified the Crusades not through the pathological desire of making war on one's neighbours but through the desire to emerge out of this dead end in order to recover the ports of access to the Silk Road, in order not to be stewed in an isolation that leads to implosion. This is confirmed besides by the great contemporary German specialist on the history of Armenia, Tessa Hofmann.[366]

---

[364] [Uncharted and unowned territory.]

[365] [William of Malmesbury (ca.1095-ca.1143) was a British historian whose chronicles include *Gesta Regum Anglorum* (*Deeds of the English Kings*) and *Gesta Pontificum Anglorum* (*Deeds of the English Bishops*).]

[366] Tessa Hofmann, *Annäherung an Armenien – Geschichte und Gegenwart*, Munich: Verlag C. H. Beck, 1997-2006.

when she evokes the Armenian kingdoms of Sicily in the 13th and 14th centuries. After having received the friendly agreement of the great emperor Friedrich I Barbarossa, the latter connected, through the crusader elements that structured and protected the region, western Europe of the Middle Ages to the commerce of Asia, the first attempt to break the encirclement, the enclave which stifled Europe by occupying lastingly the region of Antioch, by holding the Seljuk elements at bay who intended to cut off their communications. The Armenians of the County of Edessa initiated the Italian caravans on the Silk Roads; it was from the Sicilian ports in the hands of the Armenians and the crusaders that Nicola and Marco Polo undertook their travels to the vast Asiatic spaces and to the court of the Great Khan.

"Shatterbelt" and "Gateway Regions"

When one is complacent in the mediocre idea of a "dead end Europe", one sets eastern limits to Europe, purely theoretical limits, totally deprived of relevance on the Ural mountains considering that the most elevated peak of this chain of mountains is 1600 metres, exactly like the Chasseral in the Swiss Jura. Between Europe as such, that of the mediaeval civilisational space, and the other imperial spaces of Asia, Persia and India, is a "shatterbelt" of mixed zones, of transit zones which the contemporary American geopolitician Saul B. Cohen[367] calls also the "gateway regions" or the "gateway states": Armenian Sicily of the time of the Crusades was an access point to the giant "gateway" that is the Silk Road. The Ukraine of today is another "gateway region" and it is, by the force of circumstances, a zone of strong geopolitical turbulences exactly like the north of Syria and the entire space devastated by the Islamic State, a space which is indeed the contemporary counterpart and extension towards Persia of the Sicily of the 13th and 14th centuries, but a space this time devastated from top to

---

[367] On Saul B. Cohen, see David Criekemans, *Geopolitiek – 'Geografisch geweten' van de buitenlandse politiek?*, Antwerpen/Apeldoorn: Garant, 2007.

bottom to the point of no longer being able to play the role of a "gateway". At the beginning of 2015, the clearest observers of the turmoil in gestation prognosticate already new zones of turbulence in Moldavia and Turkmenistan, that is, a programmed weakening of Europe by a new variant of the "colour revolutions" in the form of a confrontation between indigenous populations (PEGIDA operations in Germany and "Je suis Charlie" in France) and Muslim immigrants which will dangerously strain the budgets of the states and weaken the Euro following the Greek crisis and the probable victory of the Greek extreme left.

These burning events oblige us to signal the beginnings of a constant of history: the Proto-Iranian horse-riders of proto-history and their Scythian or Alain successors connected the vast "shatterbelt" between Europe and India, between Europe and China. This action aroused only nostalgias: the Roman Empire wished to re-establish the connection with India and China, we know this now as it is proved by the importance of certain ancient ports in the Red Sea, the Trans-Arab caravan routes of Petra in Jordan or the campaigns of the Roman emperors in Mesopotamia. The history of the successive waves of Indo-European horse-riding peoples towards India and China should thus be part of an indispensable learning, a worthy complement of the ancient "humanities" (sabotaged by cowardly and criminal politicians), a necessary kernel of a future renascent *paedia*[368] whose orientation has been posited by Iaroslav Lebedynsky,[369] the author of precise monographs on each of the horse-riding peoples of the "grand gateway" steppe region between Europe and China.

---

[368] [Ideal educational system.]

[369] [Iaroslav Lebedynsky (1960-) is a Ukrainian French historian of the warrior cultures of the steppes and the Caucasus.]

Attila Penetrates the Pannonian Gap

The mummies of the Tarim,[370] as well as the demonstrations of Prof. Christopher I. Beckwith and the grammatical and semantic analyses of the Tokharian language spoken by the members of this people whose mummies these are, prove the preponderant influence of these horse-riding, charioteering and textile working peoples on the initial development of the Chinese civilisation. These peoples, descendants of the Proto-Iranians, such as the Tokharians and relatives, retained a complete control of the Eurasian steppe space whose strategic quality is of a "shatterbelt" according to Cohen up to ca.200 B.C. At that time a confederation of Hunnish nomadic peoples, who in turn imitated the high degree of social organisation of the Proto-Iranians and their descendants that one can say was inspired by the typical founding values of proto-Zoroastrianism, provoked, by its violent attacks, the flow of Indo-Europeans into Central Asia. Their Hun successors rushed on the barrages of the empires: China survived, Rome collapsed as soon as the horse-riders of the leader Attila penetrated the Pannonian gap, the territory of present-day Hungary, the central point and nerve-centre of the Imperial Roman presence on the axis of the river Danube. The shock sustained in Pannonia triggered the collapse of the Roman Empire including that in the Mediterranean. The latter, even if of cardinal importance, was not sufficient to conserve its coherence and unity.

Those who hold a scholarly and restricted view of the ancient history of Rome consider that the latter is an exclusively "Mediterranean" civilisation, centred on what Mussolini, puffed up with Roman nostalgia, called the "Mare Nostrum". Rome, one forgets too often, was equally a Rhine-Moselle civilisation around Trèves and Cologne. It was deployed equally on the Danube axis. Thus along two circulation routes posited on a west-east axis, the Mediterranean and the Danube, which was nevertheless partially

---

[370] J. P. Mallory & Victor H. Mair, *The Tarim Mummies. Ancient China and the Mystery of the Earliest Peoples from the West*, London: Thames & Hudson, 2000.

interrupted at the point of the "Iron Gates"[371] (on the present-day Serbo-Romanian border) or the "cataracts of the Ister". Every empire, whether it be Persian, Roman or Chinese, is also a network of communications. Rome, and consequently Europe, was based, in antiquity.

1. On the Mediterranean maritime routes ever since Caius Julius received the title of "Caesar" for having conquered the pirates of the Mediterranean (his first triumph)

2. On the terrestrial routes of communication which the Roman roads were.

3. On the river routes starting from the western bank of the Rhine and the southern bank of the Danube.

The imperium of Rome in Europe was thus the mastery of these three modes of communication that the imperial (Carolingian) restoration of Pippin sought to put back in working order after the decline of the last Merovingians: the collapse of the later Empire had been followed by a disintegration of the system of Roman roads so much so that only the communications by waterways still permitted mass transport.

The Division of Verdun in 843

One cannot repeat enough that the famous division of Verdun in 843 in fact divided the river systems among the heirs of Charlemagne's son: to western Francia the basins of the Somme, the Seine, the Loire and the Garonne, what the historians and cartographers called henceforth the "Gallic space", to central Lothringia, bequeathed to the elder Lothair and holder of the imperial title, the basins of the Meuse, the Rhine, the Rhône and the Po; to eastern Francia, bequeathed to the young and vigorous Louis, the parallel river basins of the great northern European plain

---

[371] [See above p. 28]

and the duty of reconquering the Danube all along its length up to the Black Sea, the access to the mythic Colchis of the Argonauts[372] and port of Persia. Louis established capitals in Frankfurt on the Main between the urbanised Rhineland and the remainder of his kingdom and at Ratisbonne (Regensburg) on the Danube in order, rightly, to extend himself towards the downstream portion of the great central river. This division of Verdun was wise and the premature death of Lothair gave to the young Louis the imperial title, after some vicissitudes of war, or the dual "Lothringen and Germanic" space, to the detriment of Charles the Bald, king of Western Francia, whose successors did not cease to wish to usurp the heritage of Lothair by encroaching on it for nearly ten centuries, appeasing their territorial hunger by the illegitimate annexation of Savoy in 1861 and leaving as intact morsels only a distracted and amnesiac Belgium, Luxembourg as a safety vault, Holland isolated to the north of the Rhine and the Meuse and mentally alienated by an anti-imperial Calvinism (well described by the German philosopher Christoph Steding),[373] a Padanian[374] Italy prosperous but connected to the Adriatic and the Alpine zone, Switzerland, whose Romand extended from the Jurassic hinterland to the south of Basel and Geneva, where alone the rivers begin to be navigable, rendering the Switzerland beyond Basel and Geneva uninteresting, contrary to the network of routes of Franche Comté for the Gallic, or western Frankish, imperialists from Philip the Fair[375] and Louis XI.[376] The innumerable and incessant quarrels that followed the death of the unfortunate Lothair thus determined for more than thousand years the history of the western peninsula of the Eurasian continental mass and prevented it from making a step forward

---

[372] [Colchis is a region in the southern Caucasus which was the destination of Jason and the Argonauts in Greek mythology.]

[373] [See above p. 54]

[374] [Of the Po valley.]

[375] [Philip IV, "the Fair" (1268-1314) was King of Navarre from 1284 to 1305 and King of France from 1285 until his death.]

[376] [Louis XI, "the Prudent", "the Cunning", "the Universal Spider", (1423-83) was King of France from 1461-83.]

to recover its birthright in Central Asia, the inheritance of the comitati gathered around the energetic horse-riding princes fifteen centuries before the birth of Christ.

Toynbee and Bithynia

The objective of the elders who presided over the formulation of the Treaty of Verdun was thus to leave the Danube basin to the youngest and most vigorous of the heirs of Charlemagne's son, in order that he might oppose the Hungarians and reorganise the Danube up to its delta in order to restore there a "Roman" imperium borne this time by the Franks and/or the Germans. The aim was to reach the Black Sea and reconnect with a system of communications permitting commerce with the Byzantines and the Persians, that is, all the peoples who lived beyond this mythic Persia, this Orient that had been "Indo-European" before being recently Islamised. The Black Sea, an internal sea, is for the Europeans of the west the gate towards Eurasia, just as it is for the Russians a potential access to the eastern Mediterranean, a necessity that is postulated by their desire to be at once the heirs of the Greek civilisation (which was a north-south Pontic/eastern Mediterranean axis of which the Bosphorus was a bottle-neck in a central position) and of the Byzantine imperium. Arnold Toynbee, who was important in the Royal Institute for International Affairs, an authority compiling an immense documentation and remote-controlling the action of British diplomats and strategists, was a Byzantinist; for him the Greek civilisation, posited as the matrix of European civilisation (which is only partially true in our view) is a civilisation that connects the dry space at the tip of the Balkan peninsula washed by the Aegean but draws its vital substances, its wheat, its wood, from the control of the Pontic space. There is no Greek civilisation without the resources of the Crimea which pass through the Bosphorus. Around this Bosphorus, more particularly in Bithynia,[377] writes Toynbee, there is a territory which, if it is dominated lastingly, gives at once the key to the Mediterranean, access to the Silk Road or to the "gateway region" of Scythia (present-day Ukraine), and permits also access to Persia through the trans-Caucasian Colchis, etc. Rome inherited this power by conquering Bithynia; it was, immediately after Caesar, master of the Danube, the Crimea, and the Pontic space and entered into conflict with the Persian Empire, which sought to extend itself towards the eastern Mediterranean. Byzantium, then the Ottoman Empire, inherited this Rome/Persia division. And the Ottoman enemy of Europe between the 14th and the 18th century acquired its power and expansive force immediately after consolidating its positions in Bithynia, which permitted it to conquer western Anatolia and a good part of the Balkans even before the fall of Constantinople.

Charlemagne, the incarnation of an imperium that had become Romano-Germanic, was not at all opposed to Byzantium, the Roman Empire of the east, led by the Basileus: the model that fascinated him and that he adopted to embellish his capital of Aix-la-Chapelle was precisely Byzantine. The Dom[378] of Aix-la-Chapelle, built on an octagonal plan, reflects a Byzantine splendour, especially after its recent restoration. Charlemagne therefore respected the birthright of the eastern Roman Empire and aimed at territorially connecting his Frankish empire to that of the Basileus. In order to achieve this, it was necessary to clear the Pannonian gap at the level of the Hungarian puszta[379] and re-establish contact with the Byzantines at the height of the "Iron Gates". To realise such an imperial project it was necessary to dig a waterway between the Main and the Danube, between the Rhine basin, whose waters fall into the North Sea, and the Danubian basin, whose waters flow towards the Black Sea. In 793, Charlemagne ordered the excavation of a canal that would be called the Carolingian ditch, or fossa carolina, or Karlsgraben. It served for a rather long time during

[377] [Bithynia was a Roman province in north western Anatolia.]
[378] [Cathedral.]
[379] [The grasslands of the Great Hungarian Plain.}

the High Middle Ages before getting stuck and discouraging trade given the difficulty constituted by the system of elementary canal connections of the time, but it proved to be useful in logistic operations, first to put a definitive end to the domination of the Avars under Charlemagne, then to repulse the Magyar invaders, definitively defeated by Otto I in 955 at Lechfeld permitting the definitive establishment of the Holy Roman Empire of the German Nation. From the victory of Otto there was again an imperium in Europe, because there was no longer a hostile blockade posited by any element denying or ignoring the Roman heritage in Pannonia.

Restoring the Empire Through the Control of Pannonia

The strategic objective, from Charlemagne to Otto I, was indeed the control of the Danube and of the Pannonian plain for as soon as this plan was realised there was an automatic return to an imperium in the Roman style, for Rome maintained many legions in present-day Hungary, of which the hot baths of Budapest are a remarkable memory, in the same way as those of Aix-la-Chapelle are. Another proof of the imperial restoration: the Roman imperium was the alliance of the sedentary Latin and the horse-riding (and Eurasian) mobility of the Iazyges[380] and Roxolani[381] Foederati[382] (studied by Lebedynsky), of whom the rather frozen humanities of our former school curriculum did not tell us. In fact, Rome, like Athens earlier with its Scythian police, depended on the competition of the warlike horse-riders originating from the steppe: they were called mostly Sarmatians[383] in the classical sources but the units that

[380] [The Iazyges were a nomadic Sarmatian tribe that wandered from Central Asia into eastern Europe and settled in Dacia (Romania).]

[381] [The Roxolani were a Sarmatian tribe who settled in the 1st century B.C. in Romania. They may have been related to the Slavic Rus.]

[382] [outlying nations that were allowed to live in the Roman Empire in exchange for military assistance.]

[383] [The Sarmatians were ancient eastern Iranian tribes that spoke Scythian and worshipped fire.]

served in Pannonia bore the tribal name of Iazyges and Roxolani. These experienced horse-riders were charged with protecting this Pannonian gap against the attacks of the Dacians or Germanic tribes like the Quadi or the Marcomanni.

Through the conversion of the Hungarians, Pannonia, after the victory of Otto I, had a permanent garrison of horse-riders of the steppe, Eurasian horse-riders who promised loyalty to Europe (to Christendom, in the mediaeval language), to always be ranged on the side of the latter and to prevent every invasion coming from the steppe from disrupting the neo-Roman order. The Hungarians always kept this promise by letting the crusaders pass through, by heroically fighting against the Turks in the 15th and 16th centuries, by sacrificing themselves twice on the streets of Budapest, in 1945 (to protect Vienna) and in 1956. Today, however, Jobbik, the Hungarian nationalist party, no doubt disgusted by the criminal spinelessness and incompetence of the Eurocratic cliques (who cultivate with a patholical obstinacy the denial of all Romanness, thus of all true inherited Europeanness), wagers on a pan-Turanian Eurasianism reconnecting with some antecedents – the pan-Turanian ideas of the Hungarian defectors who had become generals in the Ottoman army after the revolt of 1847-8 subdued by the Austrians, the visions of the Jewish Hungarian Turkologist Ármin Vámbéry,[384] the theoretician of a pan-Turanianism which the Hungarians of the Habsburg Empire supported – as well as on his Jewish namesake and co-religionist from Lorraine, David Léon Cahun[385] and the pan-Turanian ideology of the geographer Pál Teleki (1879-1941 [suicide]),[386] the future minister of foreign affairs and Anglophile prime minister of the Horthy government before the Second World War. It seems that this Hungarian pan-Turanianism before the present neo-nationalism of the Jobbik

---

[384] [Ármin Vámbéry (1832-1913) was a Hungarian Jewish Turkologist.]

[385] [David Léon Cahun (1841-1900) was a Jewish Orientalist whose Introduction à l'histoire de l'Asie: Turcs et Mongols des origines à 1405 (1896) was an inspiration to the Turkish nationalists including Atatürk.]

[386] [Count Pál Teleki (1879-1941) was a geographer and politician who served as Prime Minister of the Kingdom of Hungary from 1920-21 and from 1939 to 1941.]

movement was a western Franco-British manoeuvre to dislocate the Empire of the Habsburgs, ruin any new dual Austro-Hungarian or Germano-Hungarian alliance and Balkanise Mitteleuropa, as the Treaty of Versailles of 1919 did.

From the Sicambri to Parzival

Both the Roman imperium and then the Ottonian imperium thus contain a Eurasian dimension not preserved in the sweetened and frozen humanities *ad usum Delphini*[387] or by certain Russian Eurasianists of the twenties and thirties who denounced the "Romano-Germanic" civilisation by judging it to be resistant to every dynamic of Eurasian origin or fundamentally foreign to the Byzantine civilisation. The Scythian and then the Sarmatian elements were determinative in the fashioning of the Germanic mentality, repository of the imperial title, as Prof. Beckwith well notes. Besides, new studies tend to prove that the Sicambri[388] elements of the Frankish federation, originating from Cologne and its region, from whom the Merovingians derived, had Sarmatian origins,[389] exactly like the Arthurian myths wrongly called "Celtic" in Britannia. The Sarmatian ideals, those of the proto-Iranian comitatus according to Beckwith, served, just like the Muslim "*fottowat*" impregnated with Persian and not Arab traditions (Saladin), to cause to develop, in the wake of the Crusades, the hard core of the mediaeval European civilisation, that is, the chivalric orders expressed notably by the myth of Parzival (Perceval in

---

[387] ['For the use of the Dauphin', the title of a collection of classical texts used by the Duke of Montausier for the education of the Grand Dauphin, son of Louis XIV.]

[388] [The Sicambri were a Germanic tribe that dwelt on the right bank of the Rhine during Roman times.]

[389] Reinhard Schmoeckel, *Deutschlands unbekannte Jahrhunderte-Geheimnisse aus dem Frühmittelalter*, Schnellbach: Verlag Bublies, 2013; to be read along with the work of Prof. Beckwith, Reinhard Schmoeckel, *Die Indoeuropäer - Aufbruch aus der Vorgeschichte*, Schnellbach: Verlag Bublies, n.d.

Chrétien de Troyes) in the work of Wolfram von Eschenbach, who was inspired by the Arthurian myths considered today as deriving from the Roman Sarmatians and introduced them into continental Germany. Perceval is the spiritual brother of the Persian Feirefiz, whose mother is "brown skinned". The myth forged by Wolfram von Eschenbach aimed at recalling to the minds of the knights the knightly, chivalresque tradition of the Proto-Iranian (and Eurasian) comitatus shared by the Germanic imperium and the Kurdish or Persian imperium, even though they reveal a difference of a racial sort.

To return to the Carolingian epoch. If the objective of Charlemagne and his competent successors was to restore the communication on the Danube, to reach the Black Sea and to connect the west to the east at the level of the Byzantine Bosphorus, at that time, non-Romanised European elements, very far from the Roman and Mediterranean world, undertook a breakthrough farther to the east: the Scandinavian Vikings and the Swedish Varangians whose strategic and commercial focal point was the port of Hedeby,[390] reached the Volga, and the trading post of Bulgaria, and restored in this way a Eurasian commerce at the same time on the Volga which led to the Caspian and from the Caspian to Persia and from Persia to Baghdad, and the Silk Road leading towards the centre of the Eurasian continental mass, and towards China.

Danubian Limes[391] and the Gothic Axis

Rome was certainly, since the outcome of the Punic wars, a Mediterranean power but it was present also on the west bank of the Rhine with towns like Trèves, Cologne, Bonn, Mayence, Arlon, Tongres, Metz, Strasbourg, and on the southern bank of the

---

[390] [Hedeby was a trading colony on the northern German and Danish border between the 8th and 11th centuries, during the Viking Age.]

[391] [See above p. 18]

Danube with Castra Regina (Regensburg/Ratisbonne), Vindobona (Vienna), Acquincum (Budapest) and Colonia Singidunum (Belgrade). Further, beyond the "Iron Gates", in the province of Moesia Inferior, with Novae (Svishtov), Durostorum (Silistra), etc. Jean de Brem,[392] in his Testament d'un Européen, which is Roman and Byzantine in inspiration,[393] recalls the evacuation of regions that are today Bavarian and the replacement of the Romanised Celtic population or that of Italian origin by the newcomers, the Germanic Bajuwaren. In front of this limes of the Dutch delta up to that of the Danube a mass of Romanised Europeans was grouped, the Germans principally and their allies derived from different peoples. They occupied the eastern bank of the Rhine and the northern bank of the Danube and, especially under the pressure of the Goths, controlled what it is appropriate to finally call at the time of the Late Empire the "Gothic axis" or the line that ran from the Baltic Sea to the Black Sea, up to the Volga. This was an extension of the so-called Wielbark culture, appearing on the shores of the Baltic, at the mouth of the Vistula, following an occupation by populations coming from the Swedish Gothia and from the island of Gothland and extending in the 3rd century up to the Danube delta and the mouth of the Dniestr under the name of the Chernyakhov culture.

Borne by the Goths earlier derived from present-day Sweden, the Wielbark and Chernyakhov cultures contributed to the territorial structuring of Europe outside the Roman orbit. The conflictual juxtaposition of these two blocs of which the first is established, anchored in ancient history, and the other in gestation would create beyond the Romanised space a Gothic barrier in the Ukrainian "shatterbelt", Sarmatised after having been dominated by the Scythians, and after a partial Sarmatisation of the Gothic element, creating thereby a fecund and relatively homogeneous

---

[392] [Jean de Brem (1935-63) was a French journalist and patriot who belonged to the Organisation Armée Secrète (OAS) which was founded in 1961 to defend the French presence in Algeria.]

[393] The most supercilious Russian Eurasianists will not be able to reproach us for this talk!

Germano-Eurasian fusion which however would only be of short duration and not have time to crystallise. In 369, the Huns – who had subjected the Alains, another horse-riding Indo-European people from whom the present Ossetians descend – crossed the Don, the fluvial limit of the Visigoth king Ermanarich's power. The Gothic barrier of the Ukrainian steppe "shatterbelt" was crossed: the Huns were quickly on the Danube and the Rhine. Rome vacillated and then collapsed. The Empire finally disappeared for, without a Gothic barrier and without a Roman barrier, no imperium was possible in Europe.

The Tartar/Mongol Presence Prevents any Structuring of the Gothic Axis

But if the Huns and the Alains doubtless took over the ideal of the comitatus of the Proto-Iranian horse-riders, their power over the peoples was ephemeral, no doubt on account of an imperial hypertrophy, the Hunnish horse-riders and their forced allies being too far from the original place where they had assembled. Later, the Avars took over their role in the Pannonian plain, were sometimes the allies of the Byzantines, and influenced all the Slavic and Germanic peoples of the Danubian basin of the formerly Dacian zone of the Carpathians and Bohemia. They were progressively eliminated by the followers of Pippin and Charlemagne. The Magyars were defeated by Otto I. Similarly the Mongols and Tartars, present in Russia and the Ukraine from 1235 to 1480, only demanded allegiance and tribute without occupying the terrain. Europe almost fell at the same time, for the Mongol hordes arrived on the Vistula and defeated the imperial and Polish armies at Liegnitz in Silesia and reached the Adriatic after having defeated the Hungarians and then the Croats. The death of the great Khan Ögedei[394] obliged the Mongols, respectful of their customs, to return to the bases from which they had set

[394] [Ögedei Khan (1186-1241) was the son of Genghis Khan and second Great Khan of the Mongol Empire.]

out in order to participate in the election of a new supreme leader. The Tartar yoke, as it is called by the Russians, after being imposed from 1235 to 1480, prevented a new territorial structuring on the old "Gothic axis" destroyed during its period of gestation by the first Hunnish invasion, annihilated a second time when Kievan Russia, the result of a Varangian-Slavic fusion, collapsed. The shock of the Tartar-Mongol hordes, even if not very numerous, broke the incipient development of the Varangian-Slavic partnership on the Baltic/Pontic axis turned towards Byzantium, thus towards the Pontic space, the Bosphorus, the Aegean and the eastern basin of the Mediterranean and capable, as Catherine II of all the Russias and her minister Potemkin later said, of welding a neo-Hellenic civilisation rejuvenated by Slavic, Baltic and Germanic elements. This plan was never realised. Europe then remained an enclave, it was stuck or only succeeded in limited "de-enclaving" operations,[395] of which none had any real amplitude, confirming the statement of William of Malmesbury: Europe is a besieged sub-continent defeated through breaches made by stubborn enemies. Its future expansion is not due to its malignity, to a wild desire to dominate others but to a need to de-enclave itself, to escape mortal vices set in place by adversaries who have neither scruples nor worries about the "Other" – as one says today following the reflections of the philosopher Levinas.[396]

A Single Objective: to De-Enclave Itself

For Prof. Jean-Michel Sallmann,[397] the history of Europe is constituted of a series of attempts, at first timid and then grandiose, at de-enclaving.

---

[395] Jean-Michel Sallmann, *Le Grand Désenclavement du Monde – 1200-1600*, Paris: Payot, 2011.

[396] [Emmanuel Levinas (1906-95) was a Lithuanian Jewish French philosopher who wrote on existentialism, ethics and Jewish philosophy.]

[397] [Jean-Michel Sallmann (1950-) is professor of modern history at the University of Paris X-Nanterre.]

1. The Crusades were a first attempt to get out of the vice imposed by the Seljuks and their successors after their victory against Byzantium at Manzikert in 1071. The call of Urban II (alias Eudes de Châtillon) to the Franks at Clermont-Ferrand on 27 November 1095 demanded – following the appeals of the Basileus Alexis I – the liberation of "Romania", or the space that was then Roman, from a "foreign race", but not a race in the ethnological sense of the term (a biological and Darwinian concept unknown at the time). By "race" Urban II and his contemporaries understand a group unified by the same idea and the same loyalty to the Empire or to what remained of this empire in the minds of people.[398] Finally, these expeditions towards the Levant were a geopolitical mistake, from the end of the 13th century, except that they permitted a second form of de-enclaving, that initiated in parallel with these Crusades, namely,

2. The development of Italian commercial enterprises, essentially Genoese and Venetian, that were implanted in the Crimea (in Tauris) to branch out onto the northern Silk Road thanks to a Mongol tolerance for trade which the Tartars in the Crimea and the Ukraine no longer had when they sought the protection of the Turks against the Russians in this "gateway region". There also the Italians were excluded from the Central Asian commerce to the benefit of another commerce, the trans-Atlantic, which the Atlantic powers henceforth connected to the Americas would dominate for a long time. It would be necessary to wait for the entrance of the troops of Catherine II of Russia into the Crimea to potentially restore a commerce connecting the rest of Europe to Central Asia and, beyond its immense territorial spaces, its deserts and its mountain ranges (Altai, Himalayas), to China and to India, two "markets" more accessible to maritime commerce, which was more rapid and less expensive – and dominated by the English.

---

[398] As Jean de Brem perfectly explains in his *Testament d'un Européen*.

Three Attempts to Destroy the Tartar and Ottoman Barriers

There were three major attempts to destroy the Tartar and/ or Ottoman barriers: a Russian offensive, a Portuguese desire to circumvent Africa and the long war conducted by Spain to control the entire Mediterranean. Under the impetus of the English merchants, who apparently remembered Scandinavian initiatives between the 9th and the 12th centuries, Tsar Ivan the Terrible wished to re-establish under his authority a territorial complex starting from the White Sea and ending in the Caspian, at Astrakhan, including the lands that were washed by the Volga, for the advantage of his empire which posed as the heir of Byzantium, eliminated by Sultan Mehmet II in 1453. He succeeded, but without reopening the commercial routes of Marco Polo on account of the persistence of a Tartar presence under the protection of the Sublime Ottoman Porte in the present-day Ukraine, in a zone that qualifies fully as a "gateway area". In compensation, the geopolitical work of Ivan the Terrible[399] reopened the Siberian route to the Cossacks, who reached the Pacific after a century of cavalcades. The ante litteram[400] 'geopolitical' action of Ivan the Terrible initiated the Tartar/Mongol reflux but simultaneously reinforced the Ottoman will to resistance which, paradoxically, and in spite of the Russian desire to become the "Third Rome", adopted the Byzantine "anti-Latin" and "anti-Catholic" strategies in the Mediterranean, the Black Sea, and the Danubian basin, realisations of strategies recommended in the past by Justinian[401] and his generals. There was a fusion of Byzantine geopolitics and Ottoman geopolitics ever since the capture of Constantinople: for example, the famous spectacular Turkish film relating the military work of Mehmet II directed by pro-Ottoman Greeks.

---

[399] [Ivan IV, "the Terrible" (1530-84) was Tsar from 1547. He conquered Kazan, Astrakhan and Siberia.]

[400] [Before the term was used.]

[401] [Justinian I, "the Great" (ca.482-565) was renowned for his efforts to reconquer the lost western half of the Roman Empire.]

The Portuguese attempt was grander. Under the impetus of Prince Henry the Navigator (1394-1460), an Englishman of the House of Lancaster through his mother,[402] a school was established in Sagres in Portugal that compiled the geographical knowledge available at the time attracting scholars of all origins. From the age of twenty, Prince Henry obtained permission from his father John I to launch a campaign against the Moorish pirates of Ceuta. The conquest of this nest of Barbary pirates allowed him to discover that the riches of the Moorish kingdoms of present-day Morocco and of Muslim Andalusia derived from African riches including gold from present-day Ghana brought by trans-Saharan caravans. Even while recommending a systematic harassment of the Moroccan coast in order to counter all Moorish counter-offensives, Henry conceived the plan of launching maritime expeditions through coastal navigation along the Atlantic coasts of Africa in order to circumvent these caravan routes and to ensure a more rapid transport and one quantitatively more important for the benefit of Portugal. The researches of the geographical school of Sagres permitted the initiation of the de-enclaving of Europe via the African coasts and via the oceanic expanse of the Atlantic: in 1419-20 the explorers Joao Gonçalves Zarco and Tristao Vaz Teixeira discovered Madeira; in 1427 Diego de Silves discovered the Azores; in 1434 Gil Eanes crossed Cape Bojador; in 1444, the year of the fateful battle of Varna against the Ottomans, Nuno Tristao arrived at the mouth of the river Senegal; after the death of Prince Henry, Rui de Sequeira arrived in Benin in 1472 and then, between 1482 and 1486, Diego Cam reached the mouth of the river Congo and pushed as far as the coasts of present-day Namibia. Between 1487 and 1488 Bartolomeu Dias rounded the Cape of Good Hope. In 1498 Vasco da Gama arrived at Calicut in India. The route towards the Indian sub-continent, towards the spices and towards the regions of the world that the Romans aimed at exploring, was finally accessible to the Europeans, who succeeded in de-enclaving

---

[402] [Prince Henrique, Duke of Viseu (1394-1460) was the son of King João I of Portugal and Philippa, sister of Henry IV of England.]

themselves thanks to the first impetus of Prince Henry, thanks to the intellectual work of the school of Sagres. The era of European supremacy commences.

Spain did not seek to circumvent the African continental mass, a project that it doubtless considered excessive and envisaged controlling first the two basins of the Mediterranean, against the Ottomans and the Barbaresques and then finally administering blows on the eastern coasts of the Mediterranean Sea in order to reopen the classical routes of Eurasian commerce via the Syrian ports and Alexandria. This adventure – the Alexandrian dream of Charles Quint[403] and of Philip II[404] – had begun already in the 13th and 14th centuries with the Aragonese conquests of the islands (Baleares, Sardinia, Sicily, southern Italy and parts of the Greek Peloponnese). In 1565, Philippe II took Malta. The seizure of Cyprus by the Ottomans was not compensated by the victory of Lepanto in 1571. The Spanish plans to de-enclave Europe through the "depths" of the Mediterranean did not succeed, partly on account of the alliance between the French monarchs and the Ottoman enemy, a flagrant example of civilisational treason at the origin of the irremediable decline of Europe today and the explanation of the Muslim tropism of our Masonic and secular "republic" in spite of an incompatibility of this stupid and common ideology with any religious position of great temporal depth. Spain then turned to the exploitation of the Americas and kept its conquests in the New World until the beginning of the 19th century.

This retrospect of the European attempts at de-enclaving our sub-continent shows us that the conflicts are permanent and that the key zones of geostrategy can again, after more or less long periods of appeasement, become stakes that trigger new hot

---

[403] [Charles V, also Charles I of Spain (1500-58) was the Duke of Burgundy who became King of Castile and Aragon in 1516 and, in 1519, inherited the Habsburg monarchy and was elected Holy Roman Emperor.]

[404] [Philip II (1527-98) was the son of Charles V who was King of Naples and Sicily from 1554, King of England and Ireland (through his marriage with Queen Mary I) between 1554 and 1558, King of Spain from 1556 and King of Portugal from 1581.]

conflicts. The confrontations to control these key zones are thus constants of history that no irenicist ideology, no pacifist discourse can efface or annul. We have seen that the Franco-German conflict from 1870 to 1945 (or to 1963, during the De Gaulle/Adenauer meeting that sealed the new Franco-German friendship) was a conflict to control the space called "Lorraine", then the Danube and especially the Po, because the kings of France wished a window on the Adriatic to have access precisely to the commerce that Venice was trying to re-establish. Beyond this stake of the wars of Italy, the conquest of the Franche-Comté (El camino espanol) by Louis XVI and the campaigns of Napoleon III[405] in Lombardy in the 19th century, these incessant wars also aimed in some places at establishing eastern Mediterranean or Pontic bridgeheads to gain access to the Silk Road: the French Crusades aimed at taking Alexandria, just as the Italian commerce which equally intended to conserve and consolidate its outpost advantages in the Crimea until the time when the Tartars, forgetful of the wisdom of former khans, allied themselves with the Ottomans, who blocked all the Mediterranean and Pontic accesses to the Eurasian commerce leaving the Europeans only the routes opened by the Portuguese or the exploitation of the New World.

The Plan? To Re-Enclave Europe!

Today the Levant is ravaged by the militants of the Islamic State up to Mesopotamia, preventing at the same time the development of the region to the benefit of a Eurasian synergy. The Ukrainian "gateway region" is blocked at the level of the Donbass by a permanent war that they wish to maintain and sustain for a very long period in order to install a purulent "implanted abcess" which would have as its dual function the prevention of the conduct of Russian hyrdocarbons towards the west and the debilitation of the

---

[405] [Louis-Napoleon Bonaparte (1808-73), Napoleon's nephew, was President of the French Second Republic and, as Napoleon III, Emperor of the Second French Empire between 1852 and 1870.]

Ukraine, deprived in this way of its industrial regions and placed in the hands of a European Union already financially exhausted. The Crimea will soon be squeezed between this Donbass blocked by an internal war with unpredictable consequences and a Moldavia/ Transnistria that is being readied, in certain inner circles of strategists beyond the Atlantic, to produce a turmoil to impose a new blockade which will accomplish the re-enclaving of Europe, the principal enemy of Washington. To these two centres of turbulence in the Ukrainian "gateway"and in the implosion of the Levant and Iraq is added the probable reactivation of the Chechen and Dagestan conflicts and the Russo-Georgian conflict in such a way as to create long-lasting blockades on either side of the Crimea but also between the Pontic maritime space and the Caspian. The old Portuguese maritime route, in the Indian Ocean, along the coasts of East Africa has been partially interrupted in an important oceanic zone in the sea of Somalia by piracy that is said to be combated by ultra-modern fleets of NATO but which exhibit a resilience that is finally very suspect inasmuch as and even though there are two blockades present there implicity: between Madagascar and the east coast of Africa, at the level of Kenya and at the exit of the Red Sea. One can see it: the enemy is Europe, which must be re-enclaved and which must be imploded from inside by delivering it permanently to scatterbrained politicians and by constantly discharging into it heterogeneous and inassimilable populations landing in Lampedusa and the islands of the Greek Aegean. All the advances of Europe beyond its mediaeval enclaving are rendered null and void by the American strategists, heirs of the theses and plans of Brzezinski.

A "Neo-Mongol" Chaos in Central Asia?

The essential objective of the European desires to de-enclave our sub-continent was to reconnect commercial relations with China and India, who together made up at least 35% of the world commerce up to the middle of the 19th century. In the Indian

Ocean, which became a maritime "silk road" and replaced the land routes, the British took over from the Portuguese and the Dutch but excluded the rest of Europe: the France of Louis XV was driven out of India, the Ostend company at the service of the Austrian emperor was equally sabotaged, while Russia advanced its pawns in Central Asia menacing English India eventually. The Russian control of the "central land" (before the geographer Halford John Mackinder invented the concept in 1904) was opposed to the British control of the "central ocean" in a land/sea confrontation that was stressed notably by Carl Schmitt. This dialectic induced the notion of the "great game", where the Russian protagonist sought, in the 19th century, especially under Alexander II, to complete the work of Ivan the Terrible by "gathering together the lands" south of his previous conquests of northern Siberia, a very inhospitable region through which no "silk road" passes. By pushing towards Persia and towards the Islamised and Iranised lands of Turkmenistan and Uzbekistan, tsarist Russia took possession of several routes of the ancient silk roads, connecting notably the cities of Samarkand, Merv and Bukhara. A branch of this network of land routes ran towards India on the road used in the past by the Persian and Afghan conquerors, from the Ganges valley to London, people imagined already that the Tsar's cossacks were going to set forth on the same trails and arrive at Benares and Calcutta. At the same time, especially after the completion of the trans-Siberian railway up to Vladivostok and Harbin in Manchuria, the Russians took possession of the space where were assembled, around 200 B.C., the first Hunnish and Mongol coalitions which had eliminated the Indo-European kingdoms, Tokharian and others, from Central Asia before dislocating the germinating Gothic empire in the Ukraine and, later, the Roman Empire. The Russian conquest of this ancient meeting space of Hunno-Mongols made impossible, up to our days, every new dislocation by Hunnish or Mongol attacks of this immense space reunified this time by the tsars and no longer by the Mongol khans, who too often wished for empty spaces and total "de-urbanisation" in these vast lands between Manchuria and the Ukraine. The tsars for their part accomplished a "Roman" work in constructing communication routes such as the tracks of a trans-Siberian railway and in punctuating these tracks with new urban centres. This is the reason why certain observers have not hesitated to qualify the American desire to radically change Central Asia, sometimes through planted jihad, as "neo-Mongolism" considering that it sometimes wished a generalised and lasting chaos in order to weaken the peripheral empires, Russian or Chinese. "Neo-Mongol" would henceforth be the strategy of shaking Turkmenistan and perhaps also Uzbekistan (more connected to the Shanghai Organisation) with new Talibans coming from Afghanistan left voluntarily in the most absolute chaos after the departure of the American troops, who have, of course, very subtly prepared this artificial disorder without seeming to have done so, and especially contrary to the intentions proclaimed by the media. Turkmenistan possesses immense reserves of hydrocarbons exportable to Europe, which is looking for alternatives to a too great dependence on Russia: the plan to destroy the internal peace which this country still enjoys under the pretext that its presidential power is too "strong" and therefore not "democratic" enough for the innumerable American NGOs is not only an anti-Russian plan but above all an anti-European plan that aims at further restricting the supply of hydrocarbons to our sub-continent.

Access to the Red Sea

However, it was necessary to wait until 1793 for Catherine II, Empress of all the Russias, to retake the Crimea from the Tartars indentured to the Ottomans. At one stroke, Russia, previously distanced from any useful coast, benefited from the Pontic springboard of the ancient Hellenic civilisation and the Genoese and Venetian trading posts but by shaping it forcibly in a north-south direction. This new state of affairs threatened the power of England that had become almost global since the Seven Years'

War[406] when it ousted France from India and Canada. Albion feared a permanent and dangerous pressure on the future Mediterranean artery that it indeed planned to open by taking possession of Egypt and by digging a canal between the Mediterranean and the Red Sea to reactivate the commerce with India that the Romans had maintained from the Egyptian ports of Berenice and Myos-Hormus towards Yemen and Indian Gujarat. The eastern basin of the Mediterranean and the access to the Red Sea had henceforth to remain under English control and without any European pressure, besides, neither from an Austria that discovered an Adriatic, Aegean and eastern Mediterranean vocation nor from a Russia that extended from the Pontic space towards Alexandria and the Nile valley, nor from a Revolutionary or Bonapartist France that would install itself in Egypt in the shadow of the pyramids "where forty centuries would contemplate it", nor from a France of the Restoration which would support Mehmet Ali too generously. For its germinating global power predicated the conservation of the Indian sub-continent and the control of the central ocean, the Indian Ocean. The England of the Pitts and their successors had to be the only power capable of controlling the Mediterranean corridor for its benefit to the exclusion of all other European powers. The installation of the Russians in the Crimea was thus a potential *casus belli* exactly as Bonaparte's campaign in Egypt was considered as a mortal danger for the English system between the British homeland and its Indian possessions.

The Informal Eurasianism of the 18th Century

In fact, between the end of the Seven Years' War and the French Revolution, especially under the reign of Louiz XVI, there existed a sort of Eurasian strategic unity even if, at the beginning, it was deprived of the mobility provided by fleets. Louis XVI made peace

---

[406] [The Seven Years' War, between 1756 and 1763 involved most of the great powers of Europe grouped around the two major colonial powers of Great Britain and France.]

with the Austria of Maria Theresa and Joseph II; Austria was allied to the Russians against the Ottomans in the Danubian basin and in the Black Sea. Europe experienced a leap forward in all domains given the neutralisation of the plurisecular Ottoman enemy, because the maritime explorations favoured by Louis XVI, the Tsarina and her successors went very well:[407] the powers of this informal alliance bestowed upon one another, after the Seven Years' War, fleets capable of exercising the pressure that the Pitts[408] feared in London. Today, this European and Eurasian tradition, in the sense of this informal alliance of the 18th century, is resumed by Don Sixto Enrique de Borbon,[409] heir, for the Carlist legitimists, to the throne of Spain[410] and not only through marginalised nostalgias of one form or the other of "National Bolshevism".After the break of the wars against the French Revolution and the Napoleonic Empire, Europe, this time with England, sought to restore this pacified space from the Atlantic to the Pacific by the establishment of a new system, that of the Holy Alliance born during the Congress of Vienna of 1814, which the contemporary German historian Eberhard Straub[411] considers an example of political wisdom insofar as its system of collective security obtained a century of peace in Europe, which in this way was able to impose itself on the world even while conserving its diversity.[412]

---

[407] To understand the desire of Russia to extend towards the Pacific, see Owen Matthews, *Glorious Misadventures – Nikolai Rezanov and the Dream of a Russian America*, London: Bloomsbury, 2013-2014.

[408] [William Pitt the Elder (1708-78) and William Pitt Younger (1759-1806) were major Whig statesmen, the former serving as Prime Minister from 1757 to 1761 and again from 1766 and 1768, while his son served as Prime Minister from 1783 to 1801 and again from 1804 to 1806.)

[409] [Don Sixto Enrique de Borbon (1940-) belongs to a cadet branch of the House of Bourbons is considered by Carlists as the Regent of Spain.]

[410] Cf. His interview reproduced 14 June 2014 at http://euro-synergies.hautetfort. com/archive/2014/06/14/s-a-r-don-sixto-enrique-de-borbon-la-voluntad-rusa-de-independencia-nos-ayu.html

[411] [Eberhard Straub (1940-) is a German historian who has written several works on German and Spanish history and culture.]

[412] Eberhard Straub, *Der Wiener Kongress – Das grosse Fest und die Neuordnung Europas*, Stuttgart, Klett-Cotta, 2014.

The Monroe Doctrine

The Franco-Austro-Russian alliance of the 18th century, though informal, and the Holy Alliance of the Congress of Vienna were unified, strategically unified, Eurasian spaces. However they were of short duration. The French Revolution, which some French historians like Olivier Blanc[413] consider as a fabrication of Pitt's services, overturned the European balance by deploying a debilitating and destabilising ideology that ruined all harmonious cooperation between France, Austria and Russia. Blanc has explored the archives in a meticulous manner to support his theses. Following his work one might advance the hypothesis that Pitt's services aimed at exploding the France of Louis XVI which banked on the development of a fleet capable of intervening at all points of the globe, a fleet that had beaten the English at Yorktown in 1783. Pitt's objective was also to sabotage the Austro-Russian efforts against the Ottoman Empire in order to avoid this double pressure on the Bosphorus and the eastern Mediterranean and to oblige the Austrians to confront the Revolutionary French hordes in the southern Netherlands and in the Rhineland. It was a question of generating chaos in all of Europe in order to avoid a pan-European alliance or the domination of the sub-continent by a too hegemonical power. Whence, according to Straub, the fear of Metternich and of the members of the Viennese Congress of the so-called "democratic" theories more or less derived from the Revolutionary French ideas because they suspected that they would create an endless chaos.

In a first phase, which lasted a good dozen years, the European bloc of the Holy Alliance aroused the fears of an emerging power viscerally hostile to old Europe in the name of a fundamentalist and biblical Protestantism camouflaged behind a rationalism and a superficial "deism" of circumstances detached from all concrete historical heritage: the United States of America. The latter feared

---

[413] Olivier Blanc, *Les hommes de Londres – Histoire secrète de la Terreur*, Paris, Albin Michel, 1989.

that the European powers might bring aid to Spain confronted with the new democratic nationalisms of the indigenous and creole populations of the provinces of the New World. In 1823, in reaction to the potential danger constituted by the Eurasian Holy Alliance, President James Monroe formulated his famous doctrine of "America to the Americans" forging in this way a policy that would become constant: that of the rejection of every European interference in the New World. The United States did not fear just the possible aid brought to ruined Spain and henceforth incapable of reaffirming itself in the Americas: it feared also, and particularly, the Russian presence in Alaska and in California, indeed the possible alliance between the Russians and the Spanish on the Pacific coast of North America which would have blocked the march forward of the United States towards a dual ocean status, the key to their future global power. One often forgets to mention that Monroe, when he formulated his doctrine, had the more or less secret support of Grand Britain, which also, and in spite of the war which had just opposed it to the young United States in 1812, did not wish to see other European powers intervening in the Americas, where it sought to control alone certain markets, notably in Argentina. The Monroe Doctrine would be completed by the "Roosevelt corollary" after the Hispano-American war of 1898, which wrested from Spain Cuba and the Philippines, a corollary which stipulated that every policy that the United States might consider as contrary to their interests would be considered as an act of aggression. It is this "Roosevelt corollary" which justifies even today the American interventions in the world, as well as the espionage of the ECHELON network[414] and PRISM[415] (the Snowden affair) directed essentially against Europe. The "Roosevelt corollary" is interpreted in a very broad way: the optimal development of any technology, but especially aeronautic or space, even in a "friendly" country, is considered as an aggression against the interests of the

[414] [See above p. 170]

[415] [PRISM is a surveillance programme through which the American National Security Agency collects Internet communications from major US Internet companies.]

competing American firms, thus against the interests of the United States as a power.

The Greek Crisis and the East

The Eurasian coherence of the Holy Alliance was, as we have said, of short duration. It was principally the two western powers, France and Great Britain, who would progressively scuttle it. The first cracks in the Eurasian edifice that the Holy Alliance constituted were: the support to the Greeks revolting against the Sublime Porte, the Belgian independence, the Crimean War – which confirmed the rupture between a colonial west which was no longer centred in Europe itself[416] and a Central European and Russian "east" still loyal to the initial spirit of the Holy Alliance – and the Anglo-French intervention in China during the so-called opium wars. Eberhard Straub shows that this Holy Alliance, wishing to maintain Europe in a state of durable stability, guaranteed the integrity of the Ottoman Empire. The Greek revolt and the movement of the Philhellenes (of whom Lord Byron was one) caused three powers of the Holy Alliance to break with the Metternichian and anti-revolutionary ideal of European stability: the objective was not so much to save the Greeks from the Ottoman yoke, for one was never very concerned about them, but to obtain concessions, bases to take Constantinople and extend towards the Mediterranean (the Russians) or to install oneself in the Ottoman capital and block the Bosphorus in order to prevent this very Russian extension towards Cyprus, the Aegean and Egypt. Metternich saw in this purely tactical support a beginning of the "Balkanisation" of Europe, a Balkanisation that would be not so much territorial as intellectual: the Europeans would cease to follow together, and cohesively, common stabilising policies that would constitute the essence itself of the new balanced order desired by the members of

---

[416] Cf. Our article devoted to Constantin Frantz in Jean-François Mattel, *Les Œuvres Philosophiques* (two volumes), volume III of *Encyclopédie Philosophique Universelle*, Paris: PUF, 1992.

the Congress of Vienna. Tsar Nicholas I however wished a share of the Ottoman spoils where each beneficiary would find his interest, but the two western powers which acted more in the interests of the Ottomans than in those of the Russians refused this expedient which would have been able finally to save the cohesiveness of the Holy Alliance. The English and French, Straub reminds us, were suspicious of the long-term result of a general accord which would deliberately weaken the Ottoman Empire, which would then have had no other option than to demand its alliance with to the Russian Empire, exactly as today, the Turkey of Erdogan and Davutoglu[417] plays on two boards, on the west and on Russia, in the hope of hoisting itself up to the rank of a regional power that cannot be overlooked. Metternich, faced with the first Greek crisis of the twenties of the 19th century which triggered what was called the "Eastern Question", accused Lord Palmerston of being a "tyrant" to the extent that it was England that conducted a selfish politics contrary to the interests of the continent as a whole. The English objective was for its part to control the Mediterranean without any possibility of being countered by another European power even if it meant supporting all seditious movements of a revolutionary nature (according to Metternich), as today a comparable politics is deployed in Syria in order that no support of a regional power allied to Russia or to another European power that would prove to be challenging might emerge.

Belgian Independence and the Crimean War

The second crack in the edifice of the Holy Alliance: Belgian independence. Once again it was England that feared the development of the United Kingdom of the Netherlands having at its disposal a Dutch fleet of high quality, a textile industry in Flanders (La Lys around Courtrai and Wijnegem) and in Wallonie

---

[417] [Ahmet Davutoğlu (1959-) is a Turkish politician who has been the Prime Minister of Turkey and leader of the ruling Justice and Development Party (AKP) from 2014.]

(the Vesdre valley), a double coal/steel complex in Mons, Charleroi and Liège, a presence in Indonesia and in the hinge region between the Indian Ocean and the Pacific, old colonies in South Africa, (the Cape colony) and in the Mauritius island which could have returned to the Dutch fold, and above all an influence in a North Germany that speaks dialects very close to Dutch. This United Kingdom of the Netherlands could have perfectly attracted to itself, rather than to Prussia, the regions of North Germany. To break this potential continental Germanic pillar of support, the distance of a night's navigation from the heart of London, which was in the past set on fire by the fleet of Admiral de Ruyter during the Anglo-Dutch wars of the 17th century, it was necessary to make it undergo a definitive secession that would weaken the two remaining scraps.

The third, even deeper, crack: the Crimean War. After the French support given in 1839-40 to the Khedive of Egypt, Mehmet Ali,[418] revolting against the Sublime Porte, the two western powers, France and England, changed into the protectors of the Ottoman Empire to contain Russia north of the Bosphorus. Bismarck remained neutral as also the Belgium of Leopold I, who was a former officer of the army of Tsar Alexander. This Franco-English intervention in the Black Sea aimed at the containment of Russia, the maintenance of a dislocated, weakened Ottoman Empire incapable of autonomy and at the mercy of western pressures which intended to have a completely free hand in the eastern Mediterranean and in Egypt. It equally generated the Russian anti-colonialism as is attested besides by Dostoyevsky's *A Writer's Diary* and the memoirs of Tolstoy, an officer fighting on the Crimean front. The Crimean War provoked thus a rupture between the west and Russia which would feed all the anti-western ideologies which would eventually germinate whether they were of Slavophile or Eurasianist origin, or whether this Eurasianism were tsarist or Communist (Stalinist).

---

[418] [Mehmet (Muhammad) Ali (1769-1849) was an Albanian commander of the Ottoman army who became the Khedive of Egypt and Sudan. He invaded Ottoman Syria in 1831 initiating the First Turko-Egyptian War of 1831-33.]

The Ruin of the China of the Qings[419]

Parallel to these three cracks – the Greek question, the Belgian revolution and the Crimean War – the two western powers took part in the ruin of China present in Sinkiang ("Chinese Turkmenistan") and in Tibet, two important components of the Central Asian puzzle during the glorious era of the Silk Road. The first Opium War conducted by England against the Celestial Empire was sparked because Chinese protectionism maintained by a very organised bureaucracy barred access to the commerce that the English wanted to see unrestricted. The protectionism of the Qing emperors created a commercial imbalance that was not to the benefit of the English, who imported more Chinese merchandise than they exported to the Celestial Empire. Obliged to pay in silver bars, a precious metal that they did not possess in large quantities, the English – in order to import their tea – sold Indian opium against the money that they had initially ceded to obtain the traditional beverage of London afternoons. They thereby reversed the commercial imbalance: the Emperor, sending his zealous high functionary Lin Zexu, replied by prohibiting the smoking of opium, by confiscating bundles of the drug and by imposing severe restrictions. These measures entailed the British intervention and the first Opium War (1839-42), which was ended by the Treaty of Nanking where Great Britain obtained full satisfaction. The second Opium War (1856-60) was sparked immediately after the Crimean War under the pretext of a disregard of the Treaty of Nanking of 1842. France, allied to England, participated in the scramble for the spoils and, in 1860, this war was settled by the capture of Peking and the pillage of the Summer Palace. China was constrained to accept the stipulations of the Convention of Peking (1860) which repeated the humiliating clauses of the preceding treaties. This defeat considerably diminished the prestige of the Qing emperors: China, before an economic superpower, declined into a country in debt resistant to technical modernisation and a nation enslaved

---

[419] [The Qing, or Manchu, Dynasty ruled China from 1644 to 1912.]

to the consumption of opium. The situation displeased large strata of the Chinese population, which ended in the so-called Taiping revolt which erupted in 1851. The central power took fifteen years to subdue this uprising directed by a certain Hong Xiuquan, who believed that he was the blood brother of Jesus Christ.[420]

Dislocation of the Qing Empire

The weakening of the imperial power permitted the British to progress to Burma, an ancient tributary state of China, and the French to take possession of Annam and all of Vietnam in the eighties of the 19th century. The Maoists were inspired by the Taiping revolt eighty or ninety years later, because they preached a certain egalitarianism and rejected the traditional political hierarchies which had just demonstrated their incompetence in maintaining China in its status as a great imperial power. At the same time, given the discredit into which the Qing power had fallen, other revolts shook China risking the precipitation of the Empire into an indescribable chaos where rival entities confronted one another. The Taiping revolt doubtless constituted the most murderous civil war in history: around twenty to thirty million deaths. China emerged from it demographically weakened. It went from 410 million inhabitants in 1851 to 350 million in 1873.[421] Independently of the cruel ravages that this revolt caused China to undergo, it served, in spite of a bizarre Christian and thus non-Chinese or non-indigenous inspiration, as a model to future nationalisms and Maoism (which is a Chinese nationalism with a Communist flavour). The ideology of the Chinese nationalisms and Communisms, irreducible to their European models because rendered profoundly Chinese, has as its principal foundation a refusal of "unequal treaties" similar to those imposed by the British

---

[420] Cf.:http://euro-synergies.hautetfort.com/archive/2009/12/24/a911661dab8d842f12880d2134ef6047.html

[421] John King Fairbank, *The Great Chinese Revolution 1800-1985*, 1986, p. 81.

after the two Opium Wars, which today – when China is raising itself up and is resuming the predominant place in the world economy that it possessed in the past – induces a desire to leave to each political entity the right to freely determine its choices without the latter being obliterated by universalist ideologies[422] imposed by western hegemonic powers and contrary to the principle of the *mos majorum*[423] in the Chinese manner, that is, to the cult of the ancestors and to the wise notion of perpetuating known schemes that should not be modified so as to achieve a balance and a harmony derived from an understanding of Taoist thought. The Taiping rebels, inspired by a very distorted interpretation of the Gospel, did not opt for a "known scheme", either Confucian or Taoist, because the known schemas, in their view, had indeed deceived and precipitated China into an inability to seize the keys of modern power, which had been well exploited by the British enemy. After the long civil war, the Regent Empress Cixi timidly launched China on the path of an insufficient technological modernisation, with a too slow rhythm, as the Kuomintang revolutionaries of Dr. Sun Yat Sen who proclaimed the republic in 1912 later judged.

The extroversion of the two western powers was translated, throughout the 19th century, into repeated interventions in non-European arenas, into a growing indifference and an avowed contempt for the other non-extrovert European powers (following the terminology adopted by Constantin Frantz) whose needs and aspirations they never took into consideration. They incessantly camouflaged their contempt behind pompous speeches, ideological or moralising, with the support of a hateful press discharging waves of belligerent or disdainful logorrheas, against Russia, for example, or against the Germans and the Austrians considered as coarse uncultivated "barbarians" for not sharing their revolutionary Jacobin or Manchestrian schemes. This attitude, by ruining the pentarchy of the Holy Alliance, provoked a number of strategic

---

[422] Robert Steuckers, "Les Amendements Chinois au Nouvel Ordre Mondial", at http://robertsteuckers.blogspot.be/2014/04/les-amendements-chinois-au-nouvel-ordre.html

[423] [Ancestral customs.]

disequilibriums in Europe as Frantz had foreseen, which led to the explosion of 1914. And to the end of European excellence.

Of the Perverse Dangerousness of the Modernists

However, in the eyes of Prof. Beckwith, the modernisations/ centralisations through the action of the Communists affected the big political entities of the Eurasian continental mass, especially China and Russia, masters of the vast regions of Central Asia, where seductive syncretisms had been forged by cultures that have today disappeared. These modernisations eradicated the linguistic and religious diversity, the fecund syntheses that informed the region leaving behind them a cultural desert that the present-day post-Communists have not succeeded in overcoming, that the entire planet has been undergoing since the fall of the Berlin Wall, a preoccupying "neoliberal" tropism less capable of restoring the foundations of the old Central Asian cultures than the Communisms of diverse complexions were. Beckwith concludes that modernities are perversely dangerous. The Italian explorer Giuseppe Tucci (1894-1984), polyglot and orientalist, is without doubt the one who has in the most didactic manner established a chart of the syncretic religions of this Central Asia and Tibet:[424] a file that should be consulted in order to complete the long work of restoration that one should indeed undertake to cure humanity of the evils of modernity and of false traditionalisms that it generates in its wake to perpetrate by proxy, by an uninterrupted succession of "false flag" operations, its work of destruction and death, as is demonstrated by the exploitation of the fundamentalism of the Salafists and the Wahhabis, whose poor schemes are nothing in comparison to the ancient syncretisms, mainly Muslim, born and dead in Samarkhand and Bukhara.

To draw China out of the misery into which the Opium Wars and the British pressures had plunged it the first republican

---

[424] Giuseppe Tucci, *Les religions du Tibet et de la Mongolie*, Payot, 1973.

movement, the Kuo Mintang[425] of Dr. Sun Yat Sen, was, after his accession to power in 1911-12, indirectly inspired by the theses of the German Friedrich List which wished to make widespread internal development, that is, an internal colonisation not turned outwards and towards the non-European peripheries. List inspired the development of communications through canals and railway routes in Germany (a concrete project aiming at realising the political testament of King Friedrich II of Prussia) and in Belgium (at the invitation of Leopold I). Sought after as an "expert in development" before the term was coined, he equally influenced the territorial organisation of the United States in the first half of the 19th century, recommending especially the connection of the region of the Great Lakes, fertile in cereals, to the Atlantic through a system of canals, thus impelling the agricultural power that the United States has remained since then, whose best weapon, according to Eagleburger – assistant to Kissinger and advisor to Nixon – is the overproduction of food ("Food is the best weapon in our arsenal"). Later, List was considered as the theoretician of autonomous development and of national or continental economic independence especially in the countries called "third world" that had just achieved independence. He had Chinese disciples of whom the last was certainly Deng Xiaoping, promoter of post-Maoist China. In Gaullist France, the economist François Perroux set himself in his wake and pleaded in favour of a semi-autarkic independence that others, like André Grjébine, modernised within the European framework, but without getting the attention of the Eurocrats.

---

[425] [The Kuo Min Tang was the Chinese Nationalist Party founded in 1911 by Song Jiaoren and Dr. Sun Yat-Sen. Later led by Chiang Kai-Shek, it was forced to move to Taiwan in 1949 when it was defeated by the Communist Party of China. It is still the ruling party in Taiwan.]

Kang Youwei and Liang Qichao

The ideas of List of course inspired the Chinese precursors of the national and republican movement of the Kuomintang. In a work broadly distributed in the Anglo-Saxon countries and in Germany the Indian historian of the developments, Pankaj Mishra,[426] who teaches in England, recalls the patient work of the Chinese high mandarins who did not wish to see their imperial country collapse into a definite stagnation. Among them Liang Qichao[427] and his master Kang Youwei.[428] Both intended to imitate the Japanese Meiji movement, modernise and universalise education, the state structures and the armed forces. They were met with a strong resistance from the old-fashioned elements. The statist nationalists of the Kuomintang and the Communists of Mao were both, in their own way, the heirs of this modernising legacy of Liang Qichao and Kang Youwei, pioneers of the Chinese revival inspired by the Japanese Meiji era from the end of the 19th century. The ideas of Liang Qichao and Kang Youwei were nevertheless filled with Confucianism, a catalogue of the unshakeable principles from which they would not deviate, while the attempts of the first nationalists of the Kuomintang were to reject the Confucian heritage as being responsible for the Chinese delay and defeats. Similarly, in spite of the Communist speeches during the "long march" and the seizure of power, in spite of the Maoist Cultural Revolution of the sixties of the 20th century attributed in the final analysis to the "Gang of Four" (including Mao's widow), Confucianism did not stop irrigating Chinese political thought in its desire to recover its status of a great historic empire: it marked the avatars of the Kuomintang in the administration of the island of Formosa which had become

---

[426] Pankaj Mishra, *Aus den Ruinen des Empires – Die Revolte Gegen den Westen und der Wiederaufstieg Asiens*, Frankfur:t A. M: S. Fischer, 2013.

[427] [Liang Qichao (1879-1929) was a Chinese scholar who advocated various reforms during the last days of the Qing Empire.]

[428] [Kang Youwei (1858-1927) was a Chinese political thinker who championed constitutional monarchy though it was opposed by the Dowager Empress as well as by the Nationalists who overthrew the Qing dynasty in 1912.]

"nationalist China"; it marked equally deeply the Communist administration of mainland China. It accompanied the country in its step outside the first Communist constraints to allow it to evolve to the original system which, today, has given it again a power that cannot be circumvented even though it is, in fine,[429] more quantitative than qualitative since it is based on the western and social Darwinist model – as had been foreseen by a disciple of Kang Youwei fascinated by western social Darwinism of the 19th century, Tan Sitong, who was decapitated on the orders of the Dowager Empress in 1898 following the eviction of the reformist heir of the Chinese throne, Guangxu. The latter had received Liang Qichao, Kang Youweil and Tan Sitong, without the useless formalities of the old imperial etiquette, to have modernising reforms passed in an accelerated way even though still Confucianised in their spirit following the crushing defeat experienced by China against the Japanese armies in 1895. The experiment lasted exactly 103 days, explains Pankaj Mishra, before being brutally suppressed by Cixi supported by the old mandarinate and the obtuse partisans of the old antiquated structures of the Qing dynasty. There remained nothing but the nationalist and republican, anti-Manchu path, that of a radical overthrow, as Sun Yat Sen wished. It succeeded in 1911-12.

Intellectual Rigidities of Occidentalism and Fundamentalism

In spite of the tragic fate of the unfortunate Tan Sitong – who deliberately chose martyrdom because an exceptional man, he said, must accept death to ensure the final triumph of his ideas which desired only the public welfare – the eclectic mixture of pragmatic Confucian ideas and western, liberal ideas, nationalist or Communist, provides contemporary China a political thought that is finally more supple than the present western panacea where, in spite of apparently "progressive" words, intellectual rigidities

---

[429] [Ultimately.]

derived from fundamentalist Calvinism and Puritanism, allied to Wahhabism and Salafism in the Muslim world, dominate. Such ideas obstinately reject the ideological and philosophical syncretisms and eclecticisms which, in the course of history, have brought harmony to empires and nations. It is fundamentalist para-theological blueprints that are outlined behind the rigid ideologies that the West professes and that contribute to its consequences. They are presented in different political colours though sharing implicitly the same fundamentalist postulates often disguised as "progressive" as pseudo-avatars of the ideology of the Enlightenment – it is sometimes what was rightly called "doctrinaire liberalism" in the 19th century emerging in the foreground under the name of "neoliberalism" after Thatcher and Reagan, sometimes non-Marxist Marxism (for Marx did not repeat rigid and unrealistic schemes like his mediocre disciples), sometimes the discourse on human rights where the latter serve as the standard for the "politically correct" homilies and instruments of subversion manipulated by the American services to overturn states that resist their hegemony or wish to preserve barriers of any sort to preserve their national industrial assets. These rigid and repetitive ideologies serve, through a number of NGOs, as instruments in an incessant battle against the fecund syncretisms of the Arab, Turk or Orthodox worlds. The Asian world reacted against this exploitation of the discourse on human rights from the beginning of the nineties when the diverse doctrines of Clinton had imposed this discourse as a unique and incontestable standard. In the course of time, this standard, deprived of all criticism, has become the fixed foundation of "political correctness" leading to what George Orwell had defined as "goodthink". The paradoxical alliance of "political correctness" and tele-Evangelist, Christian Zionist or Salafist fundamentalisms has led the world to the present impasse, to the chaos that agitates the geopolitical "rimland" from Libya to the borders of Iran and to Pakistan, to the total confusion that marks the minds of the West, where the political caste is no longer capable of differentiating what might consolidate the public welfare from what dislocates and ruins it.

This chaos on the Mediterranean, Middle Eastern or Muslim "rimlands", from the Tunisian border to the Indus, was born of the will of the American hegemon. Starting from the support that was given to the Afghan mujahideens against the Soviet protectors of a secular regime in Kabul, Zbigniew Brzezinski wished to make use of the Islamic lever to finally control the Silk Road in Muslim Soviet Central Asia up to the disintegration of the USSR. Islamic fundamentalism was then a pure instrument, and people in Washington did not imagine that elements of this golem with multiple heads could one day become uncontrollable and follow an agenda not dictated by a third power or show itself in an undisciplined way and commit actions unwished by their initial sponsors. In 2012, Brzezinski himself confirmed the mistake of his strategic project[430] but, in spite of this well substantiated admission, Washington reactivated in 2013-14 the strategy that he had recommended in the Ukraine.

On the Position of Iran

On what other project was this reactivation of the initial plans of Brzezinski on the Ukrainian "gateway region" deployed? The project to control the Central Asian Silk Road is at the same time a project to politically unite, under the baton of an American hegemony, the zone of virtual intervention of the USCENTCOM, the American military command at the centre of the Eurasian continental mass. The geographical space under the jurisdiction of USCENTCOM has as its centre Iran. Earlier the United States aimed at neutralising the gravitational power that this Iranian centre could eventually deploy towards its periphery, from Egypt to India. The radiance of the "Iranian civilisation" was a project of the Shah who had succeeded in making peace with the Saudis (neutralising in this way the Shiite/Sunni antagonism that has

---

[430] Robert Steuckers, «Etonnantes révisions chez les grands stratégistes américains», cf. http://robertsteuckers.blogspot.be/2013/08/etonnantes-revisions-chez-les-grands.html

returned to the foreground to ravage the Near and Middle East today), in financially supporting neighbouring Afghanistan, in creating fertile links with India, in forging industrial and energy agreements with Europe and in agreeing terms on a gas project with the USSR of Brezhnev. It was necessary to break this Iranian radiation on the "rimland" of the Indian Ocean and the new petrol Irano-Saudi partnership. The Shah, though officially "allied", had from that time on to be eliminated; the revolution of Khomeini was presented to counter him to ruin his projects and weaken his European partners who had just experienced the "Glorious Thirty".[431] But the Khomeini golem proved to be recalcitrant and the atomic projects which the Ayatollah did not wish to develop (he had launched a "fatwa" against atomic weapons) were resumed by Ahmadinejad, a figure diabolised all over the world by the American media power. Iran was declared to be a "rogue state". Its power of attraction was not altogether eliminated but seriously limited. However, Iran, on account of its centrality in the territory under the USCENTCOM or the "Greater Middle East", cannot be circumvented.

The intervention in Afghanistan has brought no other result than chaos at the end of fourteen years. Eleven years of American presence in Iraq ended in an even more spectacular explosion of violence. From which certain strategists envisaged another strategy:[432] remove from Iran the status of "rogue state" and make it an ally again in order to dominate the centre itself of the space of the "Greater Middle East". This strategy, at first completely isolated in an "American ideological landscape" dominated by the intransigent belligerence of the "neoconservatives" singing in unison around the two Bush presidents, is now envisaged as a possible solution by more strategists, no doubt because the religious divisions of

---

[431] [Les Trente Glorieuses refers to the years 1945 to 1975 when France experienced considerable economic prosperity.]

[432] Robert Baer, *Iran – l'irrésistible ascension*, Paris: J.C. Lattès, 2008; Trita Parsi, *Treacherous Alliance – The Secret Dealings of Israel, Iran, and the U.S.*, Yale University Press, 2007; Barbara Slavin, *Bitter Friends, Bosom Enemies – Iran, the U.S., and the Twisted Path to Confrontation*, New York: St. Martins Press, 2007.

the Middle East have shown themselves to be more resilient than expected. The differences between the Shiites and Sunnis had been considered as superficial, as archaic childishnesses destined to disappear. The course of events has proven the opposite: the peoples of the Middle East hold on to their religion and do not wish to drown in the ocean of men without substance and quality that the western liberalism generates. In Iraq, the Shiite power, put in place by the Americans after the elimination of the Sunni Arab nationalist Saddam Hussein, feels closer to the "Iranian civilisation" dominated by Shiite Islam than to the Saudi Sunni Wahhabism which now supports Sunni jihadist forces in Iraq in order to avoid an indirect geopolitical extension of the "Persians" by interposed Iraqi Shiites while, however, these Iraqi Shiites had been hoisted to power by the Americans, allies of the Saudis: a major contradiction of the North American strategists which will have unexpected and disastrous consequences. Similarly, Afghanistan, with an Iranian (Indo-European) language, where the dominant Pashtuns are Sunni and the Persophone Asiatic minority of Hazaras are Shiite, has not yet been pacified: the Pakistani secondary base of the Talibans, at first allied then hostile, has plunged Pakistan into chaos; Iran remains stable in a totally shattered environment. The election of Hassan Rohani in 2013 has facilitated the appeasement but the game remains complex and Irano-American relations ambiguous, especially because an alignment with the BRICS could prove to be quite as interesting for Iran as a return to the global Atlantic system aiming at the permanent containment of Russia and China. Israel, which has benefited up to now from the status of the only privileged ally of the United States, fears the Irano-American rapprochement which would considerably relativise its position in the Near and Middle East, where its most tenacious enemy remains the Lebanese Shiite Hezbollah, Iranophile through a sort of new pan-Shiite convergence little perceptible on the regional chessboard before the American intervention in Iraq. The consideration of an eventual diminished position of Israel should take into account a notable change: the Jewish tradition had always been to ally themselves with the Persians against the powers coming from the west (the

Romans, then the Byzantines) in memory of Cyrus of the Bible, which also explains the patriotism of the Jews of Iran; Netanyahu practices a "Herodian" Jewish policy favorable to the hegemonic power coming from the west, as it happens the United States, which takes over from an England that the ideological ancestors of Likud, his party, had combated either in the name of anticolonialism or favored in the name of an alliance against Fascism and Nazism.

On the Eurasian Strategy of Obama

In this troubled and disturbed context what then is the Eurasian strategy of Obama? What are its outlines and ambitions?

1. Obama aims, it seems, at controlling the Black Sea, at realising to his benefit the clauses of the Treaty of Paris of 1856: at wresting the Black Sea from all forms of Russian hegemony. Obama's objective is to control or to prevent the maximal utilisation of the "South Stream" gas- and oil- pipelines; this policy once again aims at Europe, the first competitor of the United States and its "metaphyiscal enemy" insofar as it is Germany that is the nerve-centre and any return of Germany to the foreground on the international political and economic chessboard, especially through a Germano-Russian energy partnership, is the fear of the former Trotskyists turned "Neoconservatives" and outright warmongers, for their ideology is inspired in fine by the most muddled Puritanisms, enemies of any form of harmonious diplomacy and syncretic balances.

2. The control of the Black Sea implies a return of the United States and NATO in Georgia and in Azerbaijan through the exploitation of the Turkish ally, exactly as in the time of the Crimean War.

3. This plan of the domination of the Pontic space implies also the financial support of Armenia to de-enclave itself

while it is a key ally of Russia and, in addition, of Iran in the Caucasus.

4. Even if it is not apparent today, this bundle of strategies in the Pontic space must also count on a reactivation of the Wahhabi subversion in Chechnya and Dagestan in such a way as to potentially interrupt the transit of hydocarbons not only near the Ukrainian Donbass but this time in the Transcaucasian space between the Black Sea and the Caspian. If this strategy is realised, we will be dealing with a double interruption of energy flow towards Europe.

5. The final aim of this Pontic strategy of the Obama "administration" is certainly to weaken Europe because Russia would then sell its hydrocarbons elsewhere in Asia to clients that the United States can hardly influence. For the Russians there is no loss. The North Stream conducts gas towards Germany sheltered from any subversion in the Pontic space but the rest of eastern and central Europe is weakened by the deficient working of the South Stream, which implies ipso facto a weakening of the Germanic centre of Europe and a Balkanisation of the European aspirations, *mutatis mutandi*, as Metternich feared.

6. Beyond this weakening of Europe as a whole, the present American strategy seems to wish to join the Pontic space to the Iranian precisely by acting in the Caucasus, in Georgia (the ancient Colchis), in Azerbaijan, in Armenia and on the northern flank of the Caucasian mountain chain. From Romania to Afghanistan we will then see reconstituted the containment barrier dreamed of by all Anglo-Saxon strategists since Pitt. At the same time, this geopolitical barrier on the rimland which runs from west to east would be doubled by a barrier placed on a north-south axis and would cut Europe, the principal enemy, from its Russian and Caucasian supplies, which would pass through a Turkish control while the Iranian hydrocarbons would be diverted to other state clients.

7. Another facet of this strategy between the Danube and the Indus (on the ancient territory of the Macedonian empire of Alexander the Great): to centre around Iran, become an ally once again, deprived of its infamous status of "rogue state", the territories placed in an informal and virtual manner within the orbit of the USCENTCOM; at the same time, to cut Europe and China or India from other supplies of diverse and indispensable raw materials, and then to set foot solidly in Africa by developing AFRICOM.

8. China must not only be contained in Africa, where it has deployed a diplomacy without imposing ideological restraints as the West does, but also elsewhere, especially in the Pacific. It is necessary to prevent its optimal supply of hydrocarbons, just as this had been practised against Japan in 1940-41. In order to succeed in containing China, SEATO, the equivalent of NATO in east Asia, is rehabilitated. They try to embroil Thailand and Vietnam in a policy of containment and to prevent Burma (Myanmar) from having the petrol and gas terminals from China in the Bay of Bengal end at its ports.

This warmongering international politics of Obama, which is nothing but an avatar of the belligerent strategies thought of by the Neoconservatives before his mandate, has, as expected, aroused the "Eurasian" response of Russia and China:

- The Siberian gas pipelines now conduct a good part of the Russian petrol and gas towards China and no longer towards Europe by passing through Ukraine shaken by civil troubles fabricated by American NGOs.

- Replacing the dollar by other currencies for international exchange.

- Including Iran in the Shanghai Organisation and thus in the BRICS group.

This priority, which consists, in the final analysis, in controlling the entire "rimland" from Greece to the South China Sea, is handicapped by the persistent chaos which is devastating the Near East and Iraqi Mesopotamia. This chaos prevents the optimal organisation, even if promised, of a "Greater Middle East". These bloody disorders cannot constitute a seductive model. Other actors, apparently allied with the United States, pursue other plans, like Qatar or Saudi Arabia, who are hardly worried about the establishment of a "Greater Middle East" and place their priority on the elimination of all Muslim factions that are not in line with the rigorist canons of Saudi Wahhabism. This priority induces a permanent state of war of all against all which does not authorise the installation of any solid, syncretic and pacifying power. At the same time, voices rise that say that "they miss Saddam",[433] corroborating in this way the prophetic words uttered by the defeated and crushed leader at the foot of the gallows: "Iraq", he said at this fateful moment, "was plunged into a hell". Baathism, even under the brutal fist of the Iraqi military men, was a more efficient system, more productive of order and civil peace than the chaos installed after the American invasion. Similarly, Bashar al-Assad appears as a potential ally against the uncontrollable excesses of IS in spite of the diabolisation that he underwent at the hands of the media at the beginning of the Syrian civil war. The strategy of arming imbalanced factions or those formerly defeated in old civil wars or religious and/or minorities or characterless or shady politicians aspiring at seizing a power that they cannot hold with their own force is proved to be a fiasco: it would have been better to encourage a harmonious development in the Chinese fashion.

The Confucian harmony, the Chinese, Asiatic, Confucian or Buddhist ideology contains more fertile possibilities than the American or Wahhabi fundamental Puritanisms. And when the Puritan fundamentalism is camouflaged behind a simple, media-propagated and caricatured interpretation of the ideology

---

[433] Wayne Madsen, "Missing Saddam", cf. http://euro-synergies.hautetfort.com/apps/search/?s=missing+saddam

of human rights which borders on hysteria with Carter, Bill and Hilary Clinton or even Bernard Henri-Lévy, chaos is installed and hell (paved with good intentions) descends on earth, as in Libya, Syria, Iraq, or the Donbass. Human rights, said the Chinese at the beginning of the nineties of the 20th century, must be tempered by the pacifist messages of the traditional religions, especially Confucianism, which preaches harmony. One who talks of a pacifying religion talks automatically of the capacity to forge harmonious and fertile syncretisms, as the Shah had desired with his idea of "Iranian civilisation" who succeeded in signing a peace treaty with King Faisal of Saudi Arabia reducing to nothing, in the seventies of the 20th century, the plurisecular contentions between Shiites and Sunnis. Another pacifying syncretism: the Syrian and Iraqi Baathism both of which, even though become enemies, obtained internal peace in their respective countries. As for Kemalism, based on the Turkish Alawite syncretism and on the military apparatus (hostile to the fundamentalisms and the terrible simplifications of religious zealots), it offered finally a broader margin of manoeuvre to Turkey and its last manifestations, before the fundamentalist regimentation perpetrated by Erdogan, demonstrated Eurasian desires ideologically connected to its sometimes pan-Turanian positions suited to the Pontic position of Turkey – which had been reduced territorially, following the clauses of the Treaty of Lausanne of 1923, and deprived of the energy resources of the present Iraqi Kurdistan (the deposits of Kirkuk and Mosul).

The alliance between the Puritans of Boston (with their tele-Evangelical, Christian-Zionist and other avatars), the Trotskyists of the East Coast, changed to Neoconservatives for whom the Trotksyist notion of a "permanent revolution" has been transformed practically into a "permanent war", and the Saudi jihadist Wahhabis who have plunged Libya, Syria and Iraq into chaos is an alliance that one can certainly qualify as a calamitous one given the absence of acceptable results in terms of simple decency. Compared to it, Eurasianism is thus an antidote which involves the Asiatic, Buddhist, Confucianist values not derived from the Abrahamic stem and the syncretic wills of the great Mongol khans to whom Marco Polo was an advisor for seventeen years. To this body of Asiatic religions and this choice of syncretism are added the balancing and pacifying ideals that Aristotle bequeathed to us with his idea of the "*nomos*" of the land, revived in the 20th century by Carl Schmitt. It is not at all a question of a rigid "nomos" as Scholastic Aristotelianism or Metternichian practice on the margins of the Holy Alliance might make us believe but of a dynamic "nomos" that the philosopher Heidegger, under the inspiration of the future archbishop of Fribourg, Conrad Gröber,[434] explored proving that the Greek concepts were more "fluid", more supple, than the Scholastics imagined; the latter exposed themselves to criticisms, often anti-religious, that perceived the Aristotelianism of the "ancients" as a too rigid framework rejected by the "moderns". Chinese Confucianism and Aristotelianism based on a "nomos" irrigated by fluid concepts imply the establishment of a global diplomacy diametrically different from the dominant western practice today and opposed to the anti-diplomacy of the Neoconservative Robert Kagan at the time of the famous Paris-Berlin-Moscow axis of 2003, when Europe and Russia were opposed, in concert – but alas, too briefly - to the American belligerence in Iraq. This ephemeral axis was a reactivation of the implicit Franco-Austro-Russian alliance of the 18th century created by the good naval policies of King Louis XVI and the Tsarina Catherine.

The re-emergence of a Paris-Berlin-Moscow axis, difficult to revive ever since the betrayal of Gaullism by Sarkozy and Hollande, reconnects with the best traditions of the century of the Enlightenment, when the Enlightenment was not reduced to the mediocre schemes shouted out by a Bernard-Henri Lévy. It was a question of neutralising the infernal cycle of world wars and permanent wars begun with the Seven Years' War of 1756.[435]

---

[434] [Conrad Gröber (1872-1948) was the Archbishop of Freiburg and initially a supporter of National Socialism though he gradually turned against it.]

[435] Robert Steuckers, "Historical Reflections on the Notion of "World War"", cf. http://robertsteuckers.blogspot.be/2014/02/historical-reflections-on-notion-of.html

Eurasianism is thus the necessary and balancing answer to the forces productive of criminal and destructive disorder.

THE BRZEZENSKI STRATEGY, THE PARIS-BERLIN-MOSCOW AXIS AND INDIRECT WARS[436]

My talk today consists of four parts:

1. I shall outline once again, as during the previous 2nd and 3rd meetings, the situation in which we find ourselves. Effectively the operations in the Balkans in 1999, the invasion of Afghanistan from October 2001 and the invastion of Iraq during this last spring constitute three stages of the Brzezenski strategy or of assimilable or parallel plans that can be discovered by reading the innumerable Anglo-Saxon publications on the strategic importance and the history of Central Asia, Afghanistan, Pakistan, Iran and India. It would be good to bear in mind that the events that are occurring today in the world are the application by the United States of the Brzezenski strategy that we have continuously analysed and denounced. One can only understand the American geopolitics of today and, consequently, the theses of Brzezenski if one understands the great strategic stakes of the past history of Europe and Eurasia. In the light of numerous historic facts we shall see how the victories or defeats of the preceding centuries assume a strategic topicality revived by the American strategies which are supported by well established institutes of historical studies.

---

[436] Talk delivered at the Colloquium of "Terre & Peuple/Wallonie", Château Coloma, 16 November 2003. Published in www.voxnr.com, 12 April, 2004.

2. I shall then sketch the principal elements of the European and Russian response to this strategy, which is too timid, almost absent from the daily written and televised press (often indirectly in the pay of the United States). Up to now only the work of Henri de Grossouvre[437] on the Paris-Berlin-Moscow constitutes a coherent response, contains a concrete project, especially at the level of an eventual satellite and energy policy common to the EU and the Russian Federation, eventually supported by India and China.

3. I shall then evoke in a more exhaustive manner the external dangers, already in place, which will arise before any politics of strategic unification of the Old World. These dangers are of three sorts:

- The already very tangible presence of the "two anacondas" deployed by the United States; these two anacondas are the US Navy (with its strategic aircraft carriers) and the network of satellite espionage including ECHELON, which was denounced with a certain verbal vigour in some reports of the EU but without any echoes in the daily press. The weakness of present-day Europe is thus a weakness on the sea and in the circumterrrestrial space. In the two cases a cooperation with Russia proves to be necessary if not imperative, given that the former Soviet fleet remains potentially a strategic advantage and efficient tactic and that the Russian space policy also contains considerable advantages. H. de Grossouvre is well aware of this.

Cultural War or Cognitive War

- The second category of danger is related to what is now called the "cognitive war", i.e., the network of journals and circles that the Nouvelle Droite constituted in

---

[437] [See above p. 73]

its developing and mature stages before its decline, its terrible stagnation in bad policy and the sterile solipsism of its chief author, had perfectly recognised the importance of this type of political conflictuality. At the level of internal politics, the Nouvelle Droite, after having read Gramsci, spoke of "metapolitics", or of a cultural strategy aiming at changing mentalities and, consequently, provoking a political change. At the level of external politics this network had equally evoked the "cultural war" that the United States maintained against Europe and the rest of the world. The theoretician of this "cultural war" was the contemporary French linguist and Anglicist Henri Gobard (*La guerre culturelle: Logique du désastre*, Copernic, 1979). The latter denounced rightly and precisely the manoeuvres of the American cultural war against Europe. Gobard demonstrated in this way that this war had been well planned, that it had precise strategic aims, that it was part of a global political project aiming at ensuring and perpetuating the American hegemony on all continents. We shall see how the "cultural war" or the "cognitive war" is theorised today by a new generation of French strategists and military men, especially Christian Harbulot[438] and François-Bernard Huyghe.[439]

- Third category of dangers: the indirect wars capable of being immediately deployed against Europe. These are indeed latent wars of which all the measures are in place ready to be activated. There is first the "fabricated terrorism" (or capable of being mounted in a record time), the psychological mechanisms of which the Nobel Prize winner for literature, the Anglo-

---

[438] [Christian Harbulot (1952-) is a French economist who specialises in economic and strategic intelligence.]

[439] [François-Bernard Huyghe (1951-) is a French specialist in information and strategic research.]

Indian V.S. Naipaul has clearly described. In the large agglomerations of our world, thus in the suburbs of our cities, masses of unemployed youth, without a future, turn to a hysterical and very manipulable and rapidly virulent religion. These populations, detached from their roots, create for themselves a fanatic universe precisely because of their hard life. This is an ideal terrain to recruit suicidal people with a view to terrorist actions. It is in this way that the "Talibans" were fabricated in other countries. The operation could be perfectly repeated among us, the demographic mass of these diverse immigrations, or "transient ethnies", becoming more and more manoeuvrable to such ends. Every revolt in the suburbs, with raids on more fortunate quarters, would mobilise considerable troops and means and would paralyse ipso facto our country. France, in this context, runs the greatest dangers.

The Three Enemies that Should be Ruthlessly Eliminated

Then, as Xavier Raufer has recently demonstrated to us, the Mafias at work in the heart of our societies, especially the Italian and Turkish Mafias, have for a long time been connected to certain American services; they can also be activated at any time against the European states. Finally, the neo-liberal ideology and practice, declares Raufer, allow these Mafias to prosper. The formula of the strategy that will allow Europe to implode from within is thus the following: concerted actions of the disoriented masses of the suburbs, extremist religious groups which try to structure them, Mafias and neo-liberal (political and banking) networks. Religious/terrorist integrism that is purely fabricated, organised banditism and manipulating and perverse inner circles of neo-liberal economists are the three enemies of present-day Europe, those that it would be good to eliminate ruthlessly to ensure the future of our children.

Translated into a clear political programme that means: restoring justice by applying the principle of zero tolerance, purging the magistracy of all permissive elements (with the creation of a new system of "bailiffs"of public security who would proceed to the immediate arrest of lax judges of policemen for complicity with the mafias, their being brought to justice without appeal before emergency courts, their immediate punishment), returning to the principles of a regulated economy (based on theories of regulation) no longer neo-liberal but ordoliberal with the possibility of handing over without delay the neoliberal propagandists to the bailiff tribunals in order to judge the bankers and financiers who have imposed neoliberalism on our societies and have made themselves in this way the accomplices of the mafias and of banditism while weakening our industrial structures. The application of these two policies would rapidly allow the elimination *manu militari*[440] of the helping hands of these mafias recruited from among the young delinquents and the little neighbourhood hooligans. This policy of an "iron hand" can be read implicitly in the work of X. Raufer who cannot certainly be classified as an extremist. He merely underlines certain necessities of our times.

The Collusion Between Neoliberalism, Terrorism and Criminality

And that they may not come and tell us that it is a question of "extreme right" theories or "neofascist" speeches: the "2nd March Foundation", hardly suspected of sympathy with regard to these theories and speeches, has produced very clear works on the neoliberal/terrorism collusion under the authorship of Jean de Maillard (*Le marché fait sa loi : De l'usage du crime par la mondialisation*, 1001 nuits, 2001) and Michel Kotouzis (*L'argent du djihad*, 1001 nuits, 2002), former director of

---

[440] [With military aid.]

research at the Geopolitical Observatory of Drugs (OGD) and today a consultant with the United Nations and the Brussels Commission (the pro-drug "anti-fascist" lobby will, it seems to us, have some difficulty in treating these institutions as "fascist"; any anti-fascism that holds positions in favour of drugs, and therefore the Mafias that commercialise them already place themselves outside the future European law; let us specify finally that all those who, deriving from the parties of the former "rainbow" majority, do not share our positions do not share either those of the United Nations. For his part, the economist René Passet, who is a member of the scientific council of Attac,[441] has just published *Mondialisation Financière et Terrorisme*, which has the same import. The reading of all these works together is obligatory for the political scientist, whose mission it is to make his fellow citizens aware and mobilise; as well as for the politician, who has only one duty, that of acting rapidly and efficiently; these books originate from a "left" which is finally waking up, painfully and timidly, from its dogmatic sleep and its dreamlike trips, results of laxism, eudaimonism, delirium and lack of realism. The katechonical legislator could gather there the future arsenal of his restorative action capable of satisfying a people whose sensibilities, of right or left, populist in all cases, are more of less shared in equal proportions. For, the fundamental division that is outlined, beyond the usual left/right dichotomy, is the following: on the one side, laxism, having as a result rot and a return to the law of the jungle; on the other, rigour, having as a result a return to growth in the social order (a skilful dose of ordoliberalism, Keynesianism and economic heterodoxy).

4. In the fourth part, I shall turn to two aspects of the philosophy of history in Toynbee: the notions of "challenge and response" and of "withdrawal and return". The first of these notions contains an obvious voluntarism: in

---

[441] [René Passet (1926-) is a French economist who focuses on "bioeconomics" or the relation between economics and the environment.]

the system of challenge and response there is no form of geographical or racial determinism; which does not mean that Toynbee rejects the racial or geographical factors. The second of these notions implies the necessity of withdrawing oneself from the "worldy present" without for all that withdrawing from the world ("withdrawal"), without wishing to remove oneself from the laws of time and space in order to arm oneself with knowledge, activate fruitful retrospectives and to return then to the "real" ("return") stronger, better armed, more perceptive. In the system of the "withdrawal and return", shaping the future is possible in an optimal manner only if one has at first plunged oneself into the past. Toynbee's method is in this sense "archaeofuturist". All Anglo-Saxon politics functions on the basis of the works of meticulous historians, as one can perceive by consulting the catalogues of the publishing houses which teem with works on the ancient, mediaeval and modern history of the "hot spots" of the planet. The Europeans and Russians will win the "cultural war" or the "cognitive war" if they work in the same fashion, if they adopt the system of "withdrawal and return" as Toynbee has described it.

FIRST PART - THE BRZEZINSKI STRATEGY

Theorised from the middle of the nineties, the strategy of Zbiegniew Brzezinski was actualised definitively on the ground from 1999, when the American armies really gained a foothold in the European Balkans and installed military bases of large dimensions there, the most important since the Vietnam war. The second stage, preceded by an American installation in Uzbekistan, was constituted by the bombing and invasion of Afghanistan in October 2001. This second stage led to the control of the "Eurasian Balkans", following Brzezinski's terminology. The third stage, not exactly recommended by Brzezinski, aims at the control of Mesopotamia (Iraq). It constitutes a desire to put an end to the famous "Eastern Question" which has agitated the international chessboard since the last decade of the 19th century. The United States takes up here in turn the strategic plans of the defunct British Empire, that is, a) to prevent any European power (including Russia) from gaining a window on the Indian Ocean and above all the Persian Gulf; b) to prevent the economic and infrastructual organisation of the region by a European power or by an alliance of several European powers (including Russia). For the observers of the international chessboard between 1890 and 1914, as for the America strategies today, the "Eastern Question" concerns the European Balkans as much as the Near East and Mesopotamia.

France Ousted from Mosul

Immediately before 1914, the first objective was to prevent any organisation and any modernisation of the Arab territory under Ottoman domination through the Germano-Turk partnership of which the principal axis of communication would have been the Berlin/Baghdad railway. Is it "naïve Germanism" to recall today this adventure of the Berlin/Baghdad railway as certain "French sovereignists" sometimes accuse us of doing? No, for at that time, the German authorities had appealed to other European powers, including France, to exploit together the advantages of this region of the world. In the framework of the planned exploitation of Mesopotamia, the Germany of Wilhelm II, in spite of its shortcomings and insufficiencies, had a positive outstretched hand policy. This cannot be denied. The obsession with "revenge" had prevented Paris from joining this potential system. This refusal contributed to the outburst of the carnages of 1914. But from the beginning of the end of hostilities in 1918 the British, who had discovered petrol deposits in the region of Mosul, proposed a modification of the outline provided for the protectorate zones by allotting to itself, of course, this petrol zone earlier allotted to France. In this way the British killed two birds with one stone: they took away from Turkey all possibility of independence with regard to energy and wrested from France the deposits that would have permitted them to consolidate their presence in the Near East. After the bleeding of 1914-18, there remained to France two Near Eastern protectorates, Lebanon and Syria, economically not very viable and, what is more important, cost the homeland a lot.

In 1922, the Treaty of Washington imposed by the Anglo-Saxon maritime powers obliged France, theoretically victorious but in reality totally defeated, deprived of blood, deprived of its rural demographic reserves, to reduce in a drastic manner the tonnage of its war fleet; the objective pursued by London and Washington was that France might no longer really hold the two basins of the Mediterranean nor conduct any adventures in the Atlantic. The British and American "allies" cut the "fins" of the power which, through carelessness and rigid dogmatism, sacrificed its children in hundreds of thousands in combating the principal enemy of London which approached the Persian Gulf too closely. Passing before each of these moving monuments to the dead of France one must think of the blood shed by these brave peasants in order that the British enterprise may be consolidated in the region of the Gulf, a blood that was not even paid for by the petrol of Mosul... The noisy patriotism after 1918 served as a diversion to mask, behind unreal refrains, the actual double defeat of France: in the Near East and on the seas. The clique of secular belligerents screamed out this raucous patriotism in order not to admit having been wrapped in flour by the London and New York financiers. The people of France, if it had not been blinded, would definitely have sought redress ...

In 1941, the French troops of General Dentz, stationed in Lebanon and Syria, were dislodged by the British. Since that time, France of course retains a certain cultural presence in this region, which is becoming increasingly tenuous, but it no longer has a military presence. Out of shame, the dominant media in France since 1918 avoid recalling the clauses of the Treaty of Washington of 1922, the ceding of Mosul and the events of 1941 in Syria and Lebanon. People might begin to ask certain questions...

Balkanising the Near East, Cutting the Mediterranean Coasts from their Hinterland

Today, Israel serves in the region as an American pawn, an outpost in the strategy of the thalassocracies. With the British presence in Cyprus and the alliance with Turkey, this situation allows an easy control of the region concentrating the Arab resentment against Israel alone, which is, in the final analysis, never anything but an instrument that is deified to flatter a certain Jewish pride and to hide the subordinate status of the Hebrew state, a mere pawn. Now, past history had retained only one hypothesis: before 1914, the Zionism of Theodor Herzl[442] served as an idea in the service of Wilhelmine Germany seeking to anchor itself in the eastern Mediterranean space. The English and American strategy was different at that time: it spoke to Arab independence and financed in Lebanon and Syria the outbreak of an anti-Turkish "Arab conscience". The Ottoman power responded with a ferocious repression sending to the gallows twenty Arab intellectuals alienating indirectly the Arab populations of the Near East. The objective was to fragment the territory under Ottoman domination, to eventually Balkanise the Near East, to cut the Mediterranean coasts from the Syrian and Iraqi hinterland, to seize the petrol layers, to plunge the Near Eastern zone into a permanent chaos in such a way that it would never again recover its geopolitical coherence. The practical result of the Arab "cultural" missions financed by American missionary organisations ended later in the revolt of the nomadic and horse-riding tribes controlled by Lawrence during the First World War; Lawrence no doubt believed sincerely that he was working for

---

[442] [Theodor Herzl (1860-1904) was a Jewish Austro-Hungarian political activist who established the World Zionist Organisation in Basel, in 1897, and is one of the founders of political Zionism.]

the independence of the Bedouin peoples whose mode of life he admired. However, let us not forget that the English archaeological societies active in Mesopotamia included among their members prospectors and geologists charged with secretly discovering the underground petrol. Lawrence had been part of that.

After having adroitly manipulated the Arabs of Syria and Lebanon, and then those of the Arabian peninsula and the Jordanian desert, the British made all the concessions desired to the Zionists, who changed camp, very cleverly, since the collapse of the Russian front and the American intervention in 1917. The Bolshevik Revolution removed the Russian armed masses from the Turkish straits on the one hand, and from Armenia, Kurdistan and the region of Mosul, on the other. By weakening Russia through the organisation and the financing of a wild revolution the British and American services conjured up the menace of a Russian invasion of the Near East from the Caucasus which could end in an occupation of the Mediterranean coasts and threaten Egypt (in 1916 the Russian armies had largely penetrated into the Kurdish territory to the east of present-day Turkey). In this case, Zionism would perhaps have become an idea in the service of Russian aims...

A Turkey Without any Independence in Energy Resources

In Turkey, the ideology of Mustafa Kemal, the future "Atatürk", suited the British equally: by developing his "Hittite myth", by wishing to "Europeanise" Turkey, it relinquished ipso facto any claim on Arab territories that contained petrol. Kemalist Turkey is a Turkey without any independence in energy resources condemned to being nothing more than a plaything in the hands of Anglo-Saxon imperialism. An attentive observation of the events of the time confirm this view: in fact, when the positions of Atatürk and of Inönü[443] were not yet clearly defined, the British

---

[443] [Ismet Inönü (1884-1973) was a Turkish general who served, after Kemal Atatürk, as second President of Turkey from 1938 and Prime Minister of Turkey three times, between 1923 and 1965.]

distrusted any eventual Turkish awakening and armed Greece, which invaded Ionia and pushed its regiments in the direction of the centre of Anatolia. As soon as the Turks declared that they would rather follow the "Hittite geopolitics" of Mustafa Kemal, that they would relinquish forever all pretensions to the Arab territories that they had formerly dominated, London (and Washington) released Greece, for Hellenic and Orthodox presence in the proximity of the Straits and on the coast of the Black Sea could, in the case of a change of order in Russia, create a pan-Orthodox space surrounding the Black Sea and the eastern basin of the Mediterranean. London, loyal to its policy established from the time of Pitt, did not want this at any cost. This pan-Orthodox remains latent, especially with the Greek nationalist principle of "Enosis"(the reattachment of Cyprus to the Greek motherland), with the secret investments of Russian private firms in Cyprus (especially in property), with the supply of Russian missiles to the Greek forces of the island, with the designing of a Greco-Serbian, Greco-Armenian, Greco-Syrian, Greco-Iranian, etc. solidarity during the NATO attack against Serbia so much so that one reminded the United States with a certain anxiety of the possible emergence of an Athens/Erevan/Teheran axis. If one recalls all these facts one may conclude therefrom that the new Kemalist Turkey has as its function, since the twenties of the 20th century, to blockade the Straits, to keep Russia far from the eastern basin of the Mediterranean, to keep the Greeks at bay, to ruin the idea of "Enosis" for Cyprus (with the evident complicity of the English), to abandon any idea of solidarity between Turks and Arabs in such a way that no strategic space could be reconstituted between the Straits and the Persian Gulf.

The Idea of the "Greater Middle East"

As for the pan-Turanian idea which developed in the inter-war period in a good number of Turkish nationalist inner circles, it was held in reserve in order to be utilised against Russia if the need arose. During the collapse of the Soviet Union this ideology served to create television channels in a Turkish language unified for the needs of the cause, which conveyed the American vision forged in the offices of Brzezinski of a "Greater Middle East" encompassing all the Muslim and Turkophone republics of the former USSR. Another concrete and practical aspect of the pan-Turanian ideology: any Turkophone citizen of the former USSR and of Chinese Sinkiang automatically obtained Turkish nationality. If Turkey becomes a member of the European Union it is not only the 70 million Turkish citizens of the Republic of Turkey who will obtain free access to the territories of our countries but also the hundred or so million Turkophones of Central Asia. Pan-Turanianism aims at drowning Europe in demographic waves of Greater Turkey and in avenging in this way the defeats of Attila in the Catalaunian Plains, of the Avars in the 7th century, of the Hungarians in Lechfeld in 955, of the Ottomans before Vienna in 1529 and in 1683. The pan-Turanian memory is a long memory for which the old events of several centuries retain their full significance and are still valid. Compared to the post-Christian ideologies of the *tabula rasa*, of amnesia considered as election, which handicap Europe, it is a considerable strength and an advantage. Through the artifice of a bestowal of Turkish nationality on the Turkophones of Central Asia Ankara certainly intends to establish Turkish colonies up to Britanny and Ireland, far beyond the plains of Champagne, where Atilla rushed upon the Roman legions and the Germanic armies to retreat, defeated, towards Hungary. We should reflect on that, for the notion of time among the Orientals is not of a segmented time where each past segment is considered as definitively dead but of an eternal time where each event of the past is still considered as living, as calling forth an adequate response adapted to the new circumstances. This living vision of time past in the Orient shows us well into what a permanent structural weakness the ideology of the Enlightenment, the ideology of voluntary and admitted amnesia, has plunged Europe.

Let us recapitulate now the events of the past five years taking into consideration the lessons of history that we have just recalled:

The Conquest of the European Balkans

Bosnia, as you all remember, was the object of much solicitude on the part of the trendy intellectuals of Parisian high society, who were never anything but vile propagandists in the pay of Washington and who took their orders from Brzezinski. How did we claim a right to this permanent delirium in favour of a Muslim Bosnia, relic of the Ottoman presence in the Balkans? A brief glance at the physical map of the region will make us understand. Bosnia is part of the Dinaric Alps. It is an elevated region easy to maintain once one is anchored there and allows one to threaten the Adriatic coast and the valleys of the Save, whose numerous tributaries descend from the Dinaric heights of Bosnia such as the Vrbas, the Bosna (which has given its name to the region), the Drina and the Una. These geographic and hydrographic facts allow us to understand that the power that Bosnia possesses is possessed automatically by the entire Balkan peninsula, at least its western part on the edge of the Adriatic. Ever since Bosnia fell into the hands of the Ottomans in the 15th century, the latter anchored themselves solidly in the region. It took 400 years to dislodge them from there. As soon as the Ottomans abandoned Bosnia to Austro-Hungary in 1878 and then, more formally, in 1908, we witness a veritable domino effect, the remaining pieces of the Ottoman Empire in the Balkans fall one after the other, so much so that on the eve of the First World War the Turks are no longer present except in Thrace some dozen kilometres from Istanbul, threatened by the Bulgarians.

When the Parisian Intellectuals Work at the Emergence of an "Islamic Rear"

Our publicised (and vaguely telegenic) intellectuals are going to manipulate a mixture of:

1. Philo-Islamism, due to multicultural deliriums

2. The ideology of human rights (under the reign of the

democrat Clinton, this ideology was used rather than any other; with Bush Jr., the conquests and punitive expeditions were justified with an imperial discourse not embellished with eudaimonism as one observes in authors like Kagan and Kaplan),

3. Neo-Ottomanism, in order to justify in advance the installation of formidable American bases in the region, right in the centre of this Bosnia, whose strategic importance is primordial.

This is what the at once tearful and vindictive discourse of the Parisian clique of the Glucksmanns, the Lévys and Finkelkrauts[444] served; the installation of American soldiers, tanks, bombers and missiles on the high Dinaric hills of Bosnia and then of Kosovo pointed at Italy, Austria, Germany, Hungary, the eastern Mediterranean, etc. For the Serbian geopoliticians it was a matter of consolidating an "Islamic rear" allied to the United States and territorially close to Turkey, which is totally tied to Washington and deprived, since Atatürk, of all independent energy resources. The loud and chauvinist Kemalist nationalism and militarism only served to camouflage a state of terrible political weakness and impotence similar to that of a kept woman.

In the context of the American control of the peninsula that the European Balkans form, Bosnia and Kosovo constitute a central strategic territory situated on the most elevated points of the Dinaric Alps, while Serbia constitutes an excellent strategic point on the Danube, the principal fluvial artery of Europe, as I have had occasion to explain many times. Mediaeval Serbia withered after the death of the grand king Duchan in 1355 and after the defeat of his successors at Adrianopolis (Edirne) on the river Maritza in Thrace in 1371 because it lost its southern territories with the highest altitude. But Belgrade, in the Danube plain, fell only in 1439 giving the Ottomans a very important place on the Danube.

---

[444] [Alain Finkelkraut (1949-) is a Jewish French intellectual historian who has written several works on modern society and Jewish identity.]

Two years later, in 1441, they were able to subjugate Wallachia and control in this way all of the European south-east south of the Danube. The attack on Constantinople was not undertaken until after all these operations. We shall return to it; one had to wait until 1718 for the soldiers of our region, the Hutois,[445] to retake Belgrade for the Holy Empire and under the orders of Prince Eugene. The conquest of Belgrade after 277 years of Ottoman occupation marks the beginning of the end for the Sublime Porte in the south-east of Europe; never again did the Ottomans constitute a serious threat to Europe, even with a French or English alliance. Incidentally, the spread of the cultivation of potatoes in northern Europe allowed the raising of permanent armies without having the need to organise reserves of wheat, which France and the Ottoman Empire possessed in abundance. This "cereal power" constituted the basis of their military power. With the spread of the cultivation of potatoes, Prussia, Austria, Poland-Lithuania and Russia could henceforth organise troops numerically stronger than the Ottoman Empire and its Islamic hinterland.

One Does Not Take Constantinople from Anatolia

The most important lesson that we should draw from our reading of the Balkan history and the Euro-Ottoman front is that the Balkan peninsula has always constituted an indispensable springboard for the conquest of Asia Minor, the Middle East, Persia, Central Asia and Egypt. Philip of Macedonia and Alexander the Great inaugurated this strategy in antiquity. When they had secured to their advantage the Balkan periphery of their native Macedonia they could dominate Greece and its ports and then set out in the direction of the Indus. The Balkans should therefore be conquered in order to be able to control the territories which, at that time, were subjected to Alexander the Great. The Serbian geopolitician Sasha Papovic reminds us that the Seljuks, the first Turks to penetrate Asia Minor, present-day Anatolia, deeply never succeeded in taking

---

[445] [Deriving from Huy, in Belgium.]

Constantinople. In fact, the Seljuks failed at Byzantium. Papovic concludes from this that one can take Constantinople only from the Balkans, the "Anatolian path" proving too difficult. The Ottomans applied this strategy which we can call a "Macedonian" one.

The "Macedonian" or "Alexandrian" strategy of the Ottomans consisted in taking and occupying the Balkan bases before seizing Byzantium, which fell like a ripe fruit into their basket. After the Serbian defeat in Edirne (Adrianopolis) in 1371, the Ottomans advanced in the direction of the Dinaric core of the Balkan mountain range and fought the Serbs at the famous battle of Kosovo Polje[446] in 1389. Mediaeval Serbia, the centre of an unequaled culture, was erased from the map. Only the total control of the Balkans allowed the Ottomans to control the Middle East and Egypt totally (already the Hittites and the Hyskos had followed the same path in distant antiquity). Following the same "Alexandrian" logic, the Ottomans opposed the Persians in geographic and strategic conditions similar to those that prevailed during the long struggle between Rome and the Parthians (a parallel study of the battles between Romans and Parthians, and then between Ottomans and Persians, to control the Caucasus and Mesopotamia could prove to be very instructive).

Faced with this double Serbian defeat in the 14th century, in 1371 and in 1389, only some Europeans were aware of the stake: Jean de Vienne, a knight of Franche-Comté in the service of France, admiral of its fleet in the English Channel – who was not heeded when he asked to destroy the nests of English pirates in the Channel – advocated the crusades, but was barely listened to. The Order of the Golden Fleece founded by the Duke of Burgundy in 1430, and then the famous "Voeu du Faisan"[447] of Philippe the Good in 1454, just after the fall of Constantinople, constituted the Burgundian

[446] [The Battle of Kosovo Polje took place in 1389 between the Serbian forces led by Prince Lazar Hrebeljanović and the invading Ottomans, who annihilated the Serbian army.]

[447] [The Banquet of the Oath of the Pheasant was a banquet given by Philippe the Good, Duke of Burgundy, in 1454 to prepare for a Crusade against the Turks after the Fall of Constantinople. The crusade did not take place.]

(and thus our) responses to this menace. Finally, two Hungarian crusades were raised to ward off the danger, but in vain.

Whole Sections of European Memory have Definitively Disappeared

To return to the context: King Lazarus of Serbia fell in combat in 1389 during the battle of Kosovo Polje, anxious at seeing the Ottomans approaching the Danube, Emperor Sigismund called for a crusade, French, Burgundian and German knights, including the admiral Jean de Vienne, the Count of Nevers, the future Duke of Burgundy under the name of Jean sans Peur, responded to his call. But the army that set off in 1396 in the direction of present-day Bulgaria was heterogeneous and badly commanded. Against it: a Turkish military genius, Sultan Bayazid II Yildirim (the lightning) who was victorious. The massacre was frightful. Thousands of German and Franco-Burgundian prisoners were slaughtered (their deaths cry for vengeance!). To avenge the good welcome given by the Bulgarians to the western crusades, the Turks ravaged Nicopolis and the interior from end to end.

After Serbia, mediaeval Bulgaria was in turn eradicated, all of its monastic culture, including the large monastery of Tarnovo, was reduced to ashes. One does not realise it sufficiently today but this astonishing culture of monasteries of Bulgaria, Orthodox Kosovo and mediaeval Serbia and later of Catholic and renascent Croatia was totally destroyed. Whole sections of European memory, and not the least, thus disappeared forever. Many Slavs and Bulgarians emigrated to Russia and the Ukraine to avoid the Ottoman fury. These historic facts should be taken into consideration when one calls for the candidature of Turkey in the EU.

After the resounding defeat of Nicopolis, the Europeans experienced a respite. Tamerlane's Mongols moved into the route formerly used by the Seljuks: they penetrated Anatolia and crushed the Ottomans at Ankara in 1402 but, like their predecessors, they did not succeed in taking Byzantium or in reaching the Ionian shores. Blocked in Asia Minor, in spite of their victory, the

Mongols ravaged the east of Anatolia, present-day Kurdistan. The traces of these destructions are still visible today. The systems of aqueducts which nourished the towns disappeared, sapping in this way the hydraulic bases of all urbanisation and, consequently, of all imperium, Roman as well as Chinese, the two models of Leibniz. The Genoese and the Venetians were silent about this defeat and did not refer to the presence of the Mongol hordes in Asia Minor for fear of alarming their clients and donors in the west. We owe a description of these events to a Bavarian, Hans Schiltberger, prisoner of the Ottomans since the disastrous battle of Nicopolis in 1396. Schiltberger, other Germans and Franco-Burgundians as well as 10,000 Serbian cavalrymen were forced to fight in the Ottoman ranks (to defend Byzantium against the Mongols!). He has left us a narrative of this Ottoman defeat: it gave 20 years of respite to Europe, which however did not profit from it to confront in a good condition the mortal threat which menaced it in the south-east.

After the departure of the Mongols, the Anatolian background, impoverished, ruined, survived in a miserable condition. The Ottoman power, in its attempts at recovery, encountered a popular opposition that has been called the "revolt of the dervishes" whose religious competence was mystical, or pantheistic and ascetic. This revolt took place under the leadership of Sheikh Bedreddin and Bürklüce Mustafa; it had the support of Turkmen groups arrived from beyond the Caspian, as well as of the sect of Torlak Kemal. The peasant masses revolted in this way against the central and Sunni power of the Ottomans, exactly as there were also peasant revolts, more or less mystical and ascetic, in Central and Western Europe. In three battles Sultan Mehmet I beat the rebels in 1420 and had the leaders of the insurrection hanged or impaled. The Balkano-Anatolian unity of the Ottoman Empire was saved, the Ottoman territorial bloc corresponded henceforth to the ancient Byzantine bloc.

This expansion can be resumed. The lesson to be drawn today from the "revolt of the dervishes" of 1420, which gave a respite to Europe too, is that the weight of the Ottoman power and the present Turkish military power incited and could incite in the future every intelligent European power to foment social revolts in Anatolia or Kurdistan in order to oblige Turkey to withdraw from the Balkans and Cyprus and render the Turkish instrument of the American hegemony inoperative.

The Ancient Ottoman Power More Powerful Than the Americans of Today!

From 1422, the Ottomans returned to the Balkans, took advantage of the quarrels among the Slavs and consolidated there their geopolitical and strategic advantages. The Serbs allied themselves with the Hungarians proving thereby that an alliance between the Danubian powers can contain the Ottoman advance while every opposition between Serbs and Hungarians leads, on the contrary, to the encouragement of the Turkish expansion. But this alliance was not sufficient: the Turks took Belgrade (more precisely the stronghold of Smederevo on the Danube) in 1439, which confirms the thesis of our Serbian colleague Sasha Papovic: to take Constantinople it is necessary to first install oneself in the Balkans, control all its strategic points both in the mountain zones and along the course of the Danube.

In 1441, the Ottomans invaded Transylvania and defended in this way the course of the Danube to their advantage. The Balkans formed, from this annexation of Transylvania, the ancient Dacia of the Romans, a coherent unit under Turkish control. The big port of the Aegean, Thessaloniki, taken in 1423, obtained a homogeneous hinterland, which is no longer the case today, given the destruction of all coherence in the potential communications on the Belgrade/Thessaloniki line, the shortest between the Danube and the Mediterranean, as one was able to confirm during the First World War, in the wake of the offensive of von Mackensen[448] through the Serbian territory in the direction of the Aegean. In this sense, the Ottoman power was more coherent than the American project

[448] [August von Mackensen (1849-1945) was a Prussian field marshal who led the German-Austro-Hungarian-Bulgarian campaign against Serbia in 1915.]

of today which aims at an extreme territorial partition rendering impossible any economic development in this region for it cuts there the fluvial, railway and road communications, which remain thereby dismantled and inoperative.

The Burgundian Project merged with the Imperial Germanic project, with the Spanish Desire to Control all of the Mediterranean and with the Adventurous and Knightly Spirit of the Order of Malta

The invasion of Transylvania provoked in Hungary the call for a second anti-Ottoman Crusade. Contrary to that of 1396, it was well organised by an unmatched captain, János Hunyadi.[449] His armies had at their disposal artillery. They entered Transylvania and advanced towards Adrianopolis. At the head of this crusade: King Vladislav I of Poland-Hungary, who reigned over a vast hinterland corresponding to Bush's "New Europe" territory. In the present American strategy developed by Luttwak,[450] Brzezinski and Bagnall, America should control both Turkey and the "Islamic rear" and the territories that served as the meeting area in the second Hungarian crusade. Thus the Americans intend to control two offensive zones situated between Germany and Russia, recreate the cordon sanitaire of Lord Curzon,[451] prevent all territorial and strategic continuity between Germany and Russia (as the contemporary Russian geopolitician, Colonel Morozov,[452] saw very well), cut the

---

[449] [János Hunyadi (1406-56) was a noted Romanian-Hungarian general who led several campaigns against the Ottomans in south eastern Europe.]

[450] [Edward Luttwak (1942-) is a Jewish Romanian geopolitical and military strategist who provides consulting services to the U.S. government and military.]

[451] [George Nathaniel, Lord Curzon (1859-1925) was a British Conservative statesman who served as Viceroy of India from 1899 to 1905 and British Foreign Secretary in 1919, when he established the boundary line between Poland and Soviet Russia known as the Curzon Line.]

[452] [Yury Morozov is a former colonel in the Russian army and professor at the Russian Military Sciences Academy who has specialised in military strategy and national security.]

Danubian axis into two sections, prevent any projection of the German power towards the Black Sea (the Burgundian project resumed by Maximilian I since the time of his marriage to Marie of Burgundy; the Burgundian project merged, from the end of the 15th century, with the Romano-Germanic imperium; there is thus a continuity between this Burgundian project and the actions of the Austro-Hungarian partnership on the one hand and with those of Spain and the Order of Malta in the Mediterranean, on the other. For us here in Brabant in this Coloma castle where before us Louis Gueuning worked, there are no other legitimacies in Europe; those who share in this project and subscribe to it are our allies, those who do not share it, those who stutter shoddy excuses hostile to this sublime vision are our enemies and the enemies of our civilisation; here is a clear definition of the enemy – and the friend – who, as Carl Schmitt and Otto Koelreutter taught us, permits politics).

Always Divisions Among the Europeans!

The call to a crusade made by Janos Hunyadi and Vladislav I, to which German and Czech soldiers responded, aroused much enthusiasm: Albania arose under Skanderberg, Wallachia similarly under the authority of Vlad Dracul (Vlad the Impaler/Dracula); the Byzantine Basileus, isolated in Constantinople, accepted the union of all Christians; Venice advanced its warships as far as the Sea of Marmara. But, in spite of the strategic faculty of Janos Hunyadi, the Hungarian armies were crushed in 1444 at Varna in Bulgaria. The ardent king Vladislav I did not heed the counsels of moderation of Hunyadi; he charged into the Turkish apparatus well buttressed in its positions and was torn to pieces. Hunyadi escaped disaster and became the regent of the Hungarian kingdom. In 1448, a second Hungarian offensive was ended similarly on account of a mistake in Kosovo because the Wallachs of Vlad Dracul changed camps in the middle of the battle. Always divisions among the Europeans!

The son of Janos Hunyadi, Matthias Corvinus, became the king of Hungary in 1458. In 1456, he had retaken Belgrade with a modern army constituted of peasants recruited in large numbers and well trained. In the battle, the Sultan was wounded. Bells pealed all over Europe. But this brilliant victory proving the tactical care of an army of mercenaries of peasant origin had only ephemeral results: in 1459, the Serbian prince Georg Brankovic submitted to the Sultan. The Bosnians of King Stephen called to Rome and the west for help but the Bogomil nobility, victim of Inquisitions in the preceding centuries, passed to the Turks; 70% of the Bosnian population converted through hatred of the Catholics and the Orthodox Christians. Elsewhere in the Balkans (as in Greece and Bulgaria, where Islamised indigenous peoples survive) the conversions to Islam never exceeded 10%. The conversion of the Bogomil nobility to Islam constitutes the core of the present Bosnian problem.

A Danubian and Pontic Geopolitical Ambition

After the capture of Thessaloniki in 1423, and given the uninterrupted Turkish advance, the dukes of Burgundy, our sovereigns, formulated plans of reconquest which they could not realise on account of the events of the Hundred Years' War, on account of the potential French pressure on our southern borders and on the Duke of Burgundy. From 1429, Philippe the Good became aware of the danger. He founded the Order of the Golden Fleece on 10 January 1430 the spiritual inspiration of which was based on the Greek myth of the Argonauts, that is, the navigators and adventurers who explored the Black Sea. The objective of the order, at the beginning, was to reconnect with the knightly ideals of antique Persia and traditional Armenia. However, this ideal was coupled with a very concrete geopolitical perspective: to get a foothold once again in the Black Sea by going along the Danube, as the European army of 1396 had done.

John the Fearless, father of Philip the Good, had brought back from his captivity under Bayazid the Lightning (Yildirim) a clear knowledge of the geopolitical facts of the Balkan and Pontic region.

Husband of Marguerite of Bavaria from 1385, he had knowledge of the Danubian space, Bavaria being situated on the big river and consequently connected to the geopolitical outlay of this vast region which extends from the Alps to the Black Sea. Numerous Bavarian cavalry and infantrymen had besides fought at the side of John the Fearless at Nicopolis. It was the Flemish villages that paid his enormous ransom demanded by Bayazid. Murdered by the French in 1419, John the Fearless bequeathed to his son, Philip the Good, half Bavarian and quarter Flemish, the Burgundian legacy which he increased to the extent that it became the future "Circle of Burgundy" in the Holy Empire of Charles V. From 1442, Philip the Good prepared for the crusade that was announced on the appeal of Pope Eugene IV. He did not take part in it given the defeat of Varna in 1444. However, in spite of this disaster, a Burgundian flotilla, under the command of Walleran de Wavrin, departed for the Black Sea. Another Burgundian noble, Geoffroi de Thoisy, entered the combat on the same waters. These operations hardly succeeded. But they nevertheless remain indices of a Danubian and Pontic geopolitical ambition, that is, an ambition to contest the Ottoman power on the Danube, in the Black Sea and in the Crimea. We see in them the premises of the Holy Alliance of Eugene of Savoy and of Maximilian-Emanuel of Bavaria (the "Blue King") and the alliance between Spain, Austria and Russia forged in Vienna in 1725-26.

Our "National and Imperial" Mission

As Philip the Good intended to reconstitute the Lotharingian rear to better unify Europe, and as the Order of the Golden Fleece was destined to become the instrument of this policy, the spiritual and military dorsal spine of a future unified Europe, the "Burgundian affair", in its sparkling diversity, contains *in toto* the lineaments of our "national and imperial mission". There is no other. Another colloquium will be necessary to determine its nature and explore the possibilities of its revival. The events of the two Hungarian crusades of 1396 and 1444 constitute its foundational epic.

The lesson to be drawn today from the entire history of the Ottoman conquest of the Balkans, the Hungarian plains and Transylvania is the following: as Sasha Papovic has clearly taught us, one should begin by controlling the Balkans to control the Middle East (High Mesopotamia in 1515, Syria in 1516, Egypt in 1517), the Gulf region (capture of Baghdad in 1534) and Central Asia (Alexander the Great). The objective of the Anglo-Saxon politics is to imitate Alexander the Great and the Ottomans, to control the territories that they controlled in the past to hold the neighbouring civilisational spaces in check (Holy Empire/Europe/Russia/India/China). The plans of a Greater Middle Eastern "common market" extending from Egypt to Tajikistan that is formulated today in the United States move indeed in this direction. This vast space is conflated with one of the five structures of American military command in the world, the USCENTCOM, which encompasses equally the horn of Africa and Sudan. People speak equally of a "New East of energy resources" which includes also Libya (in the process of normalisation) and Pakistan. It is a matter of removing the enormous potentialities of these regions from European and Russian influence and, ipso facto, of removing the demographic masses of these regions from the future commerce of the European Union and the Russian Federation. The events confirm this "Alexandrian" procedure: the preliminaries of the conquest of the "Greater Middle East" began in Bosnia in 1993-94 and later in Macedonia. To destabilise the region from top to bottom the initial lever was the Bosnian or Albanian Muslim population and the Mafia networks that they shelter, that were artificially and cleverly excited against their Slav and Orthodox neighbours with the complicity of the Turks, the Saudis (sponsors) and the Parisian intellectuals of the left bank (Glucksmann, Lévy, Finkelkraut and some others).

First to Bring the Historians and Philologists into Line

This American strategy was shouldered by good historical knowledge, by a precise knowledge of the geopolitical and strategic dynamic that has informed the history of these regions, knowledge better supported than the wobbly formulations of the prefabricated ideas served to us by the Parisian intellectuals and the American media ad nauseam. In Europe, the universities never received an order to produce precise works on the key regions of world history. The contempt that the show business politicians and the indecent boors of the mercantile class flaunt for historians in particular, for the graduates of the faculties of philosophy and humanities in general, will be paid for dearly, very dearly. The politicians will lose the meager bribes for power which they still hold on to come what may under the American hegemony, and the venal businessmen will lose juicy markets. To have power and markets it is necessary to first bring into line historians and philologists, well paid and employed in prospective geopolitical research offices and institutes viewing the future and concerned about the welfare of the imperial "Great City". Without historians and philologists, without geopolitical offices and institutes, one falls into muck and mediocrity. That in which we are actually wallowing.

The Conquest of the Eurasian Balkans

The notion of "Eurasian Balkans" comes to us directly from the famous work of Zbigniew Brzezinski, *The Grand Chessboard*, where the author displays in language that is nevertheless muffled the plan of American dominance over the former Turkophone and Muslim Soviet republics. Ex-Soviet Central Asia was composed, in fact, of several republics such as Kazakhstan (16 million inhabitants including numerous Slavs), Turkmenistan (3.5 million inhabitants), Uzbekistan (19 million inhabitants), Kyrgystan (4.2 million inhabitants), Tajikistan (of Persian/Indo-European language, 5 million inhabitants). The objective of the United States, during the dissolution of the USSR, was to detach these new states from the ancient Russian metropolis and to bind them to Washington through an emphasis on Turkish/pan-Turanian or integrist Islamist relations. This Central Asian space thus found itself Balkanised right from the start of the post-Soviet era. The region henceforth contained two large American bases, Karchi Khanabad in Uzbekistan and Manas in Kyrgystan. This domination of vast zones of ex-Soviet Central Asia constitutes the realisation of the geopolitical plans of Homer Lea, educated at West Point at the end of the 19th century. In the course of the last decades of the 19th century, in fact, the Russian Empire and the British Empire pursued contradictory objectives: the Russians wished to reach the warm seas, especially the Indian Ocean, the English wished to protect the paths of access to India, the jewel of their possessions in the world, and intended to make of the Indian Ocean an internal sea entirely controlled by their navy. In order to protect India the English had to "contain" the Russians far from the shores of the Indian Ocean; thence the origin of all the strategies of "containment" applied during the Cold War. The end of the Cold War did not change anything in this. From this struggle between the land and the sea arose geopolitics properly called; if Lea did not use the term, Mackinder and the Swede Kjellén finally made it common and introduced it into political and journalistic discourse.

Does the End of the "Great Game" Announce the Arrival of the "New World Order"?

Afghanistan had been a central piece in the latent Anglo-Russian conflict which had unfolded from the twenties of the 20th century. The Afghan territory shelters in fact the central sections of the famous Silk Road. To avoid directly confronting one another, Russians and the British finally came to an agreement on the neutralisation of the Afghan territory which, from this fact, was never again colonised. London thought that the German danger in Mesopotamia was more important than the Russian presence in the Caucasus and at the Afghan borders. Russia has today been considerably weakened. The United States, which took over from the British Empire, as their geopoliticians Mahan and Lea had asked them to do, benefited from the (fabricated?) attacks of 11 September 2001 to complete the task by installing bases in Uzbekistan and in Kyrgystan and by conquering Afghanistan. On the territory of this conquered country three American bases were installed exactly at the roadway junctions of the Silk Roads (for there are many of them). These bases are Bagram, Mazar-e-Sharif and Kandahar, not counting the base of Jacobabad in Pakistan. On the basis of geostrategies elaborated by Mahan and Lea a century ago, and on the basis of the doctrines of Brzezinski, Washington intends to put an end totally to this conflict between "land" and "sea" which Kipling had called "the great game". Of course the American messianism intends to complete the "great game" in order to put an end to history as it were and to usher in this way the "New World Order" announced by Francis Fukuyama, who has somewhat revised his idealistic positions.

The conquest of the Eurasian Balkans is now a reality. The attacks of 11 September 2001 constituted the pretext to intervene in Afghanistan and to maintain troops in Central Asia.

The Conquest of Mesopotamia

We have seen that the Ottomans did not conquer Mesopotamia from the Persians until having totally secured the Balkans, thanks especially to the complicity of François I. I have already had the occasion many times in this forum to evoke the crucial importance of the military operations in Iraq (May 1941), Libya and Syria (June-July 1941) and finally in Iran (August-September 1941). It was a question of the British response to the occupation by the Axis of the whole of the Balkan peninsula, which proves once again that the two geostrategic zones are indissolubly connected to each other.

Today the United States has begun with the Balkans, followed by Afghanistan and ended, as regards the new order, with

Mesopotamia (Iraq). If the operations in the Balkans responded to the geopolitical imperative to contain Germanic Central Europe and Russia north of the Danube (as the Ottomans did from the capture of Belgrade in 1439) and to cut the Danubian artery (another old project), if the conquest of Afghanistan responded to another geopolitical imperative, that of occupying the spaces at the eastern extremity of the ancient empire of Alexander the Great, the conquest of Iraq corresponds to several equally important imperatives. It obviously consists in occupying one of the central parts of this ancient empire of Alexander, in completing the encirclement of Iran (we shall return to this), in preventing definitively any attempt at cooperation between a modernising power in Iraq, on the one hand, and Russia and Europe, on the other.

Saddam Hussein had in fact signed contracts with Volkswagen and Renault, with Russian lorry manufacturers, with other European firms for infrastructure construction. With the American conquest all these contracts were cancelled to the benefit of the automobile manufacturers of America, and evidently, as the European press had underlined with a real bitterness, to the benefit of Haliburton, the consortium in which Dick Cheney has a lot of interests. Further, as Gerhoch Reisegger has written in his work, of which we have translated significant extracts for *Au fil de l'épée* (nos.46 and 47, June and July 2003), Saddam Hussein wished to invoice his petrol in Euros and initiate in this way a general transition of the petrodollar to the petroeuro, a transition that would have meant, in the medium term, the end of an essentially financial American hegemony.

Completing the Encirclement of Iran

The conquest of Iraq equally completed another strategic objective: the encirclement of Iran. The latter is now cornered in a vice formed by numerous American bases: to the east the three bases of Afghanistan, the three bases distributed in Uzbekistan, Kyrgyztan and Pakistan, to the east the four new bases of Iraq (Bashur, H1, Talil and Baghdad), to the south all the bases of Kuwait and the Gulf, to the north the new American base installed in Georgia. In the background, the bases of Inçirlik in Turkey, in Israel, Djibouti and Diego Garcia. Evidently Iran is the next victim; it constitutes the centre of the "Greater Middle East". The periphery is conquered, the centre is encircled: either it will fall like a ripe fruit or it will be shaken by a revolution with hysterical ideological justifications, or it will be militarily annihilated.

SECOND PART: THE EUROPEAN RESPONSE:
THE PARIS/BERLIN/MOSCOW AXIS

Doubtlessly the most consistent theoretician of the Paris/Berlin/ Moscow axis is Henri de Grossouvre. This author elicits four major reasons to forge this continental alliance:

- To give oneself some weight in the commercial war between the EU and the United States,

- To correct the perverse effects of the neo-liberal globalisation,

- To respond to the energy stakes of 2010-2030,

- To organise a common space policy.

1. Henri de Grossouvre draws up the balance-sheet of the economic state of the world in which the formation of the axis has been considered; the EU possesses now 32% of the world's GDP while the United States 28%. The EU has thus surpassed the United States. A reason why the latter is alarmed and agitated and unleashes its powerful military machine. Then, Washington has placed itself in a state of

alert since Europe and Asia made a common front against the United States during the WTO summit in Seattle in December 1999. The idea of a Euro-Asiatic bloc was manifested, against which the United States would not be able to do anything. Besides, the points of friction between the two shores of the Atlantic have accumulated: on meats, bananas, the aeronautical industry (Boeing/Airbus). The amnesiac minds did not remember that one of the implicit causes of the intervention of the United States in European affairs during the Second World War had as its objective the destruction of the national aeronautical industries, those of Germany principally, but also those of the other European countries. The Franco-German cooperation for Airbus was thus viewed very negatively in Washington. The EU and the United States then confronted each other on the problem of the sanctions against the European firms that traded or tried to trade with Iran or Cuba. Wallonie suffered a resistance in its metallurgical industry ever since the rupture of commercial relations with Iran. From our point of view this is unacceptable. The growing cooperation between the EU and Russia thus aimed at consolidating our reciprocal positions in the face of the American economic aggressiveness and at amalgamating the expertise in aeronautical matters.

Correcting the Perverse Effects of the Liberal Globalisation

2. When H. de Grossouvre speaks of "correcting the perverse effects of the liberal globalisation" he rightly incriminates the general phenomenon of "*bougism*",[453] that is, of acquisitive restlessness, of unrestrained consumerism, of permanent mobility without rest, of a dissolution of the social fabric under the effect of the incessant appeals to "innovation". The

---

[453] [A neologism roughly translatable as "restlessness".]

inventor of this new word *"bougism"* is none other than Pierre-André Taguieff,[454] active in the "March 2nd Foundation". By comprehending with the precision of a philosopher this defect of our contemporary world Taguieff laid the foundations, doubtlessly unwillingly, of a new "conservative revolution" in the French manner. For, whether he wishes to or not, the ancient quest for permanences, or the wish to preserve them in all their "tranquil force", a wish that one finds in a founding father of conservatism like Chateaubriand,[455] was a profound desire not to sacrifice oneself to the modern cult of perpetual change, that is, to a disintegrating progressivism from which the "bougism" of today derives. H. de Grossouvre, for his part, considers that the necessary resistance to "bougism", of which "Americanism" is a variant, has as its concrete political objective the restoration of that which this "bougism" eliminates by its frenzy – all the intermediary structures between the individual and the international market: the school, the family, the community, nationality, the state, in short all the political space, the entire space of "culture", everything that is related to the "long term". Without these intermediate structures no political authority is capable of planning anything at all for the long term, everything being left to chance and the immediate of the present. The Paris/Berlin/Moscow axis whose coming H. de Grossouvre waits for, can help us get out of the "bougism" of which Americanism has for a long time been the principal paradigm by distancing the international economy from wild Manchesterism and speculation in order to return to an economy that Michel Albert at the beginning of the nineties qualified as "Rhineland", that is, patrimonial, based principally on infrastructural investments (means and routes of communication, etc.) while cultivating a concern to preserve the quality of the institutions of education, counting on the

---

[454] [Pierre-André Taguieff (1946-) is a French sociologist who has written works on anti-Semitism and anti-racism.]

[455] [The 'Fondation du 2 Mars' is a French republican think-tank established in 1998 by the journalist Élisabeth Lévy.]

good functioning of the schools and universities, which can evidently not be developed or even ensure their functioning if the perverse system of "bougism" persists. The Paris/Berlin/Moscow axis, by obtaining for Europe a territorial base and a mass of considerable productivity, allows one to disengage from the speculative economy of the American model and thereby put an end to this "bougism" which dislocates our societies.

3. H. de Grossouvre thinks that the constitution of the Paris/Berlin/Moscow axis will allow us to confront the energy stakes of the future, those of 2010-2030. The conquest of Iraq will entail, by the force of circumstances, the burdensome installation of an American monopoly of the immense reserves of petrol in this region. Between 2010 and 2020, the world, experts foresee, will experience the apogee of the production of petrol. Afterwards, it will be its decline. In this context, the objective of the Americans is to be present before the others, to grab the maximum of petrol to conserve their hegemony in the world. The occupation of gigantic Mesopotamian and Arab deposits renders the Euro-Russian partnership necessary in energy matters. For de Grossouvre, as for me, there is no other solution. H. de Grossouvre then analyses the total import of the Schroeder/Putin rapprochement. He reminds us that the Germano-Russian accords have a bearing precisely on energy and security (i.e. a revaluation of the role of the OSCE,[456] which the Americans have always sought to minimalise in favour of NATO, especially its civil component). H. de Grossouvre confirms the good functioning of this Germano-Russian partnership: around it, the other European powers, including France, should be united in order to avoid a dependence in energy matters that the American hyper-power is going to impose on us.

---

[456] [The Organisation for Security and Co-operation in Europe is an inter-governmental security organisation established in 1995.]

THIRD PART:

THE EXTERNAL HAZARDS OF A FUTURE PARIS/BERLIN/
MOSCOW AXIS

Three groups of hazards seem at present to hamper the process of European construction and the appearance of a true "Paris/Berlin/Moscow axis". They are the following:

1. The American information systems and the control satellites which they align in circumterrestrial space allow the Pentagon strategists to have an almost complete domination of media information in the entire world. François-Bernard Huyghe took this situation into consideration in a very important work, L'ennemi à l'ère Numérique : Chaos, Information, Domination (PUF, 2001). This book will become a classic of contemporary strategic thought. It is important to read it, reread it, meditate on it, and to make it well-known to teach our citizens to decipher the traps of the universal media propaganda which aims at taking away from all the peoples of the earth, and therefore also from the European peoples the sense of the real, of the historical and geopolitical reality in which they have found themselves for thousands of years. The loss of this sense of historical realities leads to political failure and to total decline.

The Weapons of Historical Knowledge are Essential

2. Our Europe has effectively been subjected to a systematic "cognitive war" whose first imperative is to forge "weapons of knowledge". The Anglo-Saxon schools excel in this field: they succeed, on the basis of very serious and well substantiated university studies, in developing simplistic

propagandas swallowed very rapidly by the public opinion of all the countries of the world. Europe today, which has resigned, lags behind. The political personnel that manage it, without really governing it, do not think it is opportune to give themselves historical institutions of the same value capable of forging, for Europe, a coherent and pragmatic vision of history. On the contrary, the dominant ideologies which operate within the European institutions think that history is a burden of the past which it would be good to get rid of, especially by no longer teaching it correctly in the schools. Now, in politics, and much more in "grand politics", the weapons of knowledge are essentially the weapons of historical knowledge; eventually it is these which, well mastered, obtain victory. Eugene of Savoy defeated the Turks and saved Europe thanks to his excellent historical knowledge. Clausewitz and his disciples insisted equally on the necessity of knowing history to forge efficient strategies.

The United States: Mafia Orientation

3. The Europe of Brussels and Strasbourg is not sufficiently attentive to the phenomena of indirect war. Xavier Raufer, in this context, insists very strongly on the role of the Mafia and of fabricated terrorism in his last work, *Le Grand Réveil des Mafias* (JC Lattès, 2003). Raufer teaches us to identify the Mafia enemy thanks to a clear and succint *vade mecum*; he shows us that the Mafia dangers are hidden, especially by the United States, which has undergone, and accepted, a "truly Mafia orientation" which allows us to speak without hesitation and without any useless paranoia of a veritable fusion between the American politics and the Mafias of Sicilian origin; apart from drugs and prostitution, the American pornographic industry feeds the cash boxes of the Mafia and, consequently, the slush funds of certain

"special services". The pages that Raufer devotes to the Turkish Mafias are very instructive and demonstrate well the Americano-Turkish collaboration in this field. And indicates to us two paths to contest the Turkish presence within the EU and its maintenance in NATO.

On the First Group of Hazards

The American media systems use what François-Bernard Huyghe calls the "four martial arts", which are:

1. The art of appearing, of talking war, of showing it, of narrating it (while excluding all other possible narrations), of twisting the narrative in the desired sense; it is a question of organising "psyops" (psychological operations) aimed at spreading the "good doctrine" throughout the world by adroitly combining narratives, photographs and films, as we saw during the Timisoara affair in Romania in 1989 or during the Kosovo conflict in 1999.

2. The art of deceiving, in other words, the art of using disinformation, of spreading slander against the enemy, who has been designated as such in the complex of the "global village"; it is essentially a matter of applying to the contemporary strategy the "art of illusions" already recommended by the strategist of Chinese antiquity, Sun Tzu;[457] the objective is to alter the perception of reality in the enemy and to provoke in him an erroneous decision; in this sense "disinformation consists in deliberately propagating false information to influence an opinion and to weaken an adversary".

3. The art of knowing, that is, of exercising a ubiquitous surveillance, especially through the ECHELON network, according to the avowed principle: "One who sees will

---

[457] [See above p. 182]

conquer"; the objective is to systematically collect useful information via satellites or spy software while pursuing diverse ends: to strike a less informed enemy at little risk, to keep the "good" strategic information for oneself, to intoxicate the adversary.

4. The art of concealing, or of dissimulating one's intentions behind an opaque screen of counter-information. In plain language, it is a matter of organising the proliferation of useless or redundant information in order to keep secret that which is really important and to use it, if necessary, against an adversary who is ignorant of it.

5. Exercising these four martial arts, today, implies disposing of a efficient satellite network: that is the case of the United States and not of Europe; whence the political and military dwarfism of the European Union. The latter has never applied the "four martial arts" that Huyghe has underlined.

On the Second Group of Hazards

For the team of the French army directed by Christian Harbulot cognitive supremacy derives from a doctrine of soft domination. These French officers and strategists declare that the United States does not reason, in this field, in terms of allies, enemies and neutrals but, more prosaically, more simply, in terms of "foreign audiences" whom it is good to manipulate, influence and pervert. The objective of the American "cognitive operations" are thus:

1. To create the optimal intellectual and psychological conditions to be able to take good decisions rationally at the right moment (since one has selected and separated the useful good information according to the rules of the "third martial art" analysed by Huyghe).

2. To prevent others from doing likewise after having inundated them with false information, false values, etc.

3. To see that the "targets" adopt the desired behaviour; this general method of the cognitive war, practised today by the United States, can only succeed if there is a long preparation ("shaping the mind"). It is a question of a global strategy maturely thought of for ages which aims at the total colonisation of the sphere of ideas, the conquest of the noosphere,[458] in the jargon of the initiates. The final objective is to create a normative international superstructure which will define human reality in a uniform manner agreeing with the American policy, of course. It is the application in the age of the electronic media of a cultural strategy begun with the cinema of Hollywood, from the end of the Second World War in Europe and Asia.

4. Europe, which, like the rest of the world, is the target of this strategy, can only respond by meditating on the same principles. That means, especially,

- Reappropriating one's own history, knowing its fecund principles, which allow a consolidation of one's positions, and the perverse principles which lead to implosion; this implies also,

- Exploring the history of the adversary to cause to appear on his territory paralysing conflicts. In plain language, for consistent European strategists, exploiting the anger of the American Blacks or cleverly supporting the protest movements within the United States.

The Anti-Global New Left is Trapped

Another example of a particularly successful manipulation, well highlighted by Harbulot: the media success accorded to the famous book of Toni Negri and Michael Hardt entitled Empire and considered by the New York newspapers as "the greatest alternative

---

[458] [Noetic sphere, or the realm of the intellect.]

theory of the 21st century". In fact, this work recommends the emergence of a vast network of splinter micro-protests that reject all forms of nationalism or continentalism, that is, which removes in advance any territorial base to the protest against the Amerocentric globalism. Now, without a territorial base, it is impossible to oppose Washington. The cognitive war thus allows the media system, at the service of the American imperialism and globalism, to offer the anti-globalists a ready-made theory which will lead them into error and which will condemn them to inaction. The real world power in this way sweeps the rug from beneath the feet of the contemporary protest orchestrated by the anti-globalist New Left and induces in its ranks an ideological ferment of permanent disintegration that is hard to eradicate.

On the Third Group of Hazards

Indirect wars are normally conducted according to the criteria of "low intensity warfare". The most recent textbook example is the so-called "contras" war conducted in the eighties against the Sandinista government in Nicaragua.[459] But for Xavier Raufer "low intensity wars" are not limited to the strategy of arming insurrectional groups in the targeted countries but also to the maintenance of Mafia networks which dislocate the political coherence, which serve as future networks of espionage and sabotage. Raufer calls our attention to a long history that has been softened and hidden: that of the close interconnection between the American power and the Italian Mafia networks. In fact, the Sicilian Mafia, he declares, is an integral power of the American power. Raufer shows us its mechanisms and explains that the mafia structures are marvellously deployed in the neoliberal systems, instituted precisely to allow this fluidity which suits the "services" well. In the historical part of his demonstration he recalls that the Mafia has been a representative

[459] [Ronald Reagan supported the anti-Sandinista Contrarevolución forces (Contras) against the left-wing government that had established itself in Nicaragua after ousting the dictator Anastasio Somoza in 1979.]

in Europe of American power since 1943, when the special services of Washington called on Lucky Luciano,[460] imprisoned in America, to organise the Allied landing in Sicily.

The Mafias Have as Their Objective the Destabilisation of European Societies

In Belgium, we have three other particularly efficient non-Italian Mafia networks: the Moroccan, Turkish and Albanian networks. All three are strategically connected to the United States and NATO, especially through the Mafia/army fusion that rules in Turkey and through the quasi-identity between the Albanian UCK[461] and the local Mafias. As for Morocco, old ally of the United States, it constitutes the principal pawn of the strategic plan of the United States in North Africa: the financing of this country is effected through the traffic in cannabis to Europe (70% of this narcotic consumed in Europe originates from the region of Rif).[462] The Mafias have as their objective the destabilisation of the European societies, their political structures (this is seen clearly at the level of the law), their economies. Besides, they allow the production of destabilising stock-exchange operations, their establishment in the real estate market, the accumulation of an uncontrollable amount of money, the constitution of spy networks, the arming of terrorist structures and the accomplishment of murders, if necessary.

Not eliminating such networks condemns us to being nothing more than the wretched objects of a particularly pernicious strategy of indirect war. But of which we see the total decadent result in the public sphere, with the blessing of a political personnel overtly connected to these networks. The fear of all future challenging political parties is essentially motivated by the risk of seeing the

---

[460] [Charles "Lucky" Luciano (1897-1962) was the leader of a Genovese crime family in America and he was, along with his Jewish associate Meyer Lansky, a founder of the National Crime Syndicate in 1929.]

[461] [See above p. 74]

[462] [The northern region of Morocco.]

structure in place called into question, especially if the challenging parties in place declare that they will conduct a war on drugs, the war-horse of the Moroccan and Turkish Mafias. The anti-racist back rooms, which make such a fuss in the media, do not have as their real objective the protection of citizens of foreign origin who would be the innocent victims of a gratuitous punishment on the part of xenophobic natives but, more precisely, the classification of every critical position vis-à-vis the occult, illegal but real power of the diverse Mafias anchored in Belgium as "racist". The anti-racist back rooms are a good example of the "fourth martial art" according to Huyghe: the art that consists in concealing one's real intentions behind a screen of ideological-media smoke.

FOURTH PART:
THE CONCEPTS OF TOYNBEE

From the immense work of the British philosopher of history, Arnold Joseph Toynbee, we have retained two fundamental ideas: those of "challenge and response" and "withdrawal and return". Every challenge entails a response for Toynbee, which implies that his vision of history is dynamic, free of all determinism: the field is always open for new responses borne by diverse, heterogeneous actors, individual or collective. Toynbee wagers on the creative capacities of man; he thinks that they always come out on top in the end. Every human group, just before they create civilisation, undergo challenges originating from the social environment or the geographical environment. If the challenge is too strong or too weak, we will not witness the emergence of a civilisation. For example, the Eskimos did not develop a civilisation but simply a culture made up of simple strategies of survival. The tropical cultures, in their paradisiacal climes, did not develop a civilisation either, the intensity of the challenge there being too weak.

Challenges are also, in Toynbee's language, "stimuli"; they are of five sorts in the classification that he proposes:

1. A too harsh geography,

2. Virgin lands that must be made profitable,

3. Blows directed at the group by enemies or by Nature,

4. A permanent external pressure provoking vigilance, thus organisation,

5. Internal pressures entailing the penalisation of one or several groups within a civilisation whose basic principles are different; this "penalisation" entails the emergence of a different mode of life permitting the birth of a marginal culture to which the power may or may not allocate particular social or economic functions; this was the case of the Greek Phanariots[463] in the Ottoman Empire, of the Jews in Morocco and in Arabised Spain and then in Germanophone Central Europe, of the Parsis in India, the Nestorians[464] between Mesopotamia and Chinese Turkestan.

The particularities of these cultures proceed from a challenge, one which ostracises and minoritises them; the cultural specificity of "penalised" populations thus constitutes the response to this type of challenge. For Toynbee these civilisations – or the efficiency of "penalised" cultures – are established when the multiple conditions for their emergence amount to an optimum, that is, when the degree of penalisation is neither too harsh nor too benign.

---

[463] [Phanariots were wealthy mercantile Greek families resident in Istanbul during the Ottoman Empire and serving in high administrative positions.]

[464] [Nestorians are followers of the doctrines of Nestorius, Patriarch of Constantinople (386-450) who distinguished between the human and divine natures of Jesus. They flourished mostly in Persia and Asia and are today mostly represented by the Saint Thomas Christians of India.]

Withdrawal and Return; Yin and Yang

Europe and our civilisation in general, Russia, our "penalised" ideological space, undergo challenges. These "penalising" challenges or these external (American) pressures are not at all definitive. As a "penalised" ideological space we should acquire a greater discipline, accumulate practical, historical, strategic and finally utilisable knowledge superior to that of the (im)politicians in power. We should act like a perpetual "shadow cabinet" which suggests credible political alternatives clearly drawn up and well constructed in their argument. For Toynbee the Ideal City corresponded to the Augustinian notion of *"Civitas Dei"* or a transcendental reality chosen to be incarnated, just as Christ was incarnated in the world to redeem it after its "fall". When the city no longer corresponds to its transcendental reality (and this model need not necessarily be "Augustinian" for us … it could be quite simply Greek or Roman), it sinks into the "worldly" or the "profane", into "sin" or, more simply, for Spengler, as for us, into decadence or degeneration.

For Toynbee, an ideological movement or space that is content to whine about the disappearance of the time before the degeneration, that would cultivate archaisms would be a "resigned" movement, backward looking and passive. The man of action (that of Blondel?),[465] the man informed by the spirit of service or knightliness, the man who intends to work for the City, to put himself in the service of his worldly community draws from the past the lessons for the future that he is going to forge through his vigorous action. He is not resigned but volunteers and is a futurist. He transfigures reality after a "withdrawal", a detachment from degenerate, amorphous worldliness that is complacent in its degeneration. This withdrawal is simultaneously a dive into (the longest) memory, but this withdrawal cannot be definitive;

---

[465] [Maurice Blondel (1861-1949) was a Christian philosopher who employed Neoplatonic notions of the soul in his various philosophical analyses. His first published work was called *L'Action: Essai d'une Critique de la vie et d'une Science de la Pratique*, 1893.]

it postulates a "return". The visionary becomes a prospective activist. He mounts an attack to remodel the City according to the transcendental model that had given it its former lustre. The agent of its "transfiguration" thus withdraws from the world, from the present (from presentism) without however wishing to leave it definitively; his withdrawal is provisional and cannot be compared to the refusal of the world that certain Gnostics of the Late Empire cultivated; he remains connected to time and space; he has a positive goal.

Toynbee also utilises the Chinese concepts of "yin" and "yang". As soon as the City finds or regains a harmony, an abundance which risks falling into a deleterious peace - the matrix of all deviations, all vices - the phase of the "yang" is then a phase of necessary and positive turmoil, a phase of fecund tumult that aims at the coming of a more perfect "yin". Toynbee especially evokes the risk of an ossification of institutions, where the latter, worm-eaten, are idolised by the holders of power incapable of arresting the course of the decline. A phase of "yang" is then necessary, borne by new forces that have effected a "return" in order to better resume business.

The task of metapolitics, the object of the ongoing "cognitive war" is precisely to generate finally what Toynbee understood by "transfiguration" or by "yang". It is up to us to be the agents of this transfiguration, to join the forces bearing the coming "yang", forces still dispersed, disparate, but which it will be necessary to unite into an invincible phalanx!

BIBLIOGRAPHY

Jacques BAUD, *La guerre asymétrique ou la défaite du vainqueur*, Rocher, 2003.

Wim BLOCKMANS, *Keizer Karel - 1500-1558: De utopie van het keizerscha*p, Uitgeverij: Van Halewyck, 2001 (2de uitgave).

William BLUM, *Killing Hope: US Military & CIA Interventions since World War II*, Zed Books, London, 2003.

Gérard CHALIAND, *Atlas du nouvel ordre mondial*, Robert Laffont, 2003.

Aymeric CHAUPRADE, *Géopolitique : Constantes et changements dans l'histoire*, Ellipses, 2003 ([2nd] revised and augmented ed.).

Hellmut DIWALD, « Prinz Eugen, der edle Ritter», in :*Mut*, Nr. 224, April 1986.

DRION du CHAPOIS, *La vocation européenne des Belges*, Ed. Universitaires, Bruxelles, 1958.

Edmonde CHARLES-ROUX,*Don Juan d'Autriche: Bâtard de Charles-Quint*, Ed. Racines, Bruxelles, 2003.

William HALE, *Turkish Foreign Policy 1774-2000*, Frank Cass, London, 2000-2002.

Catherine HENTIC, *Les maîtres des nefs du Moyen Âge*, Ed. Versoix, Genève, 1978.

Mark JUERGENSMEYER, *Terror in the Mind of God : The Global Rise of Religious Violence*, University of California Press, 2003 (3d ed.).

Gerd-Klaus KALTENBRUNNER, « Eugenio von Savoye, der Staatsmann und Humanist », in :*Mut*, Nr. 224, April 1986.

Sergei KARPOV, « Une ramification inattendue: les Bourguignons en Mer Noire au XVe siècle», in Michel BALARD & Alain DUCELLIER, *Coloniser au Moyen Âge*, Armand Colin, 1995.

Homer LEA, *The Day of the Saxon*, Harper & Brothers, London, 1912.

Jacques LEGRAND (ed.), *Lawrence d'Arabie*, Ed. Chronique, Bassillac, 1997.

Catherine et Jacques LEGRAND (dir.), *Atatürk*, Ed. Chronique, Bassillac, 1998.

Fabrice LÉOMY, *Tamerlan : Le "condottiere" invaincu*, France Empire, 1996.

Paul Robert MAGOCSI, *Historical Atlas of East Central Europe*, vol. I, University of Washington Press, Seattle/London, 1993.

Ferenc MAJOROS & Bernd RILL, *Das Osmanische Reich 1300-1922: Die Geschichte einer Großmacht*, F. Pustet/Styria, Graz/Wien/Köln, 1994.

Claude MUTAFIAN & Eric VAN LAUWE, *Atlas historique de l'Arménie Proche-Orient et Sud-Caucase du VIIIe siècle av. JC au XXIe siècle*, Autrement, 2001.

V. S. NAIPAUL, *Among the Believers: An Islamic Journey*, Picador, London, 2001.

V. S. NAIPAUL, *India : A Wounded Civilization*, Picador, London, 2002.

René PASSET, *Mondialisation financière et terrorisme : La donne a-t-elle changé depuis le 11 septembre?*, Enjeux Planète, 2002.

Joseph PÉREZ, *Charles-Quint, Empereur des deux mondes*, Gallimard, 1994.

Jean-Paul ROUX, *Histoire des Turcs : Deux mille ans du Pacifique à la Méditerranée*, Fayard, 1984.

Peter SCHOLL-LATOUR, *Das Schlachtfeld der Zukunft : Zwischen Kaukasus und Pamir*, Goldmann, 1996-1998.

Peter SCHOLL-LATOUR, *Allahs Schatten über Atatürk : Die Türkei in der Zerreißprobe - Zwischen Kurdistan und Kosovo*, Goldmann, 1999-2001.

Jean SELLIER, *Atlas des peuples d'Afrique*, La Découverte, 2003.

Jennifer SIEGEL, *Endgame : Britain, Russia and the Final Struggle for Central Asia*, I. B. Tauris, London, 2002.

Jean-Pierre SOISSONS, *Marguerite, princesse de Bourgogne,* Grasset, 2002.
Arnold Joseph TOYNBEE, *A Study of History,* Vol. 1 to 12, Oxford Univ. Press, 1934-54.
Michael W. WEITHMANN, *Balkan Chronik: 2000 Jahre zwischen Orient und Okzident,* F. Pustet/Styria: Graz/Wien/Köln, 1995.

FOR A GRAND EURASIAN AND
IBERO-AMERICAN ALLIANCE[466]

enri de Grossouvre recently published an important work suggesting to the readers the concrete bases of a Paris/Berlin/Moscow alliance. This necessary alliance can only be defensive, can only be the first stage in the direction of a vaster project insofar as the territories of this "Triple" alliance were deprived of buffer zones especially in Central Asia after the dissolution of the USSR, the inheritor of the Empire of the tsars in this region. To be complete, the alliance should equally include Iran, India, China and Japan. In this way, the thalassocratic power of the New World would experience immense difficulties in establishing and anchoring itself in the rimlands and in dislodging the imperial cohesions there.

The five principal powers of this alliance of seven, up to now a hypothesis, are Indo-European, that is, they have connections to an Indo-European past, in spite of the Christian or Muslim superstratum, Buddhism being a particular emanation of the Indo-European psyche of India borne at first by an Indian prince originating from the kshatriya class. Iran is Islamic today only because the United States supported Khomeini at first to eliminate the Shah and his programme of a return to the Persian roots of antiquity combined with an active diplomatic vision based on

---

[466] Taken from a talk delivered at the conference of the "Terre et Peuples" association of Nancy, November 2005.

the organisation of the rim of the Indian Ocean. The geopolitical project of the Shah was visionary and interesting. Zaki Laïdi[467] and Mohammed-Reza Jalili,[468] French speaking geopoliticians originating from the Muslim world, and, due to this fact, excellent experts on Arab, Iranian, Pakistani and Indian sources, have highlighted it well in their diverse works. The new media campaign against Iran, begun in depth from this autumn, in the name of the non-proliferation of nuclear armaments, is a pretext, yet another, to intervene in the Eurasian rimland and expand the conquests effected in Afghanistan and Iraq.

The Project of the "Greater Middle East"

As the *Corriere de la Sera* of 25 November 2005 titled it, Iran plans to treat its uranium on Russian soil avoiding in this way eventual American or Israeli reprisals. Beijing supports this project, quite simply because the supply of Iranian petrol is vital for a China that is fully expanding, an expansion that Washington attempts to thwart.

Europe, for its part, has no interest at all in having a general embargo, within the framework of sanctions decided by Washington, imposed on Iran: it would pay the cost of it, for the exchanges between the United States and Iran are minimal; because of this the losses would hit only the European exporters of technologies, who by not dealing with Iran would not benefit from sufficient funds to invest eventually in research and innovation. The Iranian affair, if it is analysed from the point of view of the eternal rules of geopolitics, could contribute to the consolidation in an effective manner of a project of common defence on the Eurasian continental mass, for, by striking Iran, the United States would

---

[467] [Zaki Laïdi is a French political scientist who has written several works on contemporary international politics and is a research director at the Centre d'études européennes of the Institut d'études politiques de Paris.]

[468] [Mohammed-Reza Jalili (1940-) is an Iranian Swiss political scientist who has written works on the geopolitics of Iran and Central Asia.]

strike the geopolitical heart of the central space of this immense territorial mass, would cause the last political obstacle to their plans to fall. In fact they wish to construct a "Greater Middle East" equivalent to the territory of the USCENTCOM and which would be the major outlet of their consumer industries while excluding all the other economic powers from this juicy market. Neither Moscow nor Beijing can tolerate this, for this geostrategic reorganisation would reduce their respective territories to a weakened periphery without access to the Central Ocean, the object of all imperial ambitions since the earliest antiquity.

In this synergy, which is being drawn at the moment, the sixth and seventh powers of the hypothetical "Grand Alliance" that we support, China and Japan, would begin by restoring the famous "sphere of East Asiatic prosperity" which would *ipso facto* give coherence to the oriental space of the Eurasian continental mass. On the spiritual and intellectual level these two powers are based on non-proselytising, non-messianic indigenous religions. One cannot therefore make use of a religion of this type in these two countries to cause disorders and revolutions as is done with Islam or to initiate a process of masochistic self-denigration, as is done with Christianity in Europe and more particularly in Germany and the Protestant countries. The religious heritage in China and in Japan is a complex of ancestral legacy, of rites and customs which resist all manipulation, for they are fixed and immutable even while permitting technological modernity.

China Defends Itself

In the East Asiatic space of co-prosperity there is certainly Indonesia agitated by certain fundamentalist Muslim sects but its nationalist networks which came to power after 1945 participated in the Japanese efforts, during the Second World War, to realise and consolidate this sphere. The project of a "Grand Alliance" – which will include also Thailand, another old ally of the Japanese considered for a long while as the "enemy of the United States" – implies the defence of the Buddhist national tradition against the subversive schemes of Muslim fanatic elements in the south who intend to destabilise the country and retard its economic momentum.

China, for its part, has always defended itself against the disorders provoked by the Hunnish and Turko-Mongol nomads; this is its *raison d'être*, the secret of its continuity for such a long duration; in spite of the western and modernist ideologies that have worked on it, it is not ready to back off in the Sinkiang, formerly called "Chinese Turkestan", or to accept the emergence of Muslim Turko-Ugric insurgent groups remote-controlled by a pan-Turkism activated in the final analysis by the United States. And which would aim at detaching this Sinkiang from the Chinese (and Russian) sphere of influence to make it an eventual appendix to the "Greater Middle East". The United States would realise through interposed persons the Arabo-Muslim project aborted in the past to conquer the Turkestan outposts of China and, in a final phase, would make use of the very abundant Muslim demographics to contain China for a long time on the western borders.

The problem of Islam, and more exactly of its most extreme factions, is that it is allied to the United States in spite of the proclamations and sabre-rattlings, the attacks and the bogeymen who are stirred up in the media. The space of the "Greater Middle East" desired by the Americans would be Muslim, if possible regressive in order to avoid all industrial and economic upsurge (as the CIA agents who placed Khomeini on the saddle planned it), preferably proselytising to encroach on the adjacent territories like Thailand but also, finally, in the valley of the Volga and the Kama on the territory of the Russian Federation, in the Sinkiang against China and among the immigrant communities in western Europe (who will, if and when necessary, serve as levers to provoke uncontrollable disorders, destablise the systems of social security and financially weaken the European competitors at all levels, as one sees today, in November 2005, in the suburbs of the big French cities).

The Lesson of Naipaul, Nobel Laureate in Literature

The ideological antidote to this virulent proselytism has today been given to us by V.S. Naipaul, Nobel laureate in literature, an Indo-British man to whom we owe many very interesting books on the destiny of the Indian civilisation undermined by Islamic proselytisation. Naipaul, especially in *India: A Wounded Civilisation* and *Among the Believers: An Islamic Journey*, demonstrates the noxiousness of all proselytism for it deeply mutilates the peoples or the civilisations who undergo it. The first of these books was written in 1975 after a third visit to India, the fatherland of his ancestors who had left it to settle in Jamaica. His peregrinations as an *emigré* who returns to his origins revealed to him the profound mutilation of Hindu India after centuries of foreign, Muslim and British, domination.

This wounding caused India not to have gained yet the ideology of its regeneration, for Gandhism, even though it *in fine* obtained the independence of the sub-continent, resulted, in the eyes of Naipaul, in failure. Gandhism does not cause the revival of the past, does not give the recipe for an efficient state that would be viable in the long term; it expresses the sentiments of an India that resists but not of an India that is recovering and reviving, that strengthens and asserts itself. Under the blows of a foreign proselytism an "old balance" was broken, Naipaul declared in 1975; the rule that he announced here being applicable to all proselytisms and all the "old balances" that they have broken in the course of history.

Islamic Proselytism and Media Proselytism

The second book, which we refer to here, shows the rage that the newly converted develop to destroy the legacy of their mother civilisation. The contribution of China and Japan would, in the "Grand Alliance", be that of a force that resists proselytism, which remains impermeable to it, which allows the retention of its original forces intact and the "old balance" to remain unbroken. In the 21st century, this force would serve to resist two forms of mutilating penetration, of contemporary proselytism, the one secular the other religious: that of the media discourse conveyed by the large American press agencies and that of Islam, on the territory, at the periphery of the "Greater Middle East".

The American media serve to stultify and distract the minds in Europe and in Russia, to obliterate the geopolitical awareness; the Islamic proselytism serves to enlarge the space of the Greater Middle East through a measured and remote-controlled application of jihad against the Muslim minorities or against neighbouring countries in order to encroach upon their borders (as was the case with the mujahideens and the Talibans: Saudi money and Americn weapons); then this proselytism serves to dislocate the internal peace in the European countries welcoming a strong Islamic immigration (the events of France in November 2005 will become for this reason a textbook example).

The two sorts of proselytism have as their object the erasure of living memories, the breaking of historic continuities, of inaugurating manipulatory systems. Without a living memory , without the feeling of living in a historic continuity, the peoples, like the Indian people, according to Naipaul, fall into apathy, fall into disorder and decay after crises of fanaticism and iconoclasm.

Eight Axes of Action

The Grand Alliance will emerge concretely if the European, Russian, Chinese, Iranian, Indian and Japanese apply eight axes of action:

1. Produce together a network independent of oil and gas pipelines in all of Eurasia.[469] The recent visit of Putin to Japan, where the talks were conclusive, is very promising in this direction. Putin aims at arbitrating a balance between China and Japan, whereas the big media agencies spur the two Asiatic powers against each

---

[469] See the articles of Gerhoch Reisegger in *Au fil de l'épée* (Arcana Imperii).

other in the name of differences originating from the thirties and forties. This policy aims at reviving old conflicts that are today deprived of relevance and at hindering all common synergy in the fields of communication and the transport of energy in this region with a very great demographic density. Our objective should be to counter this propaganda, to create the ideological conditions that would render it ineffective, to cultivate the psychological reflexes that would render it null and void.

2. Create a network of roads and railways between Russia, China, the Koreas and Japan on the one hand, Russia and India on the other. The necessity of ensuring optimal land connections between Russia and India emphasises the Tajiki and Kashmiri questions. In fact, Tajikistan and Kashmir are Indo-European lands partially Islamised but Persophone in Tajikistan, which it is good to detach from all foreign influences. The support to India, in its legitimate claims to the region of Kashmir, is an inescapable imperative of the future new geopolitics of the Grand Alliance. In no case should Tajikistan and Kashmir be included in the Greater Middle East.

The GALILEO Project

3. Under the impulsion of the EU, the Grand Alliance should be constituted around the GALILEO satellite project which should be the European, Russian, Chinese and Indian response to the American dominance in space and thus in the field of telecommunications. The request of Israel to participate in this project should be viewed with the greatest mistrust given the too close vassal relations of this small country of the Middle East to the American giant.

4. It is necessary to support and enlarge the project of the gas pipeline from the Baltic creating *de facto* a Germano-Russian economic axis. This project, in the process of being realised,

thanks to the determination of the former chancellor Schröder, permits the circumvention of the countries of the "New Europe" serving as satellites of the United States, like Ukraine after its "orange" revolution, Poland entirely subservient to NATO, and Lithuania, which follows the same detestable orientation. The gas pipeline from the Baltic has allowed the reduction to nothing of the new strategy of a *cordon sanitaire* or the creation of a string of small and medium powers between the EU (in the past Germany) and the Russian Federation (formerly the USSR) to which are granted a guarantee because they have subjected themselves to NATO. This Germano-Russian counter-strategy had an antecedent in 1986 with project to connect, through a system of ferries and large carriers, the port of Memel/Klaipeda in eastern Prussia to Kiel and, via the Kiel Canal, to the North Sea. Before these negotiations had ended, at the beginning of the Gorbachev era, the minister-president of Schleswig-Holstein was found dead, assassinated, in his bath.[470] The assassins were never found. If the future Grand Alliance cannot reach the Indian Ocean, given the presence of the American military in the waters of this "Central Ocean", it should have an outlet to the sea in the Baltic Sea. In this way Haushofer's dream will be realised: that of the Eurasian *troika* with the three horses that are Germany (EU), Russia and Japan. Another strategy of freeing from strangulation is in the process of being established in the Arctic: the Russian ice-boats of the new generation, which are at the same time floating nuclear factories generating their own energy, will soon open the Northern route and connect Hamburg and Japan.

Break the Alliance Between Washington and Turkey

5. Another objective: cause the alliance between the United States and Turkey to be destroyed. This alliance, indissoluble up to the

---

[470] Cf. *Vouloir*, no.30 and 31.

premises of the invasion of Iraq in March 2003, blocked Europe in the Balkans, aimed at the containment of the EU on the course of the Danube at the level of Belgrade, prevented a direct land route between the Hungarian plain and the Aegean, and then contained Russia in the Black Sea and in the Caucasus. Clinton, in the speeches that he held in Istanbul and Ankara during his last official visit to Turkey, fully played the card of the Americano-Turkish alliance; he exercised constant pressure to make Turkey enter the EU in such a way that the Europeans may ignore the Turkish deficiencies and welcome its abundant demographic. Bush does not follow exactly the same policy, a policy that had been dictated, certainly by human rights, but for a good part by the classical game of alliances. Bush II favours a petrol strategy quite in the tradition of his family and the lobbies that support it. The war in Iraq is, obviously, a war for petrol. The American petroleum companies wish to ensure the management of all the oil layers of the country or of the region for three reasons essentially:

- To maximise their immediate profits and cover the expenses of the military operations.

- To drill oil everywhere and diminish in this way their dependence on Saudi petrol, given the ambiguity of the Saudi politics, which proclaims on the one hand its alliance to the American alliance but, on the other, is moored in the Al Qaeda affair, a network of the Anglo-Saxon strategy of "insurgency" but which has followed its own path playing a double and triple game (see the works of Éric Laurent[471] on this subject).

- To remove the management of petrol from all the other powers of the Eurasian continental mass, to exploit the oil fields during the years of petrol peak and in the course of

---

[471] [Éric Laurent (1947-) is a French journalist specialising in international politics. He has published several works including *La Guerre des Bush* (2003) and *Le Monde Secret de Bush* (2003).]

the first decades of the predicted decline of petrol, in order to collect surpluses in order to finance the post-petrol technologies and to continue in this way to dominate the globe.

With the promises of Clinton the Turks had hoped to recuperate the region of Iraqi Kurdistan around the petrol fields of Mosul, even if it meant invading this northern province of Iraq, to liquidate there the Kurdish PKK presence and annex it *de facto* so as to acquire a certain energy independence of which they were deprived since the Lausanne accords of 1923. The American strategy would have counted in this case on its long standing ally and exploited the central position of Turkey in the arc of crises that runs from the Balkans to the Iranian border. But to cause the Turkish army to act, as the last Democrat administration wanted, implied the renunciation of particularly abundant wells. The petrol strategy of Bush II could not accept that. Making war on Saddam Hussein demanded a large mobilisation which should eventually pay off in booty. The wells of Iraqi Kurdistan constituted this ideal booty. No question therefore of leaving them to the Turks.

During the preliminaries of the war against Iraq the Americano-Turkish relations cooled considerably. Turkish public opinion felt betrayed – not compensated for its unfailing loyalty to the Atlantic Alliance since the beginning of the Cold War and the Korean War, where the Turkish troops had paid the price of blood to be accepted in the "Atlantic community".

Worse: to conserve this place that it considered valuable Turkey had created the material conditions for its rupture with the Arab countries of the Fertile Crescent. The Atatürk Dam,[472] inaugurated by the old strong man of Turkey, Özal,[473] is part of the Kemalist, western and liberal line. The construction of dams reflects a desire to cut itself off from the Arab world, from the sources of petrol,

---

[472] [The Atatürk Dam on the Euphrates River in south eastern Anatolia was completed in 1983.]

[473] [Turgut Özal (1927-93) was Prime Minister of Turkey from 1983 to 1989 and President from 1989 to 1993.]

from the Ottoman past. By cutting the course of the rivers of the Fertile Crescent, by limiting their flow, the Turks weaken ipso facto the economies and agricultures of their Arab neighbours. Which runs in the interest of the United States which, eventually, can practise its perpetual policy of Food Aid against raw materials or political concessions and in this way consolidate their hold on nations.

Total Support of Armenia

6. Destroying the Americano-Turkish alliance implies a support of Armena enclaved in the Caucasian mountain range. Last year, in 2004, hardly a few weeks before the abominable massacre of children of Beslan in Ossetia, the Armenian army had organised noticeable manoeuvres in the region with Russian support demonstrating thereby that the country constituted a solid implanted abscess preventing the pan-Turkic project from launching itself from the Aegean to the Chinese borders as Özal had hoped. One should bear in mind that the system of the pan-Turkic, pan-Turanian, project is one of the ingredients that serves the United States in creating the "Greater Middle East" or in establishing their dominance on the "new Silk Road" as Zbigniew Brzezinski ("New Silk Road Project") had theorised. The objective of any good Eurasian politics was from that time to slow down or counter all these projects by mobilising the forces hostile to pan-Turkism. The Armenian military core is of great utility in every counter-strategy of the "Grand Alliance" which we strongly desire.

7. It is good finally to organise the Pontic space, the river lands of the Black Sea. The great fluvial axes that the Danube, Dnieper and the Don are and, via the Don-Volga Canal, the Volga, as well as the basin of the Caspian, should be organised synergetically by excluding Turkey, which is alien to the Pontic space, given that no important river originates from Anatolian territory

and does not participate in the hydrographic synergy of the region. The Pontic space should be dominated by the powers which give it the water of its rivers in the perspective of the European powers that have wished to remove this civilisational space from the rule of foreign conquerors, from the Seljuks to the Ottomans. For our political tradition, the reconquest of this Pontic space for the consolidation of Europe has been part of the order of the day for more than six centuries, since the Duke of Burgundy John the Fearless and the creation of the Order of the Golden Fleece: all those who are opposed to it, beginning with the sinister Gallican sovereignists, who follow the detestable tradition of François I, are vile traitors who should be prevented from harming and be combated ruthlessly. The Pontic space will be from tomorrow the site on which the raw materials of the Caspian and the gas of Russia and of Kazakhstan will transit: no power that is not European in origin should have control of the transport of these raw materials.

Total Support of Chavez

8. Finally, it is good to defend the common interests of the principal Eurasian components of the "Grand Alliance" in Ibero-America and to include this continent in the global combat against Washington. For the moment, that implies an unfailing support of Chavez, president of Venezuela. Spain, in the name of Hispanic culture, has a key role to play in this strategy. The presence of Zapatero at the Latin American summit at the end of 2005 was a promising sign. Zapatero had affirmed there the rejection of any boycott against Cuba, which rests for us a Spanish province because we do not accept the repercussions of the Hispano-American War of 1898, sparked by a fallacious casus belli and a hysterical and mendacious press campaign orchestrated by the infamous Teddy Roosevelt. Condoleeza Rice evidently refused to end this boycott, which created a unanimity against her and made a star of Zapatero

who will evidently not keep his fashionable false socialist promises. The Spanish prime minister promised to sell arms to Venezuela so that the latter might – the American authorities say – "export its Bolivarist revolution" everywhere in Ibero-America. During this summit, whose work allowed the drawing of the broad lines of an eventual Eurasiatic-Ibero-American politics, the promise to sell Spanish arms to Chavez was a perfectly justified response to the sale of F-16s and other effective materials to Morocco just before the invasion of Perejil Island in July 2002, an act of war that can be considered as purely "symbolic". But Europe cannot allow itself to lose a supplementary "symbolic" war, especially in the western basin of the Mediterranean.

Philosophical Conclusion

The popularisation of this programme, its anchoring in diplomatic practice, is the goal of our struggle. Our combat is an identitarian one; it aims at a return to our identity, to our deep authenticity. But this authenticity cannot remain a small museum piece that is tenderly admired without any action. Hegel taught us that being a man was not done alone but that was done within "our collectives". Yesterday, these "collectives" were regional or national identities. Today, we aim at the coming of a vaster "collective we", that of the people of the European communities and peoples who reject the system of proselytism which, as Naipaul has taught us, eradicates identities and makes man unhappy. Hegel said that we could only live our freedom if we gave a meaning, our meaning, to the concrete reality of the world that surrounds us. Humanity is a word devoid of meaning, he added, if men did not return to their deep self before searching for a concrete reality, here and now, a concrete reality that ceaselessly undergoes mutations and changes that must also be confronted. And the "humanity" of our adversaries is effectively a meaningless word since it rejects this return to the deep authenticity of peoples and adopts fixed formulae deprived of a fighting dialectic, encouraging resignation, which is suggested to them by proselytes of all complexions, especially those who broadcast the media discourses. Washington represents the thesis: the present world power, rigid, devoid of any meaning for others; our Grand Alliance represents the antithesis: still fragile, still fallow, but alone invested with a real dynamism. I invite you to participate in it.

REFLECTIONS ON THE GEOPOLITICS AND HISTORY OF THE EASTERN BASIN OF THE MEDITERRANEAN[474]

Multiple Repercussions on the Margins of the Greek Crisis

The Greek crisis is mainly perceived as an economic and financial crisis detached from all historical and geopolitical context. The technocrats and the economists, generally dabblers without vision or common sense, stuck in an infertile present, have never reflected on the necessity of Europe's maintaining itself solidly in this eastern Mediterranean space whose control guarantees it peace. Without a strong presence in this space, Europe is deprived of force. This historical reasoning is however established: the Crusades, the Aragonese intervention in Greece in the 14th century (with the warrior caste of the Almogavares), etc. show clearly that it was always a vital necessity to anchor a European presence in this Hellenic archipelago threatened by Turkish and Muslim events. The absence of historical memory maintained by the members of our banking and economic technocracies has caused this incontrovertible truth of our history to be forgotten; the disastrous management of the Greek crisis demonstrates this constantly.

---

[474] *Euro-synergies*, 26 November 2015.

Erdogan, Toynbee and the Turkish Dynamic

The major regional power in this space is today the Turkey of Erdogan, even if all true power is, in our days, tributary; there to the American ambition, whose instrument is the navy that crosses the waters of the Great Sea. Too few are the European decision-makers who understand the ancient springs of the Turkish dynamic in this region which provides access to the Black Sea, the black earth of the Ukraine, the Danube, the Caucasus, the Nile (and thus to the heart of East Africa), to the Red Sea and to trade with India. To understand the geopolitics that has been at work all the time in this nerve-centre of the globe even before any Turkish presence is an imperative of political lucidity. We have behind us seven centuries of confrontation with the Turko-Ottoman phenomenon but it is rather in ancient history that one should discover how, in the region, the territory in itself confers a power, real or potential, on the one who occupies it. It was the Byzantinologist Arnold J. Toynbee, director and founder of the Royal Institute of International Affairs (RIIA) and thereby the inspirer of a good number of British (and then American) strategies, who has explained in the most lucid way this dynamic which a responsible European at high levels should not lose sight of: the domination of ancient Bithynia, a small territory situated just beyond the Bosphorus in Anatolian land, allows, if there is an adequate impetus, if there is a correct "response" to the "challenge" of the Bithynian territoriality (to use the vocabulary of Toynbee), the double mastery of the Aegean and the Black Sea. Rome became the ruler of these two maritime spaces after having ensured the control of Bithynia (at the cost of Caesar's virtues, the wicked Roman languages insinuated themselves...). Later this Bithynia became the initial territory of the clan of Osman (or Othman), who bequeathed to us the term "Ottoman".

An Ancient Pontic and Mediterranean Greece

One often speaks in a rigid way of ancient Greek civilisation creating a pedantic static classicism, imagining a Greece limited sometimes to the Athenian *areopagus*, at others to the Spartan gymnasium, sometimes to the syllogisms of its philosophers, at others to the geometry of its mathematicians, a Greece like an island isolated from its Mediterranean and Pontic environment. The nerve-centre of this civilisation, much more complex and much richer than the classicist professors imagine, was the Bosphorus, key to the Aegean/Pontus Euxinus[475] maritime space. The Bosphorus connected Aegean Greece to the Black Sea, the Crimea and the Ukraine, whence came its wheat and, in large part, its wood and its Scythian guards who ensured the policing of Athens. The Hellenic civilisation is thus a Mediterranean and Pontic composite merging diverse peoples of European and non-European origin into a living synthesis where the Balkan countries in the background – the Thracians and Scythians branched out to Finno-Ugric Northern Europe via the Russian rivers – are not at all absent. The Hellenic space, the future Greek-speaking Eastern Roman Empire, the Byzantine universe possessing thus a Pontic dimension and the actually Greek archipelago is the farthest point of this Pontic Balkan complex situated at the south of the course of the Danube. In this sense, the Greek space of today, where the majority of the city-states of classical Greece were concentrated, is the prolongation of the Danubian and Balkan Europe in the direction of the Levant, Egypt and Africa. If not for this prolongation, if this space were cut off from its European "hinterland", it becomes ipso facto a springboard for the Levant, and eventually for Egypt – if by chance it became again a power that counts, as in the time of Mehmet Ali[476] – in the direction of the Danubian heart of Europe.

Toynbee, with his Bithynian hypothesis, demonstrated that if Greece (Roman or Byzantine) were to lose Bithynia, close to the

---

[475] [Pontus or (Gk) Pontos Euxeinos is a region of Anatolia on the southern coast of the Black Sea.]

[476] [See above p. 218.]

Bosphorus and having at its disposal a Pontic façade, the power that would seize it could thereby easily extend in all directions: towards the Balkans and the Danube, towards the Crimea, the Black Sea and the course of the large Russian rivers, towards the Caucasus (Colchis), the springboard towards the Persian east, towards Egypt going along the Syrian, Lebanese, Palestinian and Sinai coasts, towards the Nile, the artery leading directly to the heart of East Africa, towards the Red Sea, which gives access to trade with India and China, towards Mesopotamia and the Persian Gulf. The Ottoman adventure from the initial base of the Bithynian and peri-Bithynian territories of Osman proves broadly the pertinence of this thesis. The Ottoman expansion created an enclave blockade against which Europe struggled for long centuries. Kemalist Turkey, by rejecting the Ottoman heritage, nevertheless conserved a real regional power and a potential global power by maintaining the Bithynian territory under its sovereignty. Even if it no longer has the technological, thus military means to resume the Ottoman expansion, contemporary, post-Kemalist Turkey retains its precious advantages simply through its geographic position which makes of it, even weakened, a regional power that cannot be overlooked.

A Turkey that is Ethnically and Religiously Fragmented Behind an Apparent Uniformity

The Turkish phenomenon consists in a particular nationalism grafted onto a population, certainly for the most part Turkish and Sunni Muslim, but heterogeneous, if one takes into consideration the fact that the Turkish citizens are not necessarily the descendants of warlike immigrants coming from Central Asia, the cradle of the Turkophone peoples; many are Greeks or Armenians superficially converted, professing a toned down Islam or an anti-religious secularism, others are the Indo-European Sunni Kurds or equally Sunni Semitic Arabs, others still are descendants of Islamised Balkan immigrants or of peoples coming from the northern shore of the Black Sea; to these ethnic divisions should be added the religious cleavages: how many Zoroastrians apparently Sunni or Alawite, how many dervishes with their rich and seductive religiosity, how many Bosnian Slavs whose ancestors professed the Bogomil Manichaeism, how many Shiite Muslims among the Kurds or the Turkified Kurds, all ancient religious options and well anchored that the average European and the stupid politicians whom he elects are incapable of understanding?

The Turkish nationalism of Kemalist manufacture wanted to base itself on an Anatolian geographic base which it hoped to render uniform and especially secularise in the name of a European tropism. The new nationalism borne by Erdogan, the man who inaugurated the post-Kemalist era, amalgamates a particular geopolitical option, that which combines the ancient Ottoman dynamic with the ideal of the Sunni Caliphate. The Kurds, in the past the symbolic enemies of the Kemalist and military power, have become sometimes, in Erdogan's discourse, potential allies in the global fight initiated by the Sunnis against Shiism or its derivatives. But all the Kurds, confronted with the recent actor, the Islamic State in Iraq and Syria, do not feel close to this virulent fundamentalism and do not wish, in the face of a militant and violent Sunnism, to cede any elements of traditional emancipation inherited from their Indo-European ethnic traditions, from a diffused Zoroastrianism visible behind a superficial and conventional Sunnism.

Erdogan, in any case, with his accomplice, the former Turkish president Gül, had advanced the hypothesis of an affable Neo-Ottomanism, promising, with the astute geopolitician Davutoglu, "zero conflicts at the borders". This geopolitics of Davutoglu presented itself – before the more or less pro-fundamentalist misdemeanours of Erdogan, and the support of the Islamic State against the pro-Shiite Alawites of the Syrian power – as a beneficial opening of the accesses that the Turkish territory, the combination of Bithynian and Anatolian geopolitical advantages, offers.

The Mistake of Neo-Ottomanism

Europe, if it had been sovereign and not governed by idiots and ignoramuses, would have been perfectly able to admit the geopolitics of Davutoglu as a sort of interface between the

European bloc (preferably freed from the NATO anachronism) and the complex and explosive complex of the Levant and the Middle East that the announced Neo-Ottomanism would have been able to appease and, thereby, it would have annihilated certain American projects to Balkanise this region permanently by arousing there the struggle of all against all according to the theory of Donald M. Snow[477] (the maximal intensification of disorder by "uncivil" wars).

However, Europe, between the appearance of the first geopolitical and Neo-Ottomanist writings of Davutoglu and the successes of the Islamic State in Syria and Iraq, experienced an additional repercussion in the form of a new enclaving: it does not have an access any longer to the Levant, the Middle East or even North Africa, following the implosion of Libya. The disappearance of the control of immigrant flows by the Libyan state causes Europe to find itself besieged as before the 16th century: it becomes the receptacle of a surplus (essentially sub-Saharan) population and ceases to be the point of departure of a surplus population towards the New World and Australasia. It is no longer a radiant civilisation but a civilisation that is hated or scorned (also because the official representatives of this civilisation encourage the results of the post-'68 carnival spirit which revolts the Turks, Africans and Arab Muslims).

Adriatic Dimensions

If this civilisation fatally struck loses all its advantages in the eastern Mediterranean and if Greece becomes a weak link in the European system, this irremediable decline will no longer be able to cease. A major reason for all minds that resist the imposed diversions to re-read European history in the light of the events that mark the history of the eastern basin of the Mediterranean, the Adriatic and the Republic of Venice (and the other commercial and thalassocratic city-states of the Italian peninsula). The Adriatic is the portion of the Mediterranean which is thrust most deeply into

---

[477] [Donald M. Snow (1943-) is a specialist in international politics and American defence policy.]

the interior of the countries and especially into the interior of non-littoral countries where German is spoken, the most specifically European language, expressing most deeply the European spirit. Styria and Carinthia are German-speaking Austrian provinces connected to the Adriatic and thus Mediterranean realities connected territorially to Venetia. Istria, today Croatian, was the naval base of the Austro-Hungarian marines up to the Treaty of Versailles. The Adriatic gives access to the eastern basin of the Mediterranean and it was the uninterrupted control of the waters which constituted the power of Venice, tenacious adversary of the Ottoman Empire. Venice was present in the eastern Mediterranean, Genoa in the Crimea, almost a connected island on the Silk Road left open by the Tartars before they subjected themselves to the Sublime Porte. This Venetian geopolitics, too little buttressed on a very vast and substantial territorial mass, is perhaps no longer structurable in this form today: no micro-state of urban dimension or not having at its disposal a mass of several dozens of millions of inhabitants could function today in an optimal manner nor restore a geopolitics or a thalassopolitics of large dimensions sufficient to release the entire European civilisation from the impasse and enclaving into which it has fallen today.

Double Advantage of a Neo-Venetian Geostrategy

The concert of European nations could deploy a new Venetian geopolitics which would be one perspective among many others equally fertile and potential to get out of the present impasse: this Venetian geopolitics should now be articulated by a coherent group informed by a necessarily convergent and no longer conflictual vision. This vision could prove to be very useful for an effective European extension towards the eastern basin of the Mediterranean and towards the Pontic space. Venice and Genoa extended towards the eastern basin of the Mediterranean and towards the Black Sea, beyond the Bosphorus as long as Byzantium remained independent. This double extension gave access to the Silk Road, from the Crimea towards China and also, but with greater difficulty as a result of the vicissitudes that affected the history of the Levant, from Antioch and the Syrian and Lebanese ports towards the land routes that passed through Mesopotamia and Persia to take the caravans to India or Cathay.

The presence of Italian trading towns in Alexandria in Egypt also gave access to the Nile, to this Nile artery which plunged, beyond the cataracts, towards the mysteries of sub-Saharan Africa and towards the Christian kingdom of Ethiopia. The analysis that an observation of the geopolitical and geostrategic facts of the Venetian and Genoese history leads us to posit should quite naturally cause a serious concert of European nations led by lucid leaders to reject any useless conflict on the territory of present-day Ukraine because this territory gives access to the new routes which lead from western Europe to China, whether the latter are railway routes (the German, Russian and Chinese projects to develop high-speed and large capacity trains) or offer transit to a network of oil- and gas pipelines. Similarly, the present Lebanese, Syrian and Iraqi territories, in the interest of a well conceived concert of European nations, should only know peace and harmony in order to restore in their plenitude the access routes to the Persian, Indian and Chinese empires. The Venetian or Genoese glance that one could cast on the eastern Mediterranean and Pontic spaces would permit the generation of de-enclaving strategies.

Europe is Re-Enclaved!

Today we live in a period of European history that is not very glorious, that which is marked by its re-enclaving, which implies that Europe has lost all the advantages that it had roughly acquired since the Iberian reconquest, the plurisecular struggle against the Ottoman phenomenon, etc. This re-enclaving is the result of the politics of the new western hegemon, the United States of America. The latter was Europe's debtor before 1914. After the disaster of the First World War, it became its creditor. For it is a matter especially of maintaining the old continent in a condition of perpetual weakness in order that it may never again regain its strength, never again become its creditor. To achieve this it is necessary to re-enclave this Europe so that it may never again be able to radiate in the way it did since the discovery of America and since the Portuguese and Spanish explorations of the 16th century. This strategy, which consists in working for the re-enclaving of Europe, is the chief of all the strategies deployed by the new hegemon after 1918.

Even if it did not sign the Treaty of Versailles, the United States attempted, from the middle of the twenties, to place Europe (and especially Germany) in tutelage through a policy of credits. Parallel to this financial policy, the United States imposed in the twenties the Wilsonian principles of international law, falsely pacifist, aiming at depriving the states of the right to make war, especially the European states – their principal rivals – and Japan, from which they wished to seize new conquests in the Pacific. Obviously, at first glance, but only at first glance, one could consider this desire to pacify the world as positive, borne by a good philanthropic project. The real objective however was not to pacify the world, as is clearly seen today in the Levant and in Mesopotamia, where the United States, through its golem which is the Islamic State, favours the "maximal intensification of disorder". The real objective is to strip every state, whichever it may be, whatever the traditions and ideologies that it advocates may be, of its sovereignty. No state, even if it were besieged and suffocated by its neighbours, whether it be placed by its historical antecedents in a situation of long-term inviability on account of a preceding mutilation of its national territory, has any longer the right to rectify dramatic situations that condemn its population to misery, emigration or to a demographic overpowering. Now sovereignty, remarked Carl Schmitt in the face of the pernicious deployment of this Wilsonianism, is the capacity to decide to make war or not to make it in order to escape unjust or unmanageable situations. Especially making war in order to break a fateful encirclement or an enclaving that would bar the path to the sea and maritime commerce was considered as legitimate. The best example, in this regard, is that of Bolivia enclaved in the centre of the South American continent after a war of the 19th century when Peru and Chile had cut its access to the Pacific: the problem has still not been resolved despite the United Nations. Similarly, Austria, conquered by Napoleon, was deprived of its access to the Adriatic by the establishment of "Illyrian counties";

in 1919, Clemenceau applied the same policy to it: the birth of the kingdom of Yugoslavia took away its naval bases of Istria (Pola), removing thereby the last access of the Germanic Central Powers to the Mediterranean. Austria imploded, was plunged into misery and finally accepted the Anschluss in 1938, whose real authorship goes back to Clemenceau.

Versailles and Wilsonianism Concretise the Intra-European Partitioning

And then, for the hegemon, it is necessary to conserve as much as possible the territorial partitioning of Europe. Already the restrictions on the sovereign right to make war solidified the traces of borders, often aberrant in Europe, now become completely absurd after the treaty of the Parisian suburb of 1919-20, which rendered impossible any imperial regroupment and, more precisely, any constitution, even peaceful, of the Austro-Hungarian Danubian complex, an entirely natural creation of vital and historic character. These treaties signed in the Parisian suburb divided the European territory into a German bloc with new militarily indefensible borders – "dismembered", to repeat the vocabulary of Richelieu and Haushofer – and a Soviet Russia which lost the buffer zones of the Tsarist Empire (the Baltic countries, Finland, Bessarabia, Volhynia, etc.). The double system of Versailles (of Trianon, Sèvres, Saint-Germain, etc.) and the so-called pacifist Wilsonian principles intended to definitively consolidate the partitioning of "intermediate Europe" between defeated Germany and the USSR weakened by an atrocious civil war.

The present situation flows from that: the creation of the unjust treaties of the Parisian suburb, still more divided after the explosion of ex-Yugoslavia and ex-Czechoslovakia, allows the United States today to support the centrifugal claims at times of one residual small power, at others of another, flattered to receive from the entire American Neoconservative and warmongering clique the flattering title of "New Europe", insolent in the face of a cowardly "Old Europe" (centred around the Gaullian/Adenauerian partnership of Franco-Germany or of Carolingian Europe), exactly as England played some of these small powers against Germany and Russia following the diplomatic measures of Lord Curzon or as France, which created bewildering alliances to "contain Germany" obliging the French taxpayer to finance Pharaonic military budgets, especially in Poland, the chief power of "intermediate Europe" considered as a replacement, in the French strategy, of what the Ottoman Empire was against the Austria of the Hapsburgs or what Russia was during the revenge politics of the Third Republic,[478] or a "steamroller" helping from behind, following the gruesome custom bequeathed by François I in the 16th century. Poland was thus this new "ally in the rear" less heavy than the Ottoman Empire or the Russia of Nicholas II but sufficiently armed to render more difficult a war on two fronts.

Since the nineties NATO has reduced the strength of the German Bundeswehr and placed it equal to that of the Polish army, which plays the anti-Russian role that Germany no longer wished to play since the beginning of the eighties. "Intermediate Europe" is mobilised for a strategy contrary to the general interests of Europe.

Some Separatisms that Suit the Hegemon

In the western part of Europe separatist movements are maintained by the media, as in Catalonia, for example, to promote neoliberal ideologies (vis-à-vis old states judged to be too protectionist or too "rigid") or inconsistent leftisms corresponding perfectly to the deconstructionist strategies of the ambient carnival spirit, strategies favoured by the hegemon since they permit the consolidation of the effects of Wilsonianism. This carnival spirit is fully favoured because it has shown itself to be the ideal instrument to bring down the traditional politics, already solidly assaulted by sixty or seventy years of stultifying media hammering but still judged too "political" to please the hegemon who, without stopping, makes debilitating cocktails on demand, each time adapted to the local

---

[478] [The French Third Republic lasted from 1870 to 1940.]

situation where exploitable dissidence is registered. This adaptation of the discourse causes one to believe, in an important portion of the masses, in the existence of a solid and unshakable "identity", which then allows the diffusion of an insidious discourse where the population imagines that it is defending this identity because all sorts of gadgets of local colour are manufactured for it; in reality, behind this puppet-theatre which captures all the attention of frivolous people, they join together important provinces of the old states, not according to a Europe of biological ethnies as the naïve imagine, but according to the international networks of universal depoliticisation that the neoliberal systems and/or the carnivals are, in order that all in fine may take communion – dressed in a Catalan or Basque, Flemish or Walloon T-shirt or straw hat – in the great neoliberal or carnival mass without ever seriously criticising their subjection to NATO.

Rendering all the Nations Rootless

In this way large parts of the old and tenacious enemy of the Anglo-American Calvinist/Puritan networks are still further Balkanised: the ancient empire of Charles Quint[479] is further dislocated to make all these splinters totally "invertebrate" (Ortega y Gasset). The Bretons and the Occitans[480] do not merit any support contrary to the others: if they demand autonomy or independence they commit an unpardonable sin, for they aim at the disintegration of westernised states whose intrinsic fundamentalism, a pure manipulative fiction, does not appeal to a biblical God as in America but to an eradicating atheism. The Bretons do not demand the dissolution of ancient imperial and European land but of a state that is already "rootless", "not of a people".[481] It is therefore necessary to combat them and to treat them as country bumpkins or worse. The strategy of the

---

[479] [See above p. 207.]

[480] [The people of Occitania (in southern France, north eastern Spain and north western Italy). Catalan is an Occitan language.]

[481] α privative + demos, 'people' in Greek, this neologism having been forged by the Italian philosopher Giorgio Agamben.

permanent partition of the territory aims, in fact, at preventing any reconstitution of an imperial reality in Europe, heir to the empire of Charles Quint or of the "Grand Alliance" highlighted by the Walloon historian Luc Hummel, specialist in the history of the Burgundians. The difference between the noxious anti-imperialist independences and the positive independences – because hostile to the renegade states which through intrinsic weakness have apostasised the ideal of a unified and combative European civilisation – should not prevent the necessary promotion of the European variety according to the principles highlighted by the Breton theoretician Yann Fouéré,[482] who spoke of the "laws of a required variety".

A Issue of Contradictions

In Flanders, it is necessary to combat all the forces, including those that call themselves "identitarian", that do not demand an absolute rejection of NATO and the alliances tying us the Anglo-Saxon powers which deploy the ECHELON network against Europe. These pseudo-identitarian are ready to fall, through crass stupidity, into all the traps of neoliberalism. In Wallonie, one should reject the Socialist tutelage which was the first to sink Belgium into the mire of NATO that the adversaries of this Atlantist policy called "Spaakistan", as Prof. Coolsaet[483] (RUG)[484] recalls.

In Wallonie, the so-called "regional" or "regionalist" forces are in favour of an endogenous development and a social project that is non-liberal but without clearly defining the position of Wallonie in the large region between the Rhine and the Seine. The Walloon literature, in the person of the missed Gaston Compère,[485] revives the Romanophone regions of the old Holy Empire within the Burgundian framework and causes them to participate in an

---

[482] [Yann Fouéré (1910-2011) was a Breton nationalist who adopted Irish citizenship in the fifties and founded the Celtic League.]

[483] [See above p. 128]

[484] [Rijksuniversiteit Gent, the State University of Ghent.]

[485] [Gaston Compère (1924-2008) was a Belgian writer and composer.]

imperial and cultural project, that of Charles the Bold,[486] even while criticising the urban (and thus non-traditional) forces (of Flanders and Alsace) for having torpedoed this project with the complicity of Louis XI, the "universelle aragne",[487] creator of the coercive modern state which came at the end of the fine France of the *Très riches heures du Duc de Berry*,[488] Villon,[489] Rutebeuf[490] and Rabelais.[491]

Compère inverts the vulgate circulated on the divisions of Belgium: he makes Flemish cities the accomplices of the French weakness and the Walloon countryside the protagonist of a glorious, ambitious and prestigious project, that of the Duke of Burgundy who died in Nancy in 1477. Certainly Compère formulates there, with magnifique panache, a utopia that present-day Wallonie, plunged into the murky waters of the political viciousness of its unworthy leaders, is today incapable of realising while Flanders forgets its own history in favour of a pseudo-nationalist mythology based on a range of contradictory myths which telescope a Catholic demand (the pious people) against the Jacobin importations of the French Revolution and an identification with the Protestantism of the 16th century, whose iconoclasts were the equivalents of the Islamic State of today and who ruined the mediaeval Flemish statuary vandalised in the summer of 1566. It is therefore amusing to see some shallow heads invoking these iconoclasts in the name of a pan-Netherlandism which existed only under other signs, more traditional and always within the imperial grouping, while harping constantly on a (justified) hostility against the derivatives of the Islamic State erroneously assimilated to all the cultural forms born on Islamic land: if one invokes the iconoclastic Calvinists of

---

[486] [Charles the Bold (1433-77) was the Duke of Burgundy from 1467.]

[487] [The Universal Spider; see above p. 194n]

[488] [*Très riches heures du Duc de Berry* is an illuminated prayer book produced around 1415 for Jean, Duke of Berry.]

[489] [François Villon (1431-?) was a famous French poet of the late Middle Ages.]

[490] [Rutebeuf (fl. 1245-85) was a mediaeval French troubadour noted for his satirical compositions.]

[491] [François Rabelais (ca.1483-1553) was a major writer of the French Renaissance whose most famous work is the collection of satirical novels called *La vie de Gargantua et de Pantagruel*.]

yesterday there is no reason not to applaud the events and gestures of the Muslim iconoclasts of today, armed and supported by the Puritan heirs of the vandals of 1566; if one does not applaud, it means that one is stupid and particularly inconsistent.

The myths of the Belgian state are also contradictory because they mix the imperial idea, the idea of the Crusades (the figure of Godefroy de Bouillon[492] and the traditional views of Marcel Lobet,[493] etc.), pro- and anti-Hollandism confused in a terrible goulash, a narrow and tight nationalism alien to the actual history of the regions that have today remained "Belgian".

In Catalonia, the journal *Nihil Obstat* published near Tarragona recalls (in no.22/1, 2014) very opportunely that all Catalanism was not anti-imperial: on the contrary, it claimed an Aragonese identity combined with a "worldly" discourse that the carnivalist independence movement which occupies the foreground today certainly does not claim because it prefers to wallow in the mire of the totally mixed fashions dictated by the back rooms of America or to participate in a demagogic leftism which will obviously bring no solution to any of the ills that affect the present-day Catalan society – exactly as the drift of the Flemish NVA[494] into genderism (made in the USA with the blessing of Hilary Clinton) and even into the panmixism so popular in Hollande's Paris will not resolve any of the ills that plague the Flemish society. This long digression on the, positive and negative, centrifugal forces that shake the European political landscape leads us to conclude that the hegemon pushes, in all possible and imaginable ways, whatever disturbs the policies, large and small, of Europe, Latin America and Asia as well as the carnival and panmixist centrifugal forces which import the elements of neoliberal dissolution permitting the strategies of stultification that aim at transforming the peoples into "populations", at metamorphosing all the classical nation-states rich with a potentially fecund *Realpolitik* into stuttering machines

---

[492] [Godefroy de Bouillon (1060-1100) was a Frankish knight who was one of the leaders of the First Crusade (1096-99).]

[493] [Marcel Lobet (1907-92) was a Belgian journalist and writer.]

[494] [Nieuw-Vlaamse Alliantie (New Flemish Alliance) is a conservative separatist Flemish political party. It currently leads the newly formed "Flemish Government".]

characterised by what the very relevant Italian philosopher Giorgio Agamben called "rootless" policies or policies that have eliminated the peoples whom they are nevertheless considered to represent and defend.

The monetary attack on Greece, which has weakened the Euro currency, in order that it can no longer be used to replace the hegemonic dollar, has shaken the will to a continental unity: one sees reappearing all the anti-civilisational independence movements, all the illusions of splendid isolation, especially in France and in Great Britain, all the petty nationalisms of "Intermediate Europe", all the forms of Germanophobia which raise the peripheries against the geographical centre of the continent and deny, as a consequence, any continental and civilisational unity. To this general centrifugal slide are added obviously the Neo-Wilsonianisms that do not recognise the real cynicism that appears behind this apparent optimism, that Carl Schmitt perfectly recognised. It seems as if one is fighting for "democracy" in Ukraine or in Syria on behalf of the ground forces, who show themselves to be very little democratic. The carnival spirit continues to obliterate aspirations and ruin in advance any revival of a political conscience. The separatisms useful to the hegemon gain in influence. The separatisms which could work to ruin the state machines that have become "people-less" are restricted in their momentum. Europe is a continent that has become "invertebrate", like the Spain described by Ortega y Gasset.[495] The Greek affair is the first sign of a phase of dissolution of large dimensions: weakened Greece, the flows of false refugees, the implosion of Germany, the centre of the continent, the lack of political and geopolitical judgment (especially regarding the eastern basin of the Mediterranean, the Black Sea and the Levant) are its logical results.

---

[495] [José Ortega y Gasset (1883-1955) was a liberal Spanish philosopher who served briefly as a deputy in the constituent assembly of the Second Spanish Republic.]

Lightning Source UK Ltd.
Milton Keynes UK
UKOW04f1820121017
310893UK00001B/84/P